W9-CZS-899

Voice
in
Social
Interaction

LANGUAGE AND LANGUAGE BEHAVIORS SERIES

Howard Giles
SERIES EDITOR
Department of Communication
University of California, Santa Barbara

This series is unique in its sociopsychological orientation to "language and language behaviors" and their communicative and miscommunicative consequences. Books in the series not only examine how biological, cognitive, emotional, and societal forces shape the use of language, but the ways in which language behaviors can create and continually revise understandings of our bodily states, the situations in which we find ourselves, and our identities within the social groups and events around us. Methodologically and ideologically eclectic, the edited and authored volumes are written to be accessible for advanced students in the social, linguistic, and communication sciences as well as to serve as valuable resources for seasoned researchers in these fields.

Volumes in this series

Volumes previously published by Multilingual Matters in the series Monographs in the Social Psychology of Language and in the series Intercommunication may be obtained through Multilingual at 8A Hill Road, Clevedon, Avon BS21 7 HH, England.

Editorial Advisory Board

Voice
in
Social
Interaction

An Interdisciplinary
Approach

JEFFERY PITTAM

**LANGUAGE
AND
LANGUAGE
BEHAVIORS**
volume 5

SAGE Publications
International Educational and Professional Publisher
Thousand Oaks   London   New Delhi

For information address:

SAGE Publications, Inc.
2455 Teller Road
Thousand Oaks, California 91320

SAGE Publications Ltd.
6 Bonhill Street
London EC2A 4PU
United Kingdom

SAGE Publications India Pvt. Ltd.
M-32 Market
Greater Kailash I
New Delhi 110 048 India

Printed in the United States of America

Library of Congress Cataloging-in-Publication Data

Pittam, Jeffery.
    Voice in social interaction: An interdisciplinary approach/
Jeffery Pittam.
        p.   cm.—(Language and language behaviors; v. 5)
        ISBN 0-8039-5750-5.—ISBN 0-8039-5751-3 (pbk.)
        1. Oral communication. 2. Voice. I. Title. II. Series
    P95.P59   1994
    302.2′242—dc20   94-10890

94 95 96 97 98   10 9 8 7 6 5 4 3 2 1

Sage Production Editor: Astrid Virding

To Cindy whose voice is always with me

To Sirikit and Patani whose voices I will never forget

Contents

Acknowledgments

My interest in the voice, its measurement and function in social interaction, goes back many years. It was the gifted Australian phonetician Bob Cochrane who guided my first steps along this road and set the scene for my Ph.D. research. My thanks go to Bob for providing me with a lifetime's interest. From those early days, I would also like to thank David Lee who so ably took the reins when Bob retired.

Over the years I have had the great good fortune to talk to, and in some cases work with, many of the leading players in the voice area. My thanks go out to all who have given their time to discuss issues with me. I hope I have not done an injustice to your work, and that you will continue to talk to me. In particular, I must name John Laver, Klaus Scherer, and Harry Hollien. Your professional advice, help, friendship, and mentorship have been central to the formulation of my ideas. One person who stands out in this regard is Howard Giles, who has been of considerable influence from the early days. Professionally, he has provided invaluable critical comment and advice. His own work has had a major impact on the way voice has been constructed here. In particular, many thanks for the support, advice, and time given so freely throughout the writing of this book, and many thanks, as editor of the series, for considering the book worthwhile.

The essential publishing phase of any book's development can be difficult. I have been fortunate in the help received from Sage Publications, who smoothed the difficulties throughout the process. In this regard, I would like to thank Sophy Craze who guided the process from an early stage in its development and, from a publishing perspective, played a major role in bringing the project to fruition. In addition, I would like to thank Miles Patterson and John Wiley and Sons for permission to reprint the figure of the Sequential Functional

Model of Nonverbal Behavior; and similarly Cindy Gallois (as first author) and Sage Publications for permission to reprint the figure of the Communication Accommodation Theory model.

One often finds toward the end of acknowledgment pages a reference to the personal support given by a spouse or partner. I am forever grateful for the fact that, in my case, there is a person who plays a dual role: colleague and spouse. From both professional and personal points of view, this book would not have existed without Cindy Gallois. Professionally, many hours were given willingly in discussing different aspects of the book and providing advice and help. It is impossible to acknowledge every instance of this, but it is certainly reflected throughout the book. At a personal level, the emotional support and the unstinting interest have made the debt immeasurable.

I have found, as many others have before, that in writing a book you engage in lots of talking with many people over many years. The consequence is that you inevitably take on board many ideas. I hope I have done justice to those ideas in applying them to the voice and vocal communication. Any mistakes or misapplications are mine. Finally, it is worth saying that there are areas of voice research conducted by many researchers that have not been covered in this book. This is not because they were not considered sufficiently important, but that the focus I have taken in the book has precluded my referring to them.

CHAPTER ONE

Introduction

When we hear someone speak, we hear not just the speech sounds themselves but the speaker's voice also, the underlying sound that seems to be present across long stretches of speech, perhaps even present all the time the person is speaking. As listeners, however, we usually do not separate voice from speech. That is, we do not consciously listen to the voice alone all that frequently, a point that led the early psychologist T. H. Pear (1933) to note that only young children and dogs do so with any regularity and consistency. Despite this, however, there are times when we do seem to listen consciously to the underlying voice sounds, and notwithstanding the infrequency of this, voice, as an important aspect of communication, deserves our close and critical attention. Even when we do not consciously separate voice from speech, it still communicates much information. This book, along with Pear's young children and dogs, focuses on the voice, its social and personal functions, its measurement, and the theoretical explanations we can bring to bear on its description and use. Above all, this book is concerned with the spoken voice in social interaction. It is not about the singing voice; neither is it a training manual; and while much of the material presented here is psychological and phonetic, the emphasis throughout will be on providing a *social* explanation for vocal communication.

When we use voice to communicate, we are engaging in social interaction. To say that voice is an important part of our communicative behavior, however, does not adequately describe the way we use it. People with whom we interact, although they may not consciously separate it from speech, nevertheless use voice to learn something about us socially and personally, just as we in turn use it to learn something of them. Voice, like speech, language, and other, nonverbal, behaviors, carries part of our social and personal identity and provides us with a flexible communicative tool that we can use to send information about our emotional state and attitudes, and from which we can make inferences and attributions about others and decisions about our subsequent behavior. The study of voice, therefore, can provide us with important insights into human social interaction. It is for this reason that this book emphasizes social explanations for vocal communication.

One of the ways we characterize people is by their voices. In an interesting and rather unusual attempt to relate the voices of several British poets to their poems, Berry (1962) provides insights into the personal identities of Alfred, Lord Tennyson, Percy Bysshe Shelley, and John Milton. Berry records the fact that writers who knew these poets personally felt impelled to characterize them by their voices. Thus we learn that Tennyson's voice was "very deep and deep-chested, but rather murmuring . . . like the sound of a far sea or of a pinewood" (p. 50), while Shelley's voice was described as "intolerably shrill, harsh and discordant" (p. 67), and Milton's was said to be delicate and tuneable. Perhaps the use of such poetic descriptions is apt for what are undeniably some of Britain's foremost poets, although some of these descriptions tell us little about the voices themselves. One of the overarching aims of the present book is to provide a comprehensive description of the voice from perceptual, articulatory, and acoustic perspectives.

Poetry was once, and to some extent still is, an oral art form. It may not be too surprising, therefore, that someone should believe it relevant to leave as part of the descriptive legacy of these famous writers, an idea of how their individual voices sounded. It is not only poets who attract such descriptions, however. Most writers of fiction use this device in attempting to describe the characters they create. Patrick White (1961), in his novel *The Tree of Man*, for example, described the character of Mrs. Parker as having a voice that "had been scrubbed clean of the emotions. It was bare and very dull" (p. 15), while the character of Gatsby in F. Scott Fitzgerald's (1958) *The Great Gatsby* referred to Daisy Buchanan as having a voice that was "full of money" causing the narrator Nick to comment "That was it . . . that was the inexhaustible charm that rose and fell in it, the jingle of it, the cymbal's song of it" (p. 113). In our everyday use of language, we may not use such creative metaphorical descriptions (although, as will be discussed later, it was the consistent use of subjective impressionistic descriptions of voice by academic writers that led one of the foremost researchers in this area, John Laver, to propose a phonetic description of voice). Writers of fiction, however, have only the written word to create their characterizations and must make use of such metaphorical devices. In social interaction, we have other channels of communication.

How can we best describe someone's voice? Informally, we are likely to use any description that seems apt to us at the time we communicate our message to our listeners. Such descriptions may not be as creative as the fictional ones noted above, but will be our attempt to communicate any number of things, from an actual description of the sound of the voice (such as reedy or booming), to our feelings about another person and the inferences we may have made about that person. To say someone has a lah-di-dah voice or a rough voice is to say something not only about the voice itself, but the person whose voice it is and, in addition, to say something about our attitudes and prejudices as well.

Human beings have long used the voice in these ways. Indeed, interest in the voice can be found in some of the earliest writings and no doubt predates even those. Throughout history Western writers have commented on the functions of voice. In this first chapter of the book, vocal function in social interaction will be introduced first by an historical account of vocal function, and then by considering how, in the 20th century, voice has been studied across academic disciplines. The chapter will end with an overview of the book and its aims.

Historical Accounts of Vocal Function

I am indebted to two works by John Laver that provided a point of departure for this historical perspective (Laver, 1977, 1978). The first of these has been reworked and extended in Laver (1981a), which has since been reprinted in Laver (1991). For a fuller description of the history of the phonetic description of voice and of articulatory settings the reader is referred to these works. Here the focus is on how the voice was thought to function in social interaction, rather than on a phonetic description as such.

As Laver (1977) points out, explicit classification of the voice on a phonetic basis did not begin before the 19th century. Writers from the classical period, however, were aware that the voice could function socially and personally in a number of ways. This interest in the voice may have stemmed in part from the developing importance of both the drama and rhetoric during this period, particularly in Greece and later throughout the Roman Empire. On the one hand, drama needed trained actors to perform the works of playwrights such as Aristophanes, Sophocles, and Euripides in the large newly developed amphitheaters. On the other, the work of Aristotle, among others, in developing rhetoric resulted in a need to train professional orators and the teachers of orators, the Sophists. In addition, in the Greek education system, pupils were taught to declaim, that is, to learn set speeches and deliver them in character. There appears to have been considerable traffic among the three institutions: education, theater, and professional oratory (Russell, 1983).

The art of deducing character from physical qualities, physiognomics, was well established in classical Greece. This practice included using the voice to help make one's deductions. As Stanford (1967) among others shows, early writers were concerned with the link between voice and personality characteristics of speakers. Deep, tense voices, for example, were thought to indicate bravery, whereas higher, lax voices (i.e., non-tense) were thought to represent cowardice.

From a sociopolitical perspective, one can see evidence of the patriarchal nature of the society reflected in these relationships between voice and personality. Such descriptions as these referred to male voices only, and there is a link being made with the fact that male voices are lower in pitch, as a general rule, than female voices. Socially constructed manly qualities such as bravery, therefore, were equated with the vocal features most associated with maleness. It is only in the last half of the 20th century that the possible effect of socialization on pitch levels used by males and females has become evident. A number of writers (Mattingly, 1969; Sachs, Lieberman, & Erickson, 1973; Spender, 1985) have suggested that the tendency for males to have lower pitched voices may not be simply anatomical and physiological in origin but may be determined in part by social factors. Additional evidence for this may be found in Laver (1975b), who proposed a cultural stereotype operating in the United States favoring lower pitch for males, and in Scherer (1979a) who found American males used significantly lower pitch than a similar group of Germans.

Relating characteristics such as bravery and cowardice to vocal features, as we find in the classical literature, can be seen as part of such a socialization process. Cowards were males with voices that had key features in common with voices perceived as characteristic of females: a higher pitch level and laxness. Bravery, on the other hand, was characterized by tense voices and lower pitch levels and, by inference, maleness. Again, it is only in the 20th century that we are starting to understand the perceived links between vocal tract tension and gender. Pittam (1987a) reported that his judges rated tense voices more favorably when used by males than females, while the reverse was found for breathiness (laxness is one of the major components of breathiness). One other voice type perceived negatively by Western cultures from classical times is nasality. Stanford (1967) goes on to show that the Greeks related this voice quality to spitefulness and moral laxity (British speakers of received pronunciation and many Americans and Australians should take note).

Notions of tenseness, laxness, and nasality, although still not defined very stringently by most users of them, either in classical times or in the 20th century, are nonetheless capable of standardization in phonetic terms in that they can be related directly to articulatory and physiological mechanisms (although we should note, as Laver [1980] points out, that there are a number of different types of nasality, each linked to different mechanisms). Other descriptions of voice used by the classical Greek writers appear to have been far more impressionistic in that they are linked to no obvious physical processes. Thus, one voice type has been referred to in translation as cracked or broken. Apparently, this was thought to indicate gluttony and violence, an odd pairing.

As noted above, one area of activity in which the voice was thought to be particularly important was rhetoric. Classical rhetoric, so esteemed in both classical Greece and Rome, and placed so centrally in Western education systems for many centuries as one of the seven liberal arts, was above all in its original form, an oral art. The actual delivery of the speech was perceived as one of the most important steps in producing a piece of persuasive rhetoric. Nonetheless, there are relatively few references in the classical literature on the specific methods used by the teachers of the day to train the voice, although Aristotle, in his *Rhetorica*, wrote of the manipulation of three vocal qualities to produce a successful piece of persuasive rhetoric: volume, rhythm, and harmony—the last having the three variants of shrill, deep, and intermediate. There were, apparently, accepted combinations of the three qualities to express different emotions.

To construct a piece of persuasive rhetoric successfully was thought to depend in part on the orator using a combination of logic, appealing to the emotions of the listeners, and presenting an appropriate personal identity. These were known as the appeals to logos, pathos, and ethos, respectively. Effective use of voice was a key tool in establishing both the appeal to pathos and ethos. The importance of voice as a carrier of affect and personality characteristics, therefore, was established early. Indeed, the two were closely related by Aristotle. Their communication by the voice was used particularly in both political and legal persuasive oratory: law and politics were the two major social institutions in which rhetorical techniques were used.

Interest in the voice through its use in rhetoric and, to a lesser extent, drama continued in Rome. Two classical Roman writers on rhetoric who stand out for the importance they place on voice in this respect were Cicero and Quintilian. Thus, Cicero, in his dialogues on *Oratory and Orators*, wrote of our ability to communicate the emotions of anger, lamentation, fear, violence, pleasure, and trouble by the voice (Watson, 1970). He suggested that anger should be communicated by an acute, vehement tone of voice with frequent breaks; while for pleasure one should use an unconstrained, mild, tender, cheerful, and languid tone. Lamentation or sorrow was expressed using a flexible, full, interrupted tone, and violence by a strained, vehement, impetuous tone with forcible excitement.

Cicero's proposals show an awareness that the voice can be used to communicate emotion. Once again, however, we see the use of impressionistic terminology to describe the voice. The lack of clear definitions for these terms makes it difficult to understand precisely what Cicero meant. All emotions were thought to be associated with a particular tone of voice—although the above examples show that by this Cicero meant a rather complex or compound vocal tone. It was the orator's task to manipulate the voice to produce these different tones. As Cicero put it, "there is none of these [tones] . . . which may not be influenced by art or management" (Watson, 1970, p. 257). Cicero seems to have been one of the first writers on the voice to suggest a universality in the expression of emotion—something still being contested two millennia later.

In the first century A.D., Quintilian, one of the foremost writers on rhetoric, commented more extensively on voice in his *Institutiones Oratoriae*. He too was aware of the importance of voice to the communication of emotions. In the Little (1951) translation, we find, "The voice is full and simple, or aroused to battle, or fierce and harsh according to its varied tasks: dignified to console, bold in exhortation, suggestive of tears in pity, raised to express violent emotion" (p. 297). A piece of advice that could be aimed at a book such as the present one is also to be found in this same translation: "Concerning the voice one must first ask about its quality and next, how it is to be used, for voices are strong or weak, clear or husky" (p. 294)—different voice types for different functions. The comment made earlier about the traffic among the Greek education system, orators, and theater is shown to be relevant also to Roman society by Quintilian's comment that the student of rhetoric should learn how to express emotions from the comic actors. This is an interesting comment. However stereotypically the comic actors may have expressed each emotion using the voice, Quintilian seems to have believed this would also be effective in persuasive oratory.

Both Cicero and Quintilian, while writing specifically about rhetoric and the training of orators, also commented on the fact that voice may function as a marker of cultural or national identity. From Cicero we get the following comment: "There is a certain tone of voice . . . peculiar to the Roman people and city, in which nothing can offend or displease" (Watson, p. 70), an observation that provides information about Cicero as a citizen of Rome as much as it does about the functions of voice. Quintilian made a somewhat more insightful statement: "Sometimes we blame whole nations for their sounds" (Little, p. 42). It is only in the last few decades that we have become aware of the role of voice in the establishment and development of prejudice.

As noted earlier, Laver (1977) asserts that phonetic descriptions of voice did not concern classical writers. While he is correct in this, some of the terms they used are more able to be linked to physical mechanisms than others, and on occasions attempts at definitions were made. Stanford (1967) shows that one Aristotelian writer, for example, probably in the fourth century B.C., attempted a description of a voice type that Stanford translates as *whetstone*. The description, at least in terms of what the voice was *not*, is something more than just a naive subjective impression. In part, the writer defines this voice type as "not a matter of vocal bulkiness, nor of relaxed and low tones, nor of close intervals of sounds, but rather of sharpness and delicacy and precision" (p. 150). The attempt to define the voice in terms of laxness, pitch level, and pitch range (close intervals of sound) moves it closer to a phonetic description, and may suggest that this writer was something of an expert auditory judge. In more recent times, similar ways of describing voices have been used. As Laver (1977) points out, the first British writer to mention vocal quality apparently was Roger Ascham in 1570 in his manual, *The Scholemaster*. Ascham's comment on voice reflects aspects of his society rather in the way the evaluative statements noted above reflected classical Greek patriarchal society. In the first book contained in his manual, titled "The Bringing Up of Youth," he writes of the favored type of voice for the young man as "a voice, not softe, weake, piping, womanishe, but audible, stronge, and manlike" (Alston, 1967b, p. 8). It is possible to interpret this in social class terms also, for Ascham was writing not for the peasant class but for the young gentlemen in British society.

In the following century, both Wallis in 1653 and Wilkins in 1668 relate voice to national identity (Kemp, 1972). Wallis seems to suggest that both articulatory vocal settings and features such as speech rate and pitch may reflect national character. Thus, he proposes that the English push forward their pronunciation into the front part of the mouth, the French place the sounds near the palate and accompany them with an indistinct, muffled murmur, while Germans retract their pronunciation toward the back of the mouth and even into the laryngeal area. In his modern English translation, Kemp argues that Wallis is not referring to articulations in these examples, but the relative lack of constriction of the airstream. Whether one focuses on the aerodynamics or articulatory nature of these comments, however, Wallis clearly believed voice could encode national identity. He also proposed that the French, as a nation, speak faster, Italians and Spaniards use a slower tempo, and the English use a tempo somewhat between these two. Writing a few years later, Wilkins (1668/ 1968, p. 381), provides the same examples as Wallis, and adds a comment echoing that of Cicero about the pleasantness of the Roman tone of voice. This time, however, the comment covers several European nations of the 17th century:

The Italian . . . is in pronunciation pleasant, but without sinews, as a still flowing water; the French delicate, but inward and nice, as a woman who dares scarce open her mouth, for fear of marring her countenance. The Spanish, majestical, but withall somewhat terrible and fulsome. . . . The Dutch manly, but withall harsh and quarrelsome. Whereas our English . . . hath what is comely and euphonical in each of these, without any of their inconveniences.

In fairness to Wilkins, he does go on to comment that everyone will prefer the sound of their own language, and that "foreigners" probably find defects in the sound of English. It is an instance of voice acting as a marker of national identity and triggering certain attitudes toward both the in-group (in this case English) and the various out-groups (in this case, other European nations).

Another 17th century writer (Cooper, 1687/1969, p. 10), as well as repeating yet again Wallis's examples, goes further than either Wallis or Wilkins at one point by linking voice to various aspects of social identity. He relates sex, age, and nationality to variations in the vocal tract and vocal organs, thus linking voice to anatomical features. He also relates these same three social variables of sex, age, and nationality to the forcefulness of articulation and airstream, thereby linking them to consciously manipulated vocal mechanisms:

> the passage of the breath from the lungs through the windpipe, larynx, or mouth is longer or shorter, broader or narrower, emitted with greater or less force. Whereby the same motion of the breath, made by the same specific organs, causing the same specific sound, may be spoken in diverse tones: as appears from the speech of persons of both sexes, young and old, healthful and sickly, and men of several countries, some speak very broad and openly, others fine and inwardly, and some others in a mean.

By the 18th century, voice teachers and writers in the area were interested in the communication of emotion by the voice. This interest developed as elocution became a central concern. Echoing the classical period, this concern stemmed in part from a desire to improve dramatic performance and parliamentary debate, but also in part from the perceived need for a standard pronunciation, including the type of voice used. John Mason, in 1748, in describing a "good" pronunciation, included instructions on how to communicate specific emotions such as anger (by a strong, vehement, and elevated voice), and joy (by a quick, sweet, and clear voice) (Alston, 1968a, p. 26). It seems likely that these descriptions were influenced by the classical writers: the nature of the terms used suggest this, echoing those by Cicero noted earlier.

In 1762, Thomas Sheridan expanded our understanding of the vocal communication of emotion. In a series of lectures on elocution, and more specifically in one particular lecture called "Tone," Sheridan showed quite clearly his belief in the universality of emotional expression communicated by the voice (Alston, 1968b, p. 101). He stated:

> it was necessary to society, and to the state of human nature in general, that the language of the animal passions of man at least, should be fixed, self-evident, and universally intelligible.

Even more clear is his comment just after this:

> All our affections therefore and emotions, belonging to man in his animal state, are so distinctly characterized, by certain marks, that they can not be mistaken; and this language of the passions, carries with it the stamp of its almighty Artificer; utterly unlike the poor workmanship of imperfect man, as it is not only understood by all the different nations of the world, without pains or study; but excites also similar emotions, or corresponding effects in all minds alike.

The universality of the vocal expression of certain fundamental emotions has been proposed more recently (Scherer, Helfrich, & Scherer, 1980). Even those who advocate such a position, however, might find Sheridan's proposition unacceptable. His concept of "all the different nations of the world" must of necessity have been different from that held in the late 20th century. Even so, it is still difficult to accept his comment uncritically.

The words "at least" in the first Sheridan quotation seem to indicate that he was aware of different types of emotion, and provide a link with his later and more insightful comments in 1781 (Alston, 1969). By this stage, he had developed the idea of two types of emotion: the natural and the instituted. The first are of the type described already: the animal passions, covering sorrow, lamentation, mirth, joy, hatred, anger, love, and pity—some of which would today be considered basic emotions and probably universally expressed. The instituted emotions are those learned within society. Their nature, however, is not clear. Sheridan does no more than propose that they mark "different operations, exertions, and emotions of the intellect and fancy, in producing their ideas" (Alston, 1969, p. 121). He does write, however, that they will vary across countries.

Noah Webster is one other 18th century writer who comments on the voice, this time from an American perspective. As well as writing dictionaries and proposing spelling reforms, Webster wrote a series of dissertations on the English language in 1789. His writings (Alston, 1967a, p. 108) contain one of the earliest overt comments on voice as a marker of social class as well as locality. In speaking of the peculiarities of the pronunciation of the country people of New England—which he saw as attracting ridicule—he commented:

> Words are drawled out in careless lazy manner, or the sound finds a passage thro the nose.
> Nothing can be so disagreeable as that drawling, whining cant that distinguishes a certain class of people.

Here we see reflected in Webster's words the feeling that certain features of accents, in this case long-term vocal features, are less pleasing or agreeable than others. The growing interest in elocution that took hold in the 19th century in Britain and the United States cemented that notion in the minds of many. It was an idea that was inevitably linked covertly, and sometimes overtly, to the class structure of the two countries.

In Western classical tradition, then, the voice has played an important role in human social interaction. As we have seen, this role covers aspects of social identity such as gender and nationality, as well as personality characteristics and the communication of emotion. These functions of the voice have continued to be studied in the 20th century. Historically, non-Western cultures seem not to have placed such emphasis on rhetoric and spoken drama (and hence on the voice). In the 20th century, however, many cultures have become interested in vocal communication in social interaction. This, coupled with the explosion of tertiary education, particularly in the West, has led to a corresponding wealth of material on the voice in academic writings.

The Study of Voice Across Academic Disciplines

The study of voice has been fragmented across a number of academic disciplines. From a social interaction point of view, the most important are phonetics, communication studies, psychology, and to a lesser extent medicine. Even within these disciplines, however, voice has not always been dealt with adequately. In later chapters, where it is thought to be relevant, the material covered will be linked to specific disciplines. The overall layout of the book, however, will not echo these disciplinary divisions. When focusing on the functions of voice it is necessary to cross such boundaries. That said, some understanding of the types of issues and concepts emphasized by these disciplines may provide a useful precursor to the later chapters. To that end an introduction is provided here. The medical account of voice will not be covered in this book, although a very brief note of the major concerns of the area will be given later in this chapter.

Phonetics

Phonetics is the discipline concerned with the physical measurement of speech and to a lesser extent the voice. During the 20th century particularly, the emphasis on physical measurement has manifested itself in four major ways: articulatory, acoustic, physiological, and aerodynamic. Articulatory phonetics is concerned primarily with describing speech sounds in terms of the way we as speakers articulate them using our vocal organs. Figure 1.1 shows a cross-section through the vocal tract; on the left, the three major vocal tract cavities are shown; on the right, the major articulatory vocal organs: the tongue, lips, teeth, lower jaw, soft palate, and larynx are shown. Once sound has been produced at the larynx, we then modify that sound in the three major cavities: the pharyngeal cavity, nasal cavity, and oral cavity.

Speech sounds are shaped mainly by the vocal organs in and around the oral cavity and traditionally have been described in terms of the positions or configurations of those organs. Thus, vowel sounds are usually described by indicating tongue height in the mouth and how much the tongue is retracted or pushed forward in the mouth, together with the shape of the lips. For example, the vowel in the English word *pit* is described as a front, high, spread vowel, while that in the word *put* is described as a back, high, rounded vowel. With the former vowel, we are describing it as articulated with the tongue high (i.e., held close to the roof of the mouth) and toward the front of the mouth and with the lips spread; in the latter case, we are describing the vowel as being articulated high in the mouth with the tongue retracted and the lips rounded.

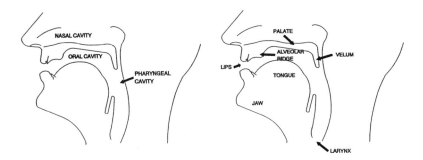

Figure 1.1. Cross-section through the human vocal tract. Major vocal cavities shown in the left-hand figure; major articulatory vocal organs shown in the right-hand figure.

Consonants are dealt with in a somewhat similar way, although describing the place of articulation alone does not distinguish all the possible consonants adequately in any language. Further parameters are needed. There are two major ones, the first is often called the manner of articulation, which effectively describes the way and extent to which we constrict the airstream with our vocal organs; the second is voicing, which refers to whether a particular type of sound is produced at the larynx or not during the production of the consonant. Thus, the consonant at the beginning of the English word *pig*—/p/—is called a labial or bilabial consonant (the place of articulation) because the major air constriction occurs at the lips. It is also called a stop consonant (the manner of articulation) referring to the way we stop the airstream completely at the designated point—in this case, the lips—before releasing the air in a burst of sound. It is also said to be voiceless because we do not vibrate our vocal folds during its production. The consonant at the end of the same word—/g/—is called a velar, voiced stop. Its major point of constriction is close to the soft palate or velum, hence the name velar. It too stops and releases the airstream in a similar way to the /p/, but sound is produced at the larynx, the vocal folds are vibrating, so it is called a voiced stop, rather than voiceless. For a more comprehensive account of vowel articulation and speech sound articulation generally, the reader is referred to Ladefoged (1993).

These concepts have been introduced here, albeit in a very brief way, because one of the main ways of describing voice has been by reference to its articulations. The same types of parameters—position of the various vocal organs, whether voicing occurs at the larynx or not, and the type of sound that is produced—have been used to describe voice types (Laver, 1980). We will return to this in more detail in Chapter 2, although it is worth pointing out here that the tongue in particular performs highly complex movements in moving from speech sound to speech sound in a continuous stream of speech. The articulatory parameters used to describe speech sounds do not do justice to this complexity. Stone (1991), using a range of imaging techniques (X ray, computed tomography, magnetic resonance imaging, and ultrasound), has shown that tongue shape and position interact in the production of vowels, and that both length and cross-section of the tongue may be divided into a number of semi-independent segments that together form highly complex and multiple shapes. This will inevitably have an impact on the production of voice as well as speech sounds.

The other major ways of physically measuring speech sounds have also been used to describe the voice. These are by reference to the physiological and aerodynamic characteristics of the sounds, and by electronically measuring the acoustic signal.

In the description of speech sounds, one important reason to consider the physiological mechanisms that underlie speech production is to account for the degree of tension present in the vocal tract during production. Although this has not been dealt with in a comprehensive way in the major forms of speech sound description, tension may be used to distinguish pairs of sounds that could not otherwise be characterized uniquely by referring to the articulations alone. Thus, the vowel in the English word *pit* may be distinguished from the vowel in the word *peat* by referring to the degree of tension. These two vowels are produced in very similar positions in the oral cavity (they are both high, front, spread vowels) so need other, non-articulatory, descriptive parameters. One is supplied by reference to the duration of the vowel, another by reference to the degree of muscular tension used in producing each vowel. The second example is called a tense vowel, while the first is called a lax (i.e., non-tense) vowel. As will be shown in Chapter 2, tension is an important parameter for describing voice. Once again, therefore, the same type of description is used in the phonetics of voice, as in the phonetics of speech sounds.

An aerodynamic account of speech and voice is concerned above all with the characteristics of the airstream, its control and efficient use. Two recent and useful references relating to an aerodynamic approach to voice are Schutte (1992) and Titze (1992). The former discusses a number of aerodynamic measurements, while the latter considers vocal efficiency—an important concept for those who use the voice professionally (see Chapter 4 for an introduction to this area) and in the voice pathology area. Figure 1.2 shows a stylized cross-section through the larynx and the top of the trachea or windpipe—the tube running between the larynx and the bronchii, which distribute the air throughout the lungs when breathing in and concentrate it into the trachea when breathing out. The figure is shown as if viewed from the front. The space between the vocal folds is usually referred to as the glottis. The cartilages surrounding the vocal folds are shaded and the soft tissue, comprising tendon, muscles, and mucous membrane, and which includes the vocal folds, is shown in white. At the top is the epiglottis, which serves to cover the larynx when swallowing food, preventing the food from entering the glottis.

Air is pushed up the trachea from the lungs by applying force from the muscles of the abdomen, diaphragm, and the intercostal muscles of the rib cage. If the vocal folds in the larynx are closed, pressure builds up in the subglottal area—the area immediately below the vocal folds. When sufficient pressure has been built up to overcome the force holding the vocal folds shut, they are forced open and a small quantity of air passes into the pharyngeal cavity. The velocity of the air passing through the glottis causes a drop in pressure in the subglottal area allowing the vocal folds to snap shut and the pressure to build up again. The cycle is repeated many times a second. This process for opening and closing the vocal folds, resulting in their vibration, is referred to as the Bernoulli effect. It was the otolaryngologist Woldmar Tonndorf who in 1925 suggested that this effect, first described by the Swiss mathematician and physicist Daniel Bernoulli, might provide an understanding of laryngeal opening and closing (Cooper, 1989). The resulting vibration of the vocal folds as they open and close sets up oscillations in the air particles in the vocal cavities. The air itself does not travel from the vocal tract to our ears. Rather, the oscillations produce a ripple effect as a stone does when dropped into a pool of water. Thus the sound travels through the air and the oscillating air particles stimulate our auditory system.

When the vocal folds vibrate and generate sound, we speak of this as voicing. The most usual type of voicing is often called modal voice, to avoid the negative implications associated with using a word such

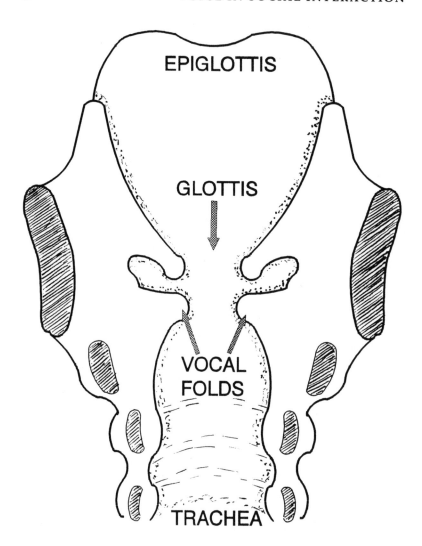

Figure 1.2. Schematized Cross-Section Through the Human Larynx Seen From the Front

as normal. We are capable of manipulating the configuration and tension of the vocal folds to produce a range of different types of "voiced" sound. Not all speech sounds or voice types utilize voicing, however. As already indicated, when the vocal folds are open and air passes through into the vocal tract without causing the folds to vibrate, we refer to this as voiceless. This does not mean that no sound is produced. The resulting sound in this instance is still audible rather like random or white noise. The ability to use both voiced and voiceless sounds, plus the various configurations, types, and degree of tension we can produce in the vocal folds, means that we have a considerable range of sounds at our disposal either for speech purposes or for more long-term communicative purposes such as those already noted: the communication of emotion and attitude, group and personal identity. This type of activity at the larynx is called phonation. Laver (1993) defines phonation as the use of the laryngeal system plus an airstream to generate an audible source of acoustic energy, and while some types of phonation, such as voicelessness, result in a continuous input into the supralaryngeal cavities, voicing creates a pulsed or vibrating input.

Finally, the electronic measurement of the acoustic signal has, in the 20th century, become one of the major ways of measuring voice and speech. The vocal mechanism is sometimes referred to as a source-filter mechanism. The sound produced by the vibration of the vocal folds in the larynx is the sound source, which is then filtered through the pharyngeal, oral, and nasal cavities. At a basic level physical measures of this filtered sound fall into three types. First, there are those underlying the perceptual feature of loudness such as amplitude; second, there are measures underlying the perceptual feature of pitch, such as fundamental frequency; and third, those related to time such as the duration of speech sounds. A detailed description of the physical measures underlying these three parameters will be provided in Chapter 3, as will a description of the more complex measures such as the spectral analysis of the voice.

The physical description of voice is of necessity phonetic, whether it be an articulatory description of the vocal organs, accounts of physiological and aerodynamic features, or values associated with various acoustic and temporal parameters. John Laver's work of the 1960s and 1970s, culminating in his 1980 book, *The Phonetic Description of Voice Quality*, demonstrates this well. One of his major contributions is at the articulatory level, however. His development of the notion of articulatory setting into a full phonetic model has changed the way phoneticians and other researchers in the speech and voice area think about voice quality. Laver's model of voice quality will be discussed in Chapter 2.

By "voice quality" Laver (1980) refers to the more-or-less permanent articulatory settings that underlie an individual's speech. The present book includes under the term *voice* not only these quasi-permanent voice qualities covered by Laver's articulatory settings, but tension settings, long-term dynamic features such as pitch and loudness, and temporal features such as duration and speech rate. We will return to this in Chapter 2 when more comprehensive accounts of these terms will be provided.

Communication Studies and Psychology

We have proposed that a phonetic description of voice is needed to describe the sound and the way that sound is formed. In this book, however, we are concerned mainly with the way the voice functions in human social interaction, as a marker of group and personal identity and as a means of communicating emotion and attitude. This takes us beyond a phonetic description. Communication studies and psychology are the disciplines where most of these other areas of voice study are to be found, although some studies of vocal function have been conducted within phonetics and sociolinguistics.

Psychology is an umbrella term covering many subdisciplines. Voice and speech have been studied mainly within developmental, cognitive, and social psychology. It is the last that mostly concerns us here. In communication studies, which also covers researchers with a vast range of diverse interests, those studying voice have tended to use psychological methodologies. As a result, we will discuss these two disciplines together.

Within social psychology and communication studies, the voice is considered to be a form of nonverbal behavior used for communication within social interaction. When human beings interact, language and nonverbal behavior usually work together as a package of behaviors that tend to reinforce one another. This often results in redundancy in the message, in the sense that interactants may be able to decode the same information on more than one channel of communication. These channels may also oppose one another, however, providing, as it were, confusing double messages. The various channels of nonverbal communication are for the most part well known. Individual writers vary in what they include in such a catalogue of behaviors, but it seems clear that most would agree on the major channels. These are: voice, gaze, facial expression, gesture, posture, personal distance and orientation, and touch.

In addition, time, clothing, body size, even body odor may be included, depending on one's definition of communication. If one accepts communication to include everything, and not to be dependent on intention, the list of communicative behaviors can become very long indeed (see, e.g., the definition developed by Watzlawick, Beavin, and Jackson [1968] as compared with the distinction made by Lyons [1977] of communicative and informative signals). Some of the more important concepts related to communication, including its scope, will be taken up in more detail in Chapter 7.

It is fast becoming a truism that to understand nonverbal communication one needs to consider the whole package of behaviors. While one would not want to argue against this per se, those who advocate such a position sometimes gloss over the roles of each channel in the package, taking little account of the complexity or otherwise of any one channel. Voice usually fares poorly in such models (as it does in most), and when included is often represented by a mix of features that lacks coherence.

When studying the voice from a psychological point of view, we need to ensure we measure a coherent set of vocal parameters. To achieve coherence, we need first to take account of the distinction between perceptual and physical features (such as pitch vs. fundamental frequency); we also need to make the distinction between speech-related features (such as speech errors or fluency) and vocal features (such as loudness or pitch). In addition, if we are making physical measurements, we need either to use a set that covers all three basic parameters of voice (measures underlying pitch, loudness, and time) or, better, to select features that we can justify theoretically as having relevance to just that aspect of the interaction with which we are concerned. The problem, then, is not that voice is not included in models of nonverbal communication or empirical studies conducted in this area (indeed, many researchers within social psychology and communication studies have included the voice in their research), but that it is often not given sufficient weight or is not broken down into its component parts, either at all or in a coherent way.

Hall (1963) proposed eight behaviors that made up his proxemic system of social behavior. Given this focus, he was mainly interested in interpersonal distance. The only mention of voice is a vocal loudness scale: loudness will usually vary depending on how far away from our interactant we are. Even in a proxemic account of interaction, however, one might have expected the inclusion of a feature such as pitch, and perhaps also speech rate, both of which may vary with the distance between interactants. Another major researcher in this area is Mehrabian (1969). He does not include voice at all in his concept of communicative immediacy, which seems to be analogous to Hall's proxemics. He does, however, discuss several features of voice under the heading of verbalizations. These include duration, rate, volume, intonation (pitch variation), halting quality, and speech errors, a mixed bag of voice dynamic features (volume, intonation, duration, and rate) and speech features (halting quality and errors). He shows how these have been related to dimensions such as arousal or positivity.

One researcher whose work we will consider in more detail later is Patterson (1983). He includes a number of features related to speech and voice in what he refers to as a tentative list. Relevant ones here are talking duration, possibly also interruptions, and paralinguistic cues (including at least speech rate and volume). As can be seen, these seem to emphasize temporal features. Finally, Argyle (1988) has the single nonverbal signal of nonverbal vocalizations, which he later expands to include duration, amplitude, fundamental frequency, plus the more complex measures of the frequency spectrum and pitch contours. This is a more coherent list than most. Argyle also shows he is aware of the difference between such objective physical measures as most of these are and their perceptual counterparts. Along with Klaus Scherer, whose work will also be considered in detail in later chapters, Argyle is one of the very few people working in the area of nonverbal communication to acknowledge not only the complexity of the voice, and the need to distinguish speech from voice, but also to recognize its various parts from both physical and perceptual points of view.

This book is concerned only with the voice. In a sense, then, one could claim it is reductionist. It is not meant to imply, however, that voice, the other nonverbal behaviors, and the verbal component do not influence one another or our perception of, for example, affect and identity. Clearly, in social interaction all channels influence perception, as indeed will the context in which the interaction takes place and the transactional nature of most interactions. In addition, the relationship among all these factors is multifaceted and not linear. One of the overarching aims of this book, however, is to provide researchers with specific information about the voice and to stimulate research into voice. To do this, it must examine the vocal channel separately.

Research in the voice area within social psychology and communication studies is, as Goldbeck, Tolkmitt, and Scherer (1988) point out, fraught with complex and practical difficulties that have not encouraged studies that combine the various vocal and nonvocal channels. One could say the same thing about the voice channel alone. Vocal communication is not only complex but compound, in the sense that a variety of features are included in this channel. The voice should not be thought of as a single item. While it is accepted that the principle of a communication package is a valid one, the voice itself is a communication package consisting of a number of independently measurable behaviors. To understand it adequately, then, it needs to be considered separately from the nonvocal channels, or, if coupled with nonvocal features, appropriate features that form a coherent set should be used. One other reason to consider the voice separately is that there are times when it is the only nonverbal channel available in an interaction, or at least is the most important: telephone calls and talk-back radio would be examples, as would a conversation where at least one of the interactants is blind. In such a case, the voice increases in importance.

Medicine

Medicine is the third major discipline that has dealt with the voice and will be covered here very briefly. *Medicine* is another umbrella term that covers many disciplines. The main ones related to the study of the voice are voice pathology and psychiatry, but we need also to consider the general practice of medicine, particularly as it concerns the diagnosis of physical illness and disease. There has been a long history of using the voice for diagnostic purposes. In Western traditions, this goes back at least to classical Greece. In addition to these areas, however, voice may mark hormonal changes occurring within the body. The voice, then, may act as a marker of anatomical and physiological abnormalities, psychiatric conditions such as schizophrenia and manic-depression, acute and chronic medical conditions, plus hormonal changes relating to, for example, sexual arousal, puberty, menstruation and pregnancy. These areas will not be considered further.

Overview of the Book

In providing an account of voice that is concerned with how it functions within the social interaction, then, we need to cover these disciplines: phonetics, communication studies, and psychology and, where appropriate, their subdisciplines. The theoretical framework we develop to account for vocal function must be drawn from these same disciplines. In particular, models of nonverbal communication that are specifically functional need to be addressed. The principal aims of the book may be stated as follows:

1. To provide an interdisciplinary account of voice
2. To provide a comprehensive exploration of the physical and perceptual measurement of voice
3. To develop a theoretical framework for the study of vocal communication
4. To provide an historical account of vocal function

Although all the disciplines discussed will be covered in the book, as noted, the layout will not follow disciplinary boundaries. That said, some chapters will relate more closely to one discipline than another. As far as possible, the structure of the book has been developed to suit both a reader who wishes to read from start to finish and one who wishes to select specific chapters. To this end, each chapter is designed to function as much as possible as an independent unit. All readers are advised, however, to consult Chapters 1, 2, and 3 before attempting to read the later chapters. These provide an introduction to the terminology necessary to understand Chapters 4 through 8. In overall terms, the layout moves from the description and physical measurement of voice on to an account of how the voice functions in social interaction. Following this is the chapter dealing with methodological issues related to the study of voice and then the proposed theoretical framework for vocal function.

Chapter 2 provides a 20th century articulatory description of voice. As such, it is largely phonetic. It looks at the work of one of the few major writers in this area—John Laver. Laver's (1980) phonetic model of voice quality is described. The main concerns of phoneticians working in the voice area are considered; namely, the standardization of terminology and the development of descriptive phonetic models. Chapter 3 also covers a phonetic account of voice but this time focuses on physical measurement. This includes an introduction to the acoustic and temporal measurement of voice, but is written for the person with little or no background in acoustics. Its aim is to provide an understanding of the basic terms and measures, to allow the reader to follow the arguments and presentations of researchers working in acoustics. Glossaries of important terms have been provided at the end of each of these two chapters.

Chapters 4 and 5 present a largely psychological account of voice; a perspective drawn mainly from social psychology and communication studies although some studies from sociolinguistics will be included. Chapter 4 is concerned with the vocal communication of identity, and is divided into two main sections. First, aspects of group identity are considered. This section is subdivided into a number of social categories such as age, gender, occupation, and language/accent group, all of which have been linked to vocal communication. The second major section is concerned with how individual, as against group, identity is reflected in the voice. This takes us into the area of personality characteristics and self-perception, as well as the vocal communication of the unique individual. Chapter 5 covers the communication of emotion and attitude. In addition to providing some detail of the communication of discrete emotions such as anger, fear, or elation, this section covers the more general affective states such as arousal and positivity/negativity. A number of research issues related to this area are also considered. The dimensional approaches related to the study of affective states and attitude are covered, and the small literature on vocal persuasion introduced.

Chapter 6 provides an introduction to a number of methodological issues concerned with the study of voice. Recording of voices will be considered, as will the construction of stimulus tapes for perceptual studies. Types of questionnaires that have been used in the study of voice will also be presented.

Chapter 7 introduces a proposed theoretical framework to explain the functions of voice in social interaction. The framework consists of four parts. The first is represented by the phonetic description of voice covered in Chapters 2 and 3. Two other parts of the framework are presented in Chapter 7. One is represented by Patterson's (1983) sequential functional model of nonverbal behavior, and communication accommodation theory (Coupland, Coupland, Giles, & Henwood, 1988; Gallois, Franklyn-Stokes, Giles, & Coupland, 1988; Giles & Coupland, 1991a). These two theories provide explanations of the dynamic aspects of social interaction; they are models of social exchange. The other part of the framework is represented by Scherer's (1978, 1979a; Goldbeck et al., 1988) modified Brunswikian lens model. This relates internalized emotions and personality traits to vocal expression, and allows the latter to be related to a listener's perceptions and that person's subsequent attributions of the speaker. The strengths and weaknesses of these models for explaining vocal function are considered. In addition, as the models are introduced other theoretical concerns are aired. These include the definition of communication itself, and the notions of indexicality and symbolism, raised by Scherer (1988) and Laver (1974, 1976).

Finally, Chapter 8 brings together the work presented in earlier chapters by constructing a taxonomy of vocal function. This provides the summary of how the voice functions in social interaction, indicating how some of the functions relate to one another. In the final section, the multidisciplinary account of voice is stressed, and a number of issues relating to our understanding of voice and its functions within social contexts are raised, including the influence on social interaction of the institutionalized structures of society and the values and norms they uphold. These issues are seen as part of the fourth dimension of the proposed theoretical framework.

This book considers vocal communication in a number of ways that together may form a rather different approach from other texts in the area. It is interdisciplinary, providing the reader with both a phonetic description of voice and the methodological insights gained from psychology and communication studies. It emphasizes the social nature of vocal communication, in particular framing the voice literature by the concept of social identity. Further, while the specific aims of the book are as listed above, at a more general level it is hoped that the following chapters help to promote an interest in the study of voice and vocal communication by indicating how to do it. Finally, a four-level theoretical framework is proposed to provide appropriate explanations (given the approach taken) for voice in social interaction.

CHAPTER TWO

The Articulatory Account of Voice

As indicated in Chapter 1, the physical description of voice is phonetic. In the next two chapters we examine the two major types of phonetic description—articulatory (this chapter) and acoustic (Chapter 3), although some account of vocal tension will also be given. Unlike in the last chapter, we are now concerned with the development of a physical description of voice in the 20th century. The present chapter concentrates on the work of John Laver in the 1960s and 1970s, and in so doing introduces some of the key issues surrounding the articulatory description of voice such as the standardization of terminology, the scope of individual terms, and the need for a coherent model based on accepted phonetic practices. The aim of this chapter (and the next), then, is to provide the reader with the means to describe the voice physically, which may then be used in interpreting the later chapters. At the end of the chapter a glossary of the most important terms that have been used and that appear throughout the book has been provided.

The Twentieth Century Articulatory Account of Voice

In the 20th century, our knowledge of vocal articulations and air stream mechanisms has been considerably expanded. In large part this has been due to the development of more sophisticated measurement techniques. The need to standardize on measurement techniques and descriptive terminology was recognized early. By the end of the 19th century, the eminent British phonetician Henry Sweet (1900) was attempting to relate voice labels such as "clear," "dull," and "gutterality" to specific modifications of the speech organs. That is, he was attempting to standardize subjective labels for voice by relating them to articulation. Sapir (1927) in his classic paper on speech and personality was aware of his own inability to classify voice types adequately, while recognizing the importance of the voice to carry both social and personal information. Since that time much work has been conducted toward voice classification. Unfortunately, the tradition of using impressionistic labels without relating them to articulatory, aerodynamic, and physiological mechanisms has continued despite the efforts of Sweet and the concerns of Sapir. As a result, a confusing use of terminology has been generated. Two writers of central concern to the measurement of voice who have made considerable efforts to avoid these problems are John Laver and Klaus Scherer (see, e.g., Laver, 1980, and Scherer, 1986a). Scherer, whose work will be dealt with in later chapters, acknowledges the important influence that Laver has had on his own approaches to voice. Much of Laver's work in this area has been concerned with overcoming the two problems of standardizing terminology and relating the subsequent labels to vocal mechanisms.

Laver's Model

Laver's model of voice is centrally concerned with voice quality, which he explains most fully in his 1980 monograph: *The Phonetic Description of Voice Quality*. As points of departure, he uses Abercrombie's (1967) notion that voice quality refers to the characteristics of the voice that are present more or less all the time an individual is speaking, and the idea of an articulatory setting, a term he adopts from Honikman (1964). This refers to the tendency for the vocal apparatus to take up particular long-term muscular adjustments underlying the movement involved in producing a sequence of speech sounds or segments.

These muscular settings can be configurations of the larynx or be supralaryngeal, involving any or all of the vocal organs above the larynx. Thus, for example, an individual may habitually adopt a laryngeal setting that produces a creaky voice quality. In this case, the muscles of the larynx configure the vocal folds in such a way that when the individual speaks, the voice quality underlying the speech segments is like, as Catford (1964, p. 32) puts it, a "rapid series of taps, like a stick being run along a railing." Another, possibly more familiar, laryngeal setting is whisper, again produced by a particular configuration of the vocal folds. Laver (1980) suggests that this setting is characterized in particular by a triangular opening of the glottis affecting about a third of the full length of the vocal folds. Examples of supralaryngeal articulatory settings would be pursed lips or a retracted tongue setting. All of these voice qualities, being habitual settings, would underlie any movement involved in producing a sequence of speech segments produced by the individual speaker. Tables 2.1 and 2.2, presented later in the chapter, provide a list of Laver's proposed articulatory settings. As will be noted below, long-term settings may refer not only to articulations but degrees of tension also.

The development of the concept of settings may be traced back through the work of Laver and Honikman to Sweet (1932), who writes of the organic basis of different languages, and perhaps even to the 17th century phonetician John Wallis, introduced in the last chapter, who wrote of different articulations characterizing different speech communities (Kemp, 1972).

Laver (1980) also follows Abercrombie (1967) in separating voice quality from what Abercrombie calls features of voice dynamics. Abercrombie includes under this term, loudness, tessitura (or pitch range characteristic of an individual or social group), register (see below for an account of this), pitch fluctuations (the melody of speech), as well as tempo, continuity, and rhythm. As the labels suggest, these correspond to the three fundamental descriptive parameters of voice and speech—loudness, pitch, and time.

Although Laver (1980) separates dynamic features from voice quality, it is interesting to note that in an earlier analysis (Laver, 1968) they were included under the heading of laryngeal setting along with laryngeal voice qualities, acknowledging the integral relationship between some elements of the two types of feature (in particular, the fact that loudness and pitch are controlled mainly by the larynx). Loudness, pitch, and temporal features of voice and speech are often grouped together under the label prosodic (rather than dynamic) features. In the present book, Abercrombie's term *dynamic* will be preferred as it seems to link these features to vocal change and to an interactive use of voice more clearly than the rather more abstract term *prosodic*, and thus is more suitable for the approach adopted here.

As a phonetician, Laver (1968, 1974, 1980) relates his concept of voice quality very closely to phonetics/linguistics. One way this is manifested is by Laver maintaining the traditional linguistic divisions of linguistic, paralinguistic, and extralinguistic when discussing the description of voice.

A linguistic level of description is concerned with the verbal rather than nonverbal aspects of speech. Of particular importance here is that it deals with the segmental elements of speech (i.e., the individual speech sounds). The term *paralinguistic*, on the other hand, seems to have been used for the first time by Hill (1958) to cover the expressive features of speech, and the nonvocal phenomena described by Birdwhistell (1952) under the name kinesics. Trager (1958) then picked it up in the same year as Hill to cover voice quality (see below) and vocalizations (noises accompanying speech). Above all, paralinguistic covers culturally determined behavior relating to long-term aspects of speech and voice rather than the short-term segmental aspects. Finally, by extralinguistic is usually meant the very long-term or permanent characteristics of an individual's voice that are, essentially, nonlinguistic in that they have no meaningful relationship with the linguistic elements of speech.

The maintenance of this tripartite division is important to Laver's (1980) phonetic model, as his concept of settings operates at all three levels. Long-term settings (articulatory and tension) can operate at the linguistic level. Thus, for example, the setting of tenseness characterizes two tones in the Vietnamese language system (Thompson, 1965). Vietnamese, like several of the world's languages, is characterized by a system of tones, two of which are distinguished by the degree of tension present in the voice when producing them. This tense-lax distinction also characterizes the vowel system of the African language of Twi (Painter, 1973), while in Gujarati a distinction between breathy voice, a laryngeal setting, and regular voicing has been noted (Firth, 1957). The major components of breathy voice are laxness (low tension) and a partial escape of air through the glottis. Regular voicing refers to the most usual type of vocal fold vibration used for speech, as described in Chapter 1, and referred to there as modal. Although all these examples refer to individual speech segments, when used in speech, that is when placed in a sequence of segments, the effect of the setting, whether it be tenseness, laxness, breathiness, or whatever, tends to influence more than the segment in question. The effect carries over to neighboring segments. This is known as coarticulation.

Settings can also operate in a somewhat longer time frame paralinguistically. Speakers manipulate settings in shifting speech style. So the laryngeal setting of whisper, for example, may be consciously adopted to indicate confidentiality or conspiracy. In such situations, sequences of speech lasting from a second or two up to several minutes will occur while the setting remains basically unchanged. At this level, Laver refers to articulatory settings as belonging to the domain of tone of voice rather than voice quality. Finally, settings can operate as the quasi-permanent features already noted, that is, an individual's habitual use of voice qualities such as creaky voice or tense voice or the habitual use of a retracted tongue, for example. This is the extralinguistic level and it is only at this level that settings are referred to as voice qualities by Laver.

The time frame represented by this tripartite division has some importance to a functional approach to voice. The quasi-permanent voice qualities will function rather differently from the more ephemeral, shorter, tones of voice. In this book, however, the close link to linguistics/phonetics will not be maintained. By opting for a phonetic description of voice quality, Laver was constrained by this, giving rise to the acknowledgment that a study of voice quality was only of secondary importance to a segmental analysis of speech. In the present book, voice has primary importance. Linguistic functions will have little importance here, and the terms *paralinguistic* and *extralinguistic* will not be used. Settings that could be said to function paralinguistically or extralinguistically will be distinguished here in terms of their role in communicating group and personal identity, emotion, and attitude in social interactions.

The distinction drawn by Laver (1980) between the dynamic features of voice and the longer term voice qualities will be maintained. Both will be included here. As we have already seen, group and personal categorization using the voice will often make use of pitch, speech rate, loudness, and so forth as well as voice qualities. Whichever we are concerned with, however, it is the common rather than distinguishing vocal features underlying any sequence of speech sounds that interests us here. It is precisely because they are common to a sequence of speech sounds, rather than being transitory features that vary over milliseconds, that they are ideally suited to function as markers of group and personal identity, to be used strategically in social interaction.

Before leaving the tripartite division of linguistic, paralinguistic, and extralinguistic, it is worthwhile noting that articulatory settings operating at the three different levels may cancel each other out. More precisely, the effect of a setting at one level may be neutralized by that at another level. A laryngeal setting such as breathiness used habitually as a quasi-permanent voice quality could be neutralized when the person adopts a whispery phonation—a different laryngeal setting—for confidentiality. Similarly, the configurations of the vocal organs at the linguistic level may also have the effect of neutralizing a longer term setting. A retracted tongue setting used habitually will be effectively neutralized perceptually during the production of vowels articulated in the front part of the mouth. The articulation of these vowels will result in the speaker's tongue being moved away from the habitual retracted setting. Thus, even the quasi-permanent voice qualities may be perceptually distinct only intermittently. There will also be times when settings will not neutralize one another, but will, rather, form a compound setting. A nasal setting, for example, could quite easily exist side by side with a laryngeal setting such as breathiness, or a supralaryngeal setting such as a retracted tongue.

In Chapter 1 a number of similarities between phonetic approaches to a segmental analysis and an analysis of voice were noted. The possibilities for neutralization and the formation of compound settings highlights another similarity. In both the domains of segmental analysis and voice we can find evidence for parametric and linear or serial relationships among features. A parametric approach is concerned with the covariation of features, whereas a linear or serial approach is concerned with abutting units of varying duration (Laver, 1993). The formation of compound settings is an example of the parametric nature of articulatory settings, whereas the neutralization of one setting by another indicates that there are times when they are manifested serially. This echoes the way segmental features may be related.

While intent on developing a phonetic description of voice quality, Laver also acknowledged a functional perspective by referring on a number of occasions to the indexicality of voice quality and the need to place this within a broader framework of semiotics (Laver, 1968, 1980; Laver & Trudgill, 1979). By indexicality, Laver meant the way the voice may refer to a characteristic of the individual's psychological or social identity. Laver (1968) outlined a scheme, indeed, based on material in Abercrombie (1967), in which voice quality functioned indexically as a marker of biological, psychological, and social information. He did not really develop this, however. Pittam (1986) took this one step further by proposing a number of functional categorizations for both voice quality and tone of voice based on the social interaction, but did not place this work within a semiotic framework as Laver had proposed.

Semiotics will not be used in the present work to provide an explanation of vocal function. For one thing, the roles of speaker and hearer in social interactions have not been adequately theorized in the semiotic framework. The concept of indexicality, however, will be taken up in more detail in Chapter 7 to allow a comparison of Laver's (1968) ideas of how voice quality functions with those of Scherer, who uses another concept found within semiotics—the symbol—to describe the vocal communication of affect. Both concepts will be discussed there.

The Standardization of Terminology

As noted, Laver's work in this area has been, at a fundamental level, an attempt to overcome the problems of impressionistic labeling of voice types that are not related to physical mechanisms, and the proliferation of confusing terminology. Unfortunately, throughout the 20th century, there has been, even within the phonetic literature, a lack of consistency in describing certain voice types. For example, voiced creak (Catford, 1964); trill plus voice (Sprigg, 1978); vocal fry (Wendahl, Moore, & Hollien, 1963), and laryngealization (Ladefoged, 1971), have all been used to describe what is apparently the same laryngeal setting. Descriptions of the physiological characteristics of voice types and of their acoustic correlates have appeared in the literature from a very early time (e.g., Catford, 1964; Pike, 1943; Zemlin, 1964). Such work is of great value. Its impact is lessened, however, not only by the inconsistency just noted, but more importantly, perhaps, by disagreements on which articulatory parameters are associated with which voice types and with which acoustic correlates. In the present chapter, we are concerned with an articulatory description of voice. Acoustics will be the concern of the next chapter. However, the ability to describe the voice accurately and consistently in some standardized way such as the articulations involved is fundamental to an interest in its acoustic (not to mention its perceptual) measurement. As Sapir (1927) rightly pointed out, we need to know what it is we are measuring.

Another area where we find little consistency is in the use of the term *register* (Colton, 1969; Hollien, 1972; Morner, Fransson, & Fant, 1964). This is a term long used to describe the singing voice but less frequently used for the speaking voice. It is above all a perceptual phenomenon that can be described from both an articulatory and an acoustic perspective. Hollien (1972) defines register in terms of the frequency of vibration of the vocal folds (see Chapter 1 for a description of frequency). A vocal register is a series of consecutive frequencies of nearly identical voice quality. He isolates three registers: vocal fry, modal, and falsetto, which he suggests are different laryngeal operations. In other words, they are laryngeal voice settings, each register consisting of a series of the same or similar setting, but each item in the register utilizing a different (but closely related) frequency. As indicated, the concept of register has found greater use in studies of the singing voice, where traditionally several registers with labels such as "chest," "middle," "head," and "falsetto" have been proposed. In terms of how the spoken voice functions within social interactions, it is not clear that the concept of register adds to other concepts we now have: articulatory setting—in particular, laryngeal setting—and frequency.

Another researcher (Titze, 1988) classifies registers in terms of the acoustic characteristics of the transitions that occur as the voice moves from one register to another. Thus, the shift in fundamental frequency (rather than the frequencies themselves) is one of the characteristics used by Titze to classify types of register. Abercrombie (1967) also applies the term to the speaking voice, but unlike Hollien (1972) he does not restrict himself to just three registers, commenting that considerably more must be distinguished. For Abercrombie, a register is not tied to any frequency or frequency range. He does see it, however, as a voice quality arising out of a particular laryngeal configuration. Despite this, as noted above, he prefers to place it in his list of voice dynamic features rather than voice qualities. Altogether, register presents a confusing picture. As Keider, Hurtig, and Titze (1987, p. 223) comment, "the nature, number, names, definitions, boundaries, and essential features of vocal registers can be characterized as a collection of conflicting opinions that often lead to ambiguity and confusion." *Register* will not be used further in the present account of vocal function in social interaction.

One other problem relating to standardization of terminology needs to be mentioned. The term *voice quality* itself has also been used inconsistently. Crystal and Quirk (1964) use it to refer only to a number of laryngeal settings (or *phonation types* to use their term) plus the general concept of resonance. Supralaryngeal settings are not included. Trager (1958) includes a number of qualitatively different phenomena. Thus, we find pitch range, vocal lip control, glottis control, articulation, and rhythm control as well as tempo and resonance included in his definition. These seem to form a mixture of dynamic features, laryngeal and supralaryngeal voice qualities. Costanzo, Markel, and Costanzo (1969) cover only pitch, loudness, and tempo, concepts that in phonetics at least would often be termed prosodic or dynamic features and, as we have seen, are usually considered separately from voice quality. Scherer (1982) covers both laryngeal and supralaryngeal features—including pitch level—and in much of his work supports Laver in linking the terms he uses to describe voice types to specific acoustic and articulatory measurements. In his earlier work (e.g., Scherer, 1970), however, he uses a range of terms such as *pleasantness* and *depth* to describe voice quality. Finally, Laver (1980), as we have noted, covers both laryngeal and supralaryngeal articulatory settings under voice quality, as well as a system of overall vocal tract tension settings (vocal tension is discussed below). He separates voice quality from dynamic features and separates both from temporal features such as speech rate and continuity.

Laver's (1980) set of supralaryngeal and laryngeal articulatory settings are shown in Tables 2.1 and 2.2, respectively. As can be seen in the first of these, Laver was intent on including all relevant supralaryngeal vocal organs (jaw, lips, tongue—including important parts of the tongue such as the tip and blade—the palate and velum) and describing relevant shapes and positions of each (thus, close jaw position; spread lips; position of the tongue against parts of the palate). He also included relevant aspects of the supralaryngeal resonating cavities (nasal and denasal voice; pharyngealized voice). For the laryngeal settings he selected those that appear most frequently in the literature, sometimes drawing a distinction between a setting with voicing and without (thus, creak and creaky voice). In addition, the two major positions of the whole larynx—raised and lowered—were included. As will be seen later, he modified this set for use by voice pathologists and therapists.

Table 2.1   Supralaryngeal Articulatory Settings

close jaw position
open jaw position
protruded jaw position
open lip rounding
close lip rounding
spread lips
labiodentalized voice
tongue tip articulation
tongue blade articulation
retroflex articulation
dentalized voice
alveolarized voice
palato-alveolarized voice
palatalized voice
velarized voice
uvularized voice
pharyngealized voice
laryngo-pharyngealized voice
nasal voice
denasal voice

SOURCE: Adapted from Laver, 1980.

In addition to providing this comprehensive set of articulatory settings, Laver allowed for at least some of these settings to be categorized by scaling conventions. Thus, researchers or practitioners trained in Laver's model can, by listening to a voice, rate it for the presence or absence of each setting and, if present, can indicate the degree of presence. This may be achieved by rating the voice on a numerical scale, using adjectives of degree such as "slight," "moderate," and "extreme," or a system of diacritics. The reader is referred to Laver (1980) for a full description of these settings and their perceptual measurement. Other researchers, some in the voice pathology area, have also been concerned with the standardization of terminology. More recent descriptions of some voice types may be found in Poyatos (1991) and Sonninen and Hurme (1992).

Vocal Tension

As noted above, in addition to the laryngeal and supralaryngeal articulatory settings, Laver (1980) allows for settings of overall mus-

Table 2.2   Laryngeal Articulatory Settings

raised larynx
lowered larynx
modal voice
falsetto
whisper
whispery voice
creak
creaky voice
breathy voice
harsh voice

SOURCE: Adapted from Laver, 1980.

cular tension affecting the whole vocal apparatus; that is, subglottal, laryngeal, and supralaryngeal tension. He includes the distinction of tense and lax voice, representing high and low degrees of overall tension. Although this chapter is concerned primarily with articulations, some account of tension needs to be given. The level of tension present in the vocal apparatus is an important element of the voice, influencing the damping characteristics or degree of absorption of sound of the voice.

Subglottal tension refers to the degree of tension present in the upper part of the trachea, just below the larynx; supralaryngeal tension to that present in the musculature of the vocal tract above the larynx including the tongue, a muscle in its own right. It is the tension in the larynx itself, however, that has attracted most attention in the literature.

Tension can be active or passive. Active tension occurs either when muscle length is decreased while holding tension constant, or by holding length constant and increasing tension; passive tension occurs when a body is acted upon by another body (Colton, 1988). In the case of laryngeal tension, these different types are particularly important for understanding the movement and type of sound produced in the larynx. The amount of passive tension present in the larynx depends on two properties of the vocal folds: elasticity and stiffness. Elasticity refers to the ability of the body in question (in this case the vocal folds), once distorted by another body, to return to its former configuration when the force is removed. Stiffness is the ability to resist distortion. The two parameters most commonly

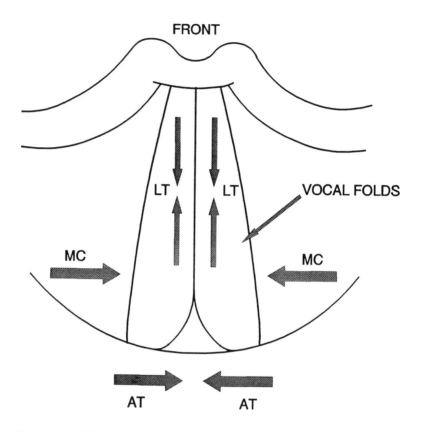

Figure 2.1. Schematized figure of the types of tension acting on the vocal folds.

SOURCE: Adapted from Laver, 1980.
NOTES: LT = Longitudinal Tension; MC = Medial Compression; AT = Adductive Tension

contributing to tenseness and laxness of the larynx and, therefore, influencing our perception of the voice, are adductive tension and medial compression. A third parameter is longitudinal tension. Figure 2.1 (modified from Laver, 1980), showing a stylized glottis viewed from above, illustrates the action of these three parameters.

One of the most important effects laryngeal tension has on the voice is to change fundamental frequency—the frequency with which the vocal folds vibrate. Both active and passive types of tension are thought to affect this, although as Colton (1988) indicates, fundamental frequency is determined not by tension alone but by length and mass of the vocal folds in combination with tension. Human vocal folds are capable of a considerable range of tension, but most of this range is useful only to produce falsetto. For modal voicing, fundamental frequency is produced by an interaction of mass and tension. The overall perceptual effect of tense and lax voice, that is, the degree of tension in the voice, is to increase and decrease pitch and loudness, respectively. However, in articulatory and aerodynamic terms, degree of tension is characterized by a profile of subglottal, laryngeal, and supralaryngeal features. Thus, what we perceive as a tense voice is made up in part by higher air pressure in the subglottal area, the whole larynx raised slightly, constriction of the laryngeal and pharyngeal cavities, a convex surface to the tongue, and vigorous activity of the lips and jaw. Lax voice, on the other hand, tends to be the reverse of these settings. For further characteristics of tense and lax voice generally, readers are referred to Laver (1980) and Colton (1988).

The Application of Laver's Model

Following the publication of his 1980 monograph, Laver became involved in the development of a protocol for the perceptual analysis of what became known as vocal profiles (Laver, Wirz, MacKenzie, & Hiller, 1981). This protocol was developed for, and used for the most part by, speech therapists and pathologists, that is, those needing to diagnose pathological conditions of the voice. This analysis aimed to provide "a statement of the speaker-characterizing long-term features of a person's overall vocal performance" (Laver et al., 1981, p. 139). As such it covered not only laryngeal and supralaryngeal aspects of voice quality, but commented on the dynamic features of pitch and loudness and temporal features such as rate and continuity. As indicated above, the settings listed in the 1980 monograph were modified for this applied setting. Thus, the supralaryngeal and laryngeal settings were divided into categories such as labial and phonation type, and the specific settings listed under these categories.

This is not the place to attempt a detailed evaluation of such a diagnostic tool. A brief comment, however, is perhaps warranted. The pathologist/therapist requires considerable training in the system to perceive accurately and consistently (and reliably when compared

Table 2.3   Simplified Example of Part of the Vocal Profile Analysis Protocol

Category	Neutral	Non-Neutral Normal	Abnormal	Setting	Scalar Degrees Normal	Abnormal
Labial features				Lip rounding	1 2 3	4 5 6
				Lip spreading	1 2 3	4 5 6
				Labiodentalization	1 2 3	4 5 6
				Extensive range	1 2 3	4 5 6
				Minimized range	1 2 3	4 5 6

SOURCE: Adapted from Laver, Wirz, MacKenzie, & Hiller, 1981.

with other therapists) the various settings in patients' voices. They must make decisions about all settings regarding neutrality or otherwise (i.e., a setting is deemed to have deviated from neutrality if the presence of that setting can be detected). If a setting is deemed nonneutral, the pathologist/therapist must then decide whether that deviation is within a normal range rating it (for most settings) on a 6-point scale, with the move from normality to abnormality occurring between scalar degrees 3 and 4. Clearly, as well as issues of accuracy, consistency, and reliability, the system must be normed for all communities for all settings, which raises nontrivial social questions about the setting of those norms. This is not to lessen the value of the work of voice pathologists and therapists, of course, but to acknowledge that decisions of normality are not made in a social vacuum. None of these issues are necessarily problematic, of course. Table 2.3 provides a simplified example from the 1981 vocal profile analysis protocol, showing how, in this case, the labial settings were formatted.

The training of pathologists/therapists in such a system has particular importance here, even though this book does not cover the area of voice pathology, mainly because it echoes in many ways the training of expert judges in numerous psychological perceptual studies of the voice. Concepts such as accuracy, consistency, and reliability, as well as the need to norm measures for the communities studied, are equally important to such expert judges.

The vocal profile analysis protocol represents a major step forward in expert perceptual judgments of the voice. Its use is not necessarily restricted to speech pathologists/therapists, but can be used for other nonapplied perceptual studies. Pittam (1986), for example, used judges trained in the method in his study of a number of laryngeal and supralaryngeal settings. In this case, the notion of normality was not used; the scalar degrees were used as a 6-point interval scale (see Chapter 6 for more details about such scales).

Summary

An articulatory account of voice is one of the most fundamental ways we can describe the long-term vocal sounds that underlie our speech patterns. Unfortunately this has been made problematic by the use of a considerable amount of nonstandard terminology. Laver's (1980) model attempts to overcome this by allowing us to describe the voice in terms of the shape and positioning of the articulatory organs, the level of tension present, the dynamic characteristics such as pitch and loudness, as well as an account of the temporal features such as speech rate and fluency. By describing the voice in this way, we can arrive at a profile of features for any voice.

As we have noted, Laver's (1980) model has been applied to the voice pathology area (Laver et al., 1981). It is essentially the perceptual measurement of the articulations of voice, requiring the training of expert judges in the recognition of each setting and dynamic feature. Perceptual measures of voice can be quantified in articulatory terms, as this one is; in attitudinal terms, in terms of personality characteristics or affect; or in terms of correlates of physical measures, such as ratings of pitch as a perceived measure of the fundamental frequency of voice, or loudness as a perceived measure of amplitude. Whatever the type of measure, there is a clear need for recognizable and standard definitions for the labels we give to voice types.

In a sense, attempting to describe voice types in the way introduced in this chapter is to give support to the anthropophonic approach to phonetic theory put forward by Lindblom (1983). This approach starts from the principle that researchers are (or should be) capable of accounting for all the sound-making potential of the human vocal apparatus. Laver's (1980) model brings us closer to achieving this principle. Lindblom proposes that in languages generally human beings underexploit the anthropophonic possibilities due to both production and perception constraints—a position that

Laver (1993) suggests is gaining ground. The inclusion of an account of voice into phonetic theory and practice may show these constraints to be less narrow than we think they are.

No matter how complex and all embracing our measurement techniques, however, we must know what it is we are measuring. This applies just as much to perceptual measurements as it does to measures of voice production. We must have reliability across judges for the terms we use to describe voice. That is, the judges must all be thinking of the same voice type when they use a particular label. This is the potential usefulness of a model such as that proposed by Laver. Within the other measurement area developed in phonetics, acoustics—a form of measurement that is abstracted away from subjective human judgments to a large extent—there is much greater agreement on terminology. It is to this area that the next chapter turns.

Glossary of Key Terms

The following are the technical terms used in this chapter that will be found in a number of places in later chapters. They are included here with their definitions to provide an easily accessible glossary.

Articulatory setting. The tendency for the vocal apparatus to take up particular long-term muscular adjustments underlying the movement involved in producing a sequence of speech segments.

Dynamic features. These refer to the features of voice related to the perceptual dimensions of pitch, loudness, and time. Sometimes referred to as prosodic features.

Fundamental frequency. The lowest frequency component of the voice. Essentially, the characteristic frequency of vibration of the vocal folds that an individual speaker adopts, usually expressed in Hertz—the number of complete cycles of vibration per second.

Glottis. The space between the vocal folds in the larynx.

Larynx. The complete framework of bones, muscles, and cartilage structures situated in the throat at the top of the windpipe or trachea and below the pharyngeal cavity. For voice, the key parts of the larynx are the two vocal folds that produce sound by vibrating.

Phonation. The production of sound in the larynx.

Tones of voice. The domain of vocal activity used by Laver to describe the longer term but culturally determined uses of voice.

Vocal tension. The degrees of muscular tension present in the vocal tract, larynx, and subglottal area.

Vocal tract. Comprises the cavities above the larynx—the major ones being the pharyngeal cavity situated immediately above the larynx at the back of the throat; the nasal cavity or rather the set of cavities and sinuses in the nose; and the oral cavity or mouth.

Voice quality. As used by Laver, this refers to the very long-term, habitual voice settings that characterize individuals.

CHAPTER THREE

The Physical Measurement of Voice

This chapter presents an overview of the physical measurement techniques that have been developed mainly within phonetics to examine voice. As with the previous chapter, the aim is to provide the reader with the means to describe voice phonetically, which may then be used in reading and interpreting the later chapters. The material covered is qualitatively different from that in other chapters in that much of it has its foundation in physics and, as such, may represent new ground for many readers. Most of the types of measure introduced in this chapter are acoustic; that is, they are electronic measurements of the actual sounds we make when we speak. The concepts used in the acoustic measurement of voice, and the measures themselves, are used widely by researchers working within psychology and communication studies as well as phonetics. To understand this work, therefore, a grounding in acoustics is just as important as the terminology used for the articulatory account of voice covered in Chapter 2. In addition to acoustic measures, other physical measures relating to the temporal dimension of speech and voice will be covered.

The chapter is divided into four sections. Three of these relate to the basic dimensions introduced in Chapter 1 and raised again in the last chapter—loudness, pitch, and time. The first two of these sections cover the acoustic measures underlying loudness and pitch; the third section deals with the measures underlying time—these are not necessarily acoustic. Acoustic measures may incorporate a temporal dimension, but basic temporal measures such as speech rate or pausing essentially involve the timing and counting of sections of the recorded signal. The fourth section introduces a number of more complex measures that utilize more than one of these parameters, including time, and that have been developed as technology has become more sophisticated. They are mostly acoustic. As with Chapter 2, a glossary of the most important terms has been provided at the end of the chapter.

Types of Physical Measure

As noted in Chapter 1, the sound produced by the vibration of the vocal folds in the larynx is often referred to as the sound source, which is then filtered through the oral, pharyngeal, and nasal cavities. By adjusting our vocal organs—the tongue, lips, lower jaw, soft palate—we are able to shape the sound to produce speech sounds (for a recent general overview of vocal tract acoustics, see Kent, 1993). In this book, we are not overly concerned with speech sounds themselves but, as will be discussed below, even these may provide us with useful measures of the voice. We are particularly interested in the measurement of long-term vocal features, those that extend over more than a single speech sound or segment. Given this, the techniques used are themselves usually long term. This does not necessarily mean we must ignore short-term measures such as those relating to individual speech sounds, but that, if used, they will need to be statistically manipulated to simulate longer time frames.

Physical measures of the voice can be used by researchers to relate to various types of perceptual measure such as psychological measures of attitude or judgments of emotion carried in the voice. Such studies can help determine which aspect of the voice carries which type of psychological information. As will be seen, it is often the case that both short-term and long-term physical measures need to be statistically manipulated for use with such perceptual analyses. Means, summations, ranges, or variances of the physical measure used, for example, may need to be calculated. It is these that are then used to relate to the perceptual measures.

Measures Underlying Loudness

In generating sound, energy is expended. When we generate the sounds we call voice and speech, the energy comes from action of the muscles of the breathing apparatus; that is, the muscles of the abdomen, diaphragm, and the intercostal muscles of the rib cage all applying force to the lungs. We have already seen in Chapter 1 how that force in turn creates vibrations of the vocal folds in the larynx which themselves create the oscillating movements of air particles we refer to as sound waves. It is these sound waves that stimulate our auditory system. The air particles themselves do not travel from the larynx to the listener's ears, however. The energy produced causes each air particle to move a certain distance from its point of rest and then return. In returning, it moves past the point of rest rather in the way a swinging pendulum does. The oscillating air particle causes adjacent air particles to oscillate and so on, forming a ripple effect that eventually reaches the listener's ears. The maximum distance these oscillating particles move from their point of rest is their amplitude. The greater the amount of energy expended, the greater their movement, the greater the amplitude and the louder we hear the sound.

These oscillations are not simple smooth movements. Voice and speech sounds are highly complex and produce very complex oscillations or sound waves. An individual's speech sounds may be characterized by the shape of the corresponding sound waves. The sound wave of each type of speech sound will be different from that of others. Some tend to be relatively periodic; that is, the shape of the wave representing each cycle of movement is very similar (essentially, the same) as the shape of the adjacent ones. This may be seen in Figure 3.1 below. Similarly, voice types may be characterized by their sound waves. Periodicity of the sound wave is not always found, however. Some speech sounds and some voice types are more periodic than others. Some voice types, such as whispery voice, have far less voicing in the sense we defined it in Chapter 1 and are basically aperiodic: each cycle of the sound wave has a different shape from all others.

Figure 3.1 shows acoustic representations of the English sentence, "Are you ready to leave yet?" At the top is the acoustic sound wave, with amplitude represented by the vertical axis and time by the horizontal axis. The words are printed below the wave form to show which word corresponds to which part of the figure. Below this is an enlargement of a very small part of the sound wave for the vowel in the first word *are*. It shows the individual oscillations or periods that represent cycles of vocal fold vibration. The periodicity of the sound wave can be seen by the way each repeated cycle is very similar to

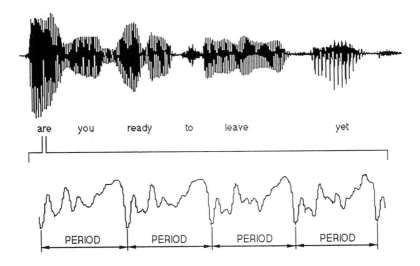

Figure 3.1. Acoustic sound wave of the sentence "Are you ready to leave, yet?" and expanded wave form of the vowel in the first word "are," showing individual periods.

the others. The complexity of each period can also be seen from the shape.

Amplitude is not the only physical correlate of loudness, however. Another measure related to both amplitude and frequency is sound intensity (Fry, 1979). This is not the place to consider the mathematics of the two concepts; the reader is directed to Fry's book *The Physics of Speech* for that. However, we can say that while the perceptual concept of loudness does depend on the amplitude of the sound, a closer and more accurate relationship exists between loudness and intensity. This is because two sounds of the same amplitude but of different frequency require different amounts of energy to produce them, and the sound of higher frequency will be perceived as louder. Sound intensity is the measure that accounts for this. The voice has energy at many different frequencies, making intensity a particularly appropriate measure for voice and speech. The unit used as the measure of intensity is the decibel (dB), designed specifically to allow comparison of two or more sounds, which is often the key issue for loudness of the voice in perceptual studies where several speakers may be compared with one another. Studies of vocal communication have commonly used the mean, variance, or range in decibels of the intensity of the voices measured (Scherer, 1984b).

Measuring intensity can be difficult. Unless we are able to keep the speaker's mouth at a constant distance from the microphone when recording, and unless we are consistent with the manipulations of the gain control on recording and playback equipment, vocal intensity can be meaningless. That is, the voice will sound louder in the recording, but this will have nothing to do with the speaker's voice, just the recording conditions. See Chapter 6 for further comment on this and other methodological issues.

Measures Underlying Pitch

The second type of physical measure is that underlying the perceptual concept we call pitch—how high or low the sound is perceived to be. The most frequently used measure is that of fundamental frequency (usually referred to as F0). This is essentially the rate at which the vocal folds oscillate or vibrate. It is measured by the number of vibrations (or cycles) per second and is expressed in Hertz (Hz). Thus, 100 Hz means the vocal folds are vibrating 100 times a second. As noted, each period in the lower part of Figure 3.1 represents one cycle of the vocal folds. It is the number of these periods in each second, then, that represents the fundamental frequency of the speaker at that point in time.

Other statistical measures based on fundamental frequency that have been used in studies of the voice are F0 range, F0 variability, and mean F0 across a whole utterance. Fundamental frequency basically varies continuously throughout speech but does so around a base level for each individual. There are normal day-to-day variations in this base level or habitual F0, however. Coleman and Markham (1991) suggest as much as 18% variation from one day to the next in speaking fundamental frequency as being within normal limits. Figure 3.2 shows a typical F0 trace; that is, the fundamental frequency of voice as a speaker speaks a sentence—in this case, the same sentence represented in Figure 3.1. The sound wave is shown above the F0 trace. The rise and fall of fundamental frequency is clearly illustrated in the lower part of the figure. As can be seen, F0 rises to a peak of about 200 Hz as the speaker says *you*; there is a drop then a slight rise half way through *leave*; and F0 drops again to about 100 Hz at the start of *yet* but rises and then falls as the sentence ends.

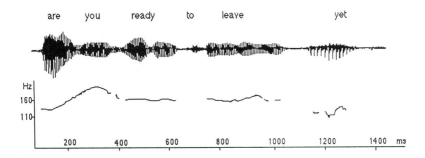

Figure 3.2. A graph of fundamental frequency for the sentence "Are you ready to leave, yet?"

During voiceless periods and periods of very low energy, the trace disappears.

For all the individuality in F0 variation, and remembering the comments made in Chapter 1 about social factors influencing the pitch used by males and females, there is an accepted link between F0 and gender (Fry, 1979). Males usually have lower fundamental frequencies than females. This is due to the vocal folds being larger, longer, and thicker for many males. Fry suggests an average F0 of 120 Hz for males and 225 Hz for females. While it is not clear where these values come from (although they are likely to be from white Western groups), they do provide an indication of the magnitude of difference often found between the two sexes. Fry also proposes an average fundamental frequency of 265 Hz for children.

One other measure relating to frequency that may be a useful vocal correlate of age or such psychological variables as emotion is *jitter*. This is the term used for perturbations in fundamental frequency. More specifically, jitter is manifested as micro-irregularities in the individual periods of the sound wave. Jitter has been found to be useful to the perception of hoarseness, harshness, and roughness in the voice (Orlikoff, 1989) and seems to be nonlinearly related to fundamental frequency, although voices with lower F0 appear to be characterized by jitter of greater magnitude while those with higher F0 display jitter of less magnitude.

A third, and more complex, type of frequency measure (it does, in fact, make use of both frequency and intensity) is one relating to a

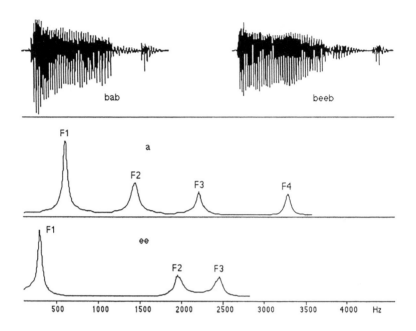

Figure 3.3. Formant spectra of the vowels in the nonsense words "Bab" and "Beeb," showing the three vowel formants.

segmental analysis of speech—that of vowel formants. Formants are the basis on which we recognize the different vowel sounds in any language. There may be other factors involved, depending on the language, such as nasality or vocal tract tension, but the formant structure remains the key perceptual feature of vowels.

The shape of the vocal tract produces increases in amplitude at a number of frequencies. These are sometimes called vocal tract resonances. When we pronounce vowels, the three "resonances" that are lowest in frequency have been shown to be the most useful for distinguishing one vowel from another. These are the formants. Two examples are illustrated in Figure 3.3, which shows the formant spectra of two vowels. The formants in each case have been marked. At the top are the sound waves: on the left is the vowel in the nonsense word *bab*, while the one on the right represents the vowel in the nonsense word *beeb*. Below this are the formant spectra. The top one is the spectrum for the vowel in *bab,* and the one at the bottom is the spectrum for the vowel in *beeb.* In each case, the spectrum is shown at a specific point in time, a "slice," as it were, cut through the acoustic signal of the vowel. The spectra shown in the figure highlight the first three formants (usually designated F1, F2, and F3), which are manifested as peaks of energy in the spectra. The figure shows that the formants for the two vowels have different frequencies. The formant peaks in the spectrum for /a/ are relatively evenly spaced with F1 (the lowest in frequency) situated at approximately 650 Hz. Formant four is also visible. The formant peaks for /ee/, however, are quite different with F1 around 300 Hz and F2 and F3 close together. Such spectra can be produced for any point in time in the continuous stream of speech.

As each vowel uses a different vocal tract shape (in particular, the tongue is positioned differently in the mouth for each vowel), the resonances produced by the vocal tract for each vowel will be different. That is, the formants for each vowel in a language will be characterized by different frequencies. As indicated, we usually characterize each vowel using the first three of these resonances or formants as shown in Figure 3.3. There is a great deal of individual variation, however, in the absolute frequencies of vowel formants. The same vowel spoken by different people will have different formant frequencies, which may vary differently throughout the duration of the vowel. Our ability to perceive vowels accurately whoever speaks them, thus, stems not from the absolute frequency values of each formant, but rather from the relationship among the three formants and in particular the changing relationship between F1 and F2 through time.

Another potentially useful measure of voice that relates to formants, and so to the segmental rather than longer term aspects of speech, may be found in the acoustic phenomena present at the transitions in the continuous stream of speech from vowel to vowel or vowel to consonant. These remain relatively stable across individuals, although they are influenced by the surrounding speech sounds. Transitional phenomena may be useful measures to relate to perceptual measurements. Ladefoged (1993) uses the words *bab, dad,* and *gag* to illustrate these transitions. The same strategy is adopted here. Figure 3.4 shows a spectrogram of the three words spoken by the author. The spectrogram is a graphic representation of speech with time along the horizontal axis and frequency along the vertical axis. Some indication of intensity can be gained by the darkness of parts of the spectrogram. The spectrograms of the three words are

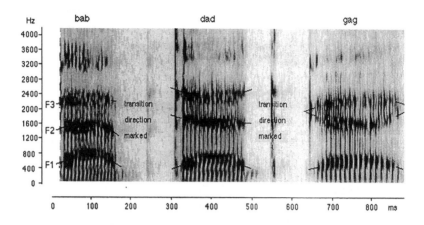

Figure 3.4. Spectrogram of the English words "Bab," "Dad," and "Gag," showing formant transition contours.

annotated and the formants and transitions of the vowels have been noted in the figure. It is the vowel in each case that is particularly noticeable; the consonants at beginning and end are not well marked. They do, however, have an effect on the vowel formant transitions. The formants appear as the dark bars in the spectrogram. The differences in the contours of the transitions can be seen: the direction of the relevant transitions have been marked with short lines. Formant one tends to rise at the beginning of each vowel and fall at the end. It is F2 and F3 that show differences across the three words, however. In each case the presence of the labial, alveolar, and velar consonants before and after the vowel result in different transitional contours. In *bab* the labial consonants produce a rise and fall at the beginning and end, respectively, of F2. In *dad*, the alveolar consonants produce falls in frequency at the beginning of F2 and F3. F2 remains relatively steady at the end, while F3 rises again. In *gag*, the velar consonants result in F2 and F3 coming together at beginning and end. In Figure 3.4 a higher fourth formant is just noticeable for each vowel. The fourth (and higher) formants are not used in vowel perception.

Spectrograms such as the ones in Figure 3.4 have proven useful to phoneticians for measuring formant characteristics and for temporal features of speech. The vertical axis of Figure 3.4 goes to 4,000 Hz only. As we have said, however, when we speak we produce sound at many frequencies. At the lowest frequency, we have F0, or our fundamental frequency. In addition, as well as the formants or vocal tract resonances that can be seen in the figure, the voice produces harmonics of F0 at higher frequencies. In the range of approximately 100 Hz to 5,000 Hz the important elements of speech are to be found. The various shapes in the spectrogram represent the way speech is superimposed over the basic sound of voice at the larynx—fundamental frequency and its harmonics. Above about 5,000 Hz the sounds of speech have little or no effect. This range may be important for voice, however. The spectrogram shown in Figure 3.4 is usually called a wideband spectrogram. It represents each pitch period, or cycle of vibration of the vocal folds, as a vertical striation. Other types can also be produced, the most useful being the narrowband spectrogram, which emphasizes the harmonics of the voice.

For more information about vowel formants the reader should consult Fry (1979) or Ladefoged (1993). For our purposes, we can note that vowel formants and their transitions are short-term measures in that they refer to a single speech sound or segment. They can be statistically manipulated to simulate a long-term measure in similar ways to the measures already noted. Once again, these may then be related to perceptual ratings such as measures of emotion, personality characteristics, and so forth. Thus, Scherer (1984b) indicates that the most common manipulation of formant frequencies used in studies of vocal communication is to take the mean frequency value across a number of vowel segments that appear in an individual's speech. This can be done for each of the three formants separately. Another measure involving formants that incorporates both intensity and frequency is to take the mean intensity value at each of the formant frequencies for a number of vowel segments.

In summary, the first two sections on acoustics have introduced two measures underlying loudness—amplitude and intensity; two underlying pitch—fundamental frequency and jitter; and two that relate to both loudness and pitch—vowel formants and formant transitions. In addition, a series of graphic representations of voice and speech have been presented: the sound wave, fundamental frequency traces, formant spectra, and spectrograms.

Measures Related to Time

The third type of physical measure uses the temporal domain and is not really an acoustic measurement as such. Neither is it strictly speaking a measure of voice. Temporal measures are included as one of the dynamic features of speech and voice and are usefully considered here as accompaniments to vocal measurement. Measures related to time that may be useful to voice include duration of the overall utterance spoken by an individual and speech rate. The former may be measured in milliseconds, seconds, or minutes; the latter may be calculated as the number of words or syllables spoken per second. Another measure involving time is the measurement of that part of speech in which voicing occurs and that in which no voicing occurs. Such measures are often given as proportions of the whole utterance.

Similar to the measurement of those portions of the speech signal where there is no voicing, but not necessarily the same, is the measurement of the amount of pausing found in an utterance. When measuring the sections where no voice occurs, we may include the nonvoiced segments of speech such as (in English) /p/, /t/, and /k/, plus any microsecond silences between words. When measuring pausing, however, we may include only longer stretches of silence that indicate lack of fluency or the speaker thinking of what next to say. Pauses in this sense may not be silent at all, but be filled with sounds such as *er* or *mm* and so forth. None of the temporal measures introduced here, including those that incorporate periods of silence, should be seen as measures of silence per se but rather as aspects of the dynamics of speech. Silence is a communicative phenomenon in its own right, functioning within social interactions in many different ways. For a functional account of silence see Jaworski (1993).

The dimension of time relates more closely to voice when more complex acoustic measures are taken. We saw above how time was one of the dimensions characterizing the spectrogram. The section below dealing with the complex measures of voice quality shows in more detail the role played by time.

Complex Measures

The measures presented so far are all (with the exception of vowel formant characteristics) measures of dynamic features of voice. Acoustic measures of long-term articulatory settings, in the Laver (1980) sense, are more difficult to make. Laver, in his review of the phonetic measurement of voice quality, provides profiles of characteristics for a large range of voice qualities. Thus, we can note that the frequency range of the laryngeal setting of creaky voice is low, with an average range for males being 24-52 Hz, and that a mean F0 of 34.6 Hz has been suggested (Michel & Hollien, 1968). Other, micro-acoustic measures, combined with articulatory and aerodynamic measures, provide a comprehensive and complex profile of this particular voice quality. It is this type of synthesis that can be found in Laver's monograph and that may be used in the study of the functions of voice. Some researchers, for example, have been able to show significant relationships between some of these types of measure and ratings of affect or personality characteristics. Again, see Scherer (1982, 1984b, 1986a) for reviews of this work.

In addition to the above three fundamental types of acoustic measure and the clusters of measures just noted, more complex acoustic measures of voice, based on two of the three fundamental parameters, have been calculated. Thus, Scherer and Oshinsky (1977) relate a measure they call the envelope to the communication of emotion. The envelope is a measure that combines the amplitude and time parameters. It refers to the amount of time taken for an auditory signal to reach maximum amplitude (the "attack"), and the time it takes for it to "decay" to zero amplitude.

Various measures of the glottal sound source (i.e., sound at the larynx before it has been modified by the vocal cavities above the larynx) have also been developed. These are useful not only for relating the physical sound source to perceptual measures but are important within the voice pathology area. Potentially they provide a measure of the laryngeal articulatory settings discussed in Chapter 2. One of these types of measure, known as electroglottography, is an impedance, rather than acoustic, method of measuring the glottal source. This measurement technique uses electrodes attached to the neck in the region of the larynx to pick up its signal. Measuring impedance at the glottis rather than an acoustic signal, electroglottography effectively removes the filtering effect of the vocal tract from the signal collected.

Other measures of the glottal sound source use the signal that emanates from the mouth. Thus, inverse filtering (Fritzell, 1992) is a way of filtering the acoustic sound signal that matches the inverse of the effect produced by the upper vocal cavities. This essentially means that the vocal tract resonances—in particular, the formants—are eliminated, thus producing a graphic representation analogous to the glottal source. Like the spectral envelope, this combines the amplitude and time parameters but, being a representation of the glottal sound wave, each repeated graphic representation of the wave form is the equivalent of one cycle of the vocal folds. Inverse filtering over a period of a second or more produces in effect, then, a measure of fundamental frequency.

Perhaps the most frequently used complex acoustic measure, and potentially the most useful, is the long-term spectrum (LTS) of voice (Pittam, 1987b; Pittam & Millar, 1989). This also uses the signal emanating from the mouth but does not try to represent the glottal sound source by eliminating the filtering effect of the vocal tract. It does, however, as explained below, try to overcome the effect of the specific speech sounds.

The LTS is a measurement of the distribution of energy in a selected frequency range of a sample of continuous speech and averaged over a time period usually of between 30 and 60 seconds. The resulting spectrum is made up of a discrete number of equally spaced points (256, for example) across the frequency range. Thus, if a 30-second sample of speech is analyzed over the frequency range 0-4,000 Hz (or 4 kHz—kilohertz—as it is more usually known), an average of the amplitude across that time period is calculated for all 256 points of frequency equispaced in the 4 kHz range.

Li, Hughes, and House (1969) suggest that after about 30 seconds of continuous speech, the effect of individual speech sounds on the spectrum is no longer significant. That is, the LTS will not change significantly regardless of how much more speech is analyzed. While shorter time periods have been suggested (Furui, Itakura, & Saito [1972], for example, propose 10 seconds to achieve a stable spectrum) many researchers seem to have accepted a speech sample of between 30 and 60 seconds (e.g., Byrne, 1977; Fritzell, Hallén, & Sundberg, 1974). If the spectrum does stabilize in this way it becomes a potentially useful tool for measuring the longer term settings.

An example of the LTS is shown in Figure 3.5. Intensity is represented along the vertical axis and frequency along the horizontal. As can be seen, the LTS is a graph with a lot of energy present in the lower frequency range that falls away in the higher frequency ranges. This drop in spectral energy allows us to refer to the slope of the spectrum. Apart from the spectral slope of the LTS, the profile of peaks and troughs may be useful for representing different voice types or relating to perceptual measures (Pittam, Gallois, & Callan,

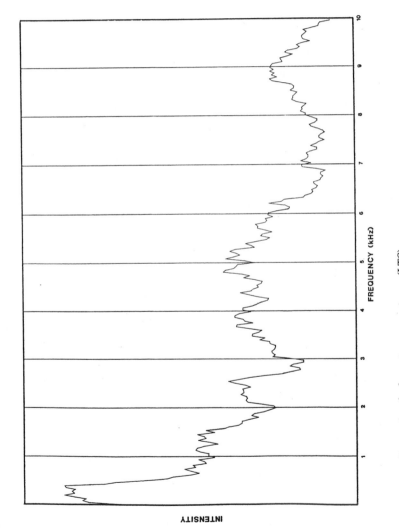

Figure 3.5. Example of a long-term spectrum (LTS).

1990). The LTS illustrated in Figure 3.5 shows that sound energy is present above the frequency range we have suggested as important for speech (100-5,000 Hz). Indeed, this particular spectrum shows energy continuing at least to 10 kHz.

An annotated bibliography of the LTS (Pittam & Millar, 1989) shows that it has been used to measure many social and personality variables including national, gender, and age identity; affect dimensions, specific emotions, personality characteristics, and individual speakers; plus psychiatric conditions and pathological voice states. It has, in addition, been used in architectural acoustics, development of aids for the deaf, and music acoustics (see Pittam [1987b] for a review of those studies dealing with social and personality variables as well as a brief historical overview of the measure).

One potential weakness of most studies that have used the LTS (including some of those by the present author) is that data have been considerably reduced. So, for example, rather than using the entire 256 points of intensity across the selected frequency range, mean intensities are taken for specified frequency bands within that range. The resulting values are then used to relate to perceptual measures of personality or social variables. This manipulation usually results in the loss of the majority of the data and inevitably leads to questions of just what these mean values represent and how meaningful they are to a listener. It also leads to a rather exploratory and subjective account of voice. A few studies, on the other hand, have tried to overcome these problems by entering all the spectral data points into statistical analyses. Pittam et al. (1990), for example, used a multimode factor analysis to do this. Other types of statistical analysis such as the use of clustering algorithms may also be useful in this way.

Another potential problem in using this measure to relate to affect has been noted by Scherer (1982) and Pittam and Scherer (1993). They point out that emotions may be difficult to distinguish in the LTS unless the lower frequency range is excluded. Large energy shifts due to the changing fundamental frequency contour and extraneous to emotion can occur in the lower frequency regions. Low-pass filtering is needed to exclude this. That is, the lower part of the spectrum needs to be removed. Even this, however, will not eliminate the effect of these shifts completely, which will be reflected in the higher harmonic structure. Statistical corrections to account for this may be necessary.

Although the influence of individual speech sounds may have been eliminated from the LTS, the overall effect of the vocal tract remains. This measure is not simply another measure of the glottal sound source, in other words. At first glance, therefore, it could be seen as a potentially useful measure of supralaryngeal articulatory settings. As yet, however, there is no convincing evidence that the LTS can successfully differentiate such settings. It is possible, however, that the LTS and the other two complex measures represented here may be more able to distinguish laryngeal settings.

This possibility stems from the development of a measure called the alpha parameter. This is a measure of the ratio of the energy in one part of the LTS to that in another. The alpha parameter achieved some popularity in the 1970s, being originally developed by Frøkjaer-Jensen and Prytz (1976) within voice pathology. As used by these researchers it was the ratio of the mean intensity above 1 kHz to the mean intensity below 1 kHz, expressed in decibels. One useful feature of such a measure as this, important when collecting and manipulating data, is that taking a ratio effectively normalizes the data, making it independent of distance from speaker to microphone and of amplification levels. Any measure of intensity must take these two factors into account.

It has been suggested that the alpha parameter is representative of vocal tract tension, specifically of medial compression (Frøkjaer-Jensen & Prytz, 1976). If so, it could be a useful discriminator of voice qualities in the Laver (1980) sense, particularly tense and lax laryngeal settings, and perhaps of all laryngeal settings. Support for this may be found in Nolan (1983). He used a modified version of the alpha parameter to discriminate many voice qualities using the Laver model, adopting 1.5-3.0 kHz expressed as a ratio of 0-1.5 kHz, after considering several cutoff points and frequency ranges. Nolan concluded that the measure was more useful as a discriminator of laryngeal settings than supralaryngeal settings. These findings, while encouraging, have not been replicated, however, and as far as is known the alpha parameter has not been used outside of the voice pathology area since that time.

Continuous measures of the glottal sound source such as electro-glottography and inverse filtering, along with measures of the averaged energy levels of the filtered voice across time, such as the LTS, take the temporal dimension into account in ways the more simple acoustic measures cannot achieve. This makes them potentially useful for measuring the long-term social and psychological correlates of voice. It is in this way that they may be useful then, as direct acoustic measures of perceived social and psychological variables.

Summary

Both recorded voices and "live" voices may be analyzed acoustically. Software and hardware packages for digitally processing speech signals on personal computers—both IBMs (and IBM compatibles) and Macintoshes—have become readily available. In addition, several larger and more powerful packages are available for workstations. To analyze speech and voice digitally, the signal from the recorder or microphone (if a live voice is used) is fed into the computer through a sound input/output (I/O) board (or "card," as they are sometimes called) attached to the computer's mother board. These are sometimes known as AD/DA boards pointing to the fact that they digitize the incoming analogue signal (A to D), and do the reverse for the output (D to A). A software package is then used to analyze the digitized signal. Such packages usually provide facilities to produce frequency and amplitude displays of the signal in addition to spectral displays of various kinds including spectrograms. A range of modifications may be made to the various analyses and stored for future use. The stored digitized signals may then be restored to analogue form via the I/O board, an amplifier, and loudspeakers, and can usually also be printed off as hard copy. The figures used in this chapter were produced in this way.

This chapter has presented only a brief overview of the major physical measures that have been found useful in the study of voice. Analysis packages, which are usually oriented to speech analysis, provide many more types of measure. For a somewhat more extended account of the measures introduced here and other, micro-acoustic, measures of voice, including the distribution characteristics that can be measured, the reader is referred to Scherer (1982, 1984b, 1986a). Scherer's chapter on methods (1982), in particular, is a very useful and comprehensive introduction to methods of vocal measurement at the acoustic as well as the physiological, phonatory, and articulatory levels in addition to providing information on how these might relate to perceptual measures.

When we hear a voice speaking, all of these acoustic cues (and many others) enter our auditory system. In interpreting that complex sound wave it is not clear how (or if) we isolate any of the cues mentioned. Neither is it always clear just what the relationship is between these physical cues and the way they are perceived. We have already noted that a basic cue such as fundamental frequency is perceived as pitch. The relationship between F0 and pitch is highly complex, however. It is not, for example, a linear relationship. Rather, it is, in part at least, closer to a logarithmic relationship. In attempting to represent this more accurately, several "perceptual" scales have been developed. The two most common ones are the Mel scale and the Bark scale, in both of which perceptually equal intervals of pitch are represented as equal distances along the scale. The just noticeable difference (JNDs) of pitch, or limens, to use the psycho-physical term, is of the order of +/− 1 Hz in the frequency range 80-160 Hz and is larger in higher ranges (Flanagan, 1957). However, as 'tHart, Collier, and Cohen (1990) point out, JNDs of pitch depend on a number of things such as F0; duration and intensity; whether the frequency is steady or changing; and the presence of accompanying noise. The relationship between frequency and pitch, in others words, is indeed complex.

The relationship between loudness and intensity remains uncertain, although it is most sensitive in the 1-5 kHz frequency range (Moore, 1982). For temporal measures, perceived duration may be dependent to some extent on F0 (van Dommelin, 1993a). The relationship between many of the other less basic acoustic cues and their perceptual counterparts has yet to be explored.

Many of the studies that have used these physical measures will be reviewed in later chapters. The voice is an extremely complex instrument of communication. As technology advances, the means devised to measure voice physically also become more complex. As was said at the end of the last chapter, however, we must know what it is we are measuring. This applies just as much to acoustic measurements as it does to measures of voice perception and articulation. One of the important questions that must always be kept in mind is whether any of our measures of voice are meaningful to a listener.

Glossary of Key Terms

As in the last chapter, a short list of the technical terms used in Chapter 3 is provided here. These two chapters provide the means of describing voice that are then used in interpreting the studies of voice covered in later chapters.

Amplitude. An acoustic correlate of loudness. The maximum distance oscillating air particles move from their point of rest.

Decibel. A measure of relative sound intensity. The difference in intensity between the quietest and loudest sounds we can hear is very large. The decibel (dB), named after Graham Bell, the inventor of the telephone, is a means of handling such large numbers. Decibels are calculated by dividing the intensity of a sound by a reference sound—supposedly the quietest sound humans with the best hearing capacity can hear. The logarithm of this is taken and multiplied by 10. The result of this calculation is the decibel (dB). In other words, the decibel is not an absolute value but a relative one. Every time the intensity of a sound doubles, we get an increase of 3 dB.

Electroglottography. An impedance method of measuring the glottal sound source.

Formants. Vocal tract resonances representing bands of high energy in the spectrum.

Fundamental frequency. The lowest frequency component of the voice. Essentially, the characteristic frequency of vibration of the vocal folds that an individual speaker adopts, usually expressed in Hertz—the number of complete cycles of vibration per second.

Glottal sound source. The sound produced at the larynx before being filtered through the vocal tract. The glottal wave is periodic, being made up of F0 and its harmonics. In shape, each period is essentially triangular.

Hertz. The measure of sound frequency. One Hertz represents one cycle of movement of the vocal folds.

Intensity. An acoustic correlate of loudness. It represents the magnitude of the sound.

Inverse Filtering. A way of filtering the sound signal that matches the inverse of the effect produced by the vocal tract, thus producing a measure that corresponds to the glottal sound source.

Jitter. Perturbations in fundamental frequency. More specifically, jitter is manifested as micro-irregularities in the periods of glottal pulses.

Long-Term Spectrum (LTS). A measurement of the distribution of energy in a selected frequency range of a sample of continuous speech and averaged over a time period usually of between 30 and 60 seconds.

Spectrogram. A graphic representation of speech with time along the horizontal axis and frequency along the vertical axis. Some indication of intensity can be gained by the darkness of parts of the spectrogram.

CHAPTER FOUR

The Vocal Communication of Identity

This chapter reviews research on the vocal communication of identity. Much of this work is conducted within psychology and communication studies, although a few researchers in sociolinguistics are concerned with the area too. This is particularly the case when the focus is on the vocal characteristics of accent. For the most part, however, the central concerns of researchers in this area tend to be psychological. We will review the work from all three disciplines, highlighting the types of vocal function proposed and introducing the major issues and concerns in each area covered. The chapter has two main sections: the first covering the vocal communication of group identity, the second dealing with the communication of personal identity. The group identity section is subdivided into areas that may be useful in Chapter 8 when the taxonomic component of the theoretical framework is constructed. The social categories of age, gender, occupation, and accent and language group are covered. The second section, dealing with the communication of personal identity, has two subsections: personality characteristics and the communication of the individuality or uniqueness of speakers. Both group and personal identity may be classed under the general heading of social identity.

The term *social identity* has been used on a number of occasions throughout this book without a full explanation being given as to what it refers. Very few, if any, people are or have been so isolated that they have experienced no contact with others. The vast majority of individuals live in social groups. The voice, along with other nonverbal behaviors and speech, has developed primarily to provide us with the ability to communicate with others (even though this may not have been the primary use of the vocal apparatus initially). It is, above all, then, a *social* communicative tool.

Social identity is a term that has been used in a variety of ways and has been explored in a number of disciplines but particularly within social psychology. One of the main traditions of research into social identity stems from the work of Henri Tajfel (1981), which has given rise to social identity theory (SIT) (Abrams & Hogg, 1990; Hogg & Abrams, 1988; Tajfel, 1981; Turner, 1987). SIT is a theory of intergroup relations that emphasizes conflict and social change, and the individual's need to distinguish in-groups—the social group(s) we feel ourselves affiliated with at any point in time—positively from out-groups—all groups with which we believe we have no affiliations. SIT incorporates, as a central tenet, the notion of social categorization, the division of the world into meaningful social units. As Giles and Coupland (1991a) point out, social categorization involves our knowledge of our membership of social groups.

Social categories and the values associated with them form major components of our social identity, but according to SIT this only has meaning in the context of social comparison. The theory assumes that we try to achieve a positive social identity, an enhanced self-esteem, by making the in-group positively distinct from other relevant groups. In other words, social identity becomes relevant when a category of comparison is one with which we identify (Abrams & Hogg, 1990). Abrams and Hogg note that "social identity is self-conception as a group member" (1990, p. 2). Social identity theory, however, provides for a continuum of identity from group to personal. That is, it allows for the possibility of communicating in interactions at a personal as well as a group level. The communication of personal identity by the voice can be considered from at least two perspectives, one of which originated in psychology—personality characteristics. These usually represent the "normal" end of another continuum. At the opposite end of this continuum are placed those voice types we categorize as abnormal or markers of neuroses. In many ways these are more extreme forms of the "normal" types.

The second perspective has been studied across several disciplines including phonetics and speech science as well as psychology: the communication of the unique individual. This may be examined by asking such questions as: "Do we each have a unique voice?" This takes us into the realm of what one group of researchers has called voiceprints, and into the areas covered by speaker identification and verification. Both of these perspectives are introduced in the second section of this chapter. For the moment, however, we will concentrate on group identity.

The Communication of Group Identity

The way the voice may communicate our membership of particular social categories or groups is the concern of this section of the chapter. The categories covered will be age, gender, occupation, and accent and language group. It is possible that membership of other groups may also be communicated by the voice. The set covered has been the main one studied, however, and form a sufficient example of the vocal communication of social categorization. Some researchers (e.g., Siegman, 1987) refer to such categories of social identity as demographic variables. This practice will not be followed here. The term *demographic*, while widely used, takes the focus away from the all-important notion of voice acting as a carrier of social identity.

Vocal communication of identity concerns both the production and perception of voice: encoding and decoding. Questions we may want to ask include both "What are the vocal correlates of social categories such as age or gender?" and "Can listeners perceive specific categories from the voice when interacting with others?" It is important to remember, however, that the salience of a particular group membership to an interaction may well change throughout the duration of the interaction. At one point age may be important, for example, at another, gender or nationality, and there may be times when group identity is not salient at all.

In addition, although categories of age, gender, and so forth are dealt with separately here, it should be remembered that voice is usually multifunctional. As will be seen, social categories interact in terms of the vocal features that characterize them. Further, any one vocal feature, such as frequency or intensity, will be important for more than one category. Thus, it is likely that degree of presence of a particular vocal feature or different parts of the total range of a feature will be what distinguishes one social category from another rather than type of feature. So, one group may use a louder voice than another (degree of presence) or be represented in one part of the frequency range rather than another (different part of the total range). We would also expect that a profile of different vocal features, rather than a single feature, would be needed to distinguish clearly one category from another. In reviewing the identity literature, the multifunctionality of vocal features will become evident. This will be particularly noticeable when studies have included more than one category as independent variables.

The Communication of Age

The first issue of the *Journal of Voice* was given over in part to the special interest area of vocal aging. The reader is referred to this issue for an overview of the aging voice from a number of perspectives. I am indebted here to an article by Harry Hollien from that issue (Hollien, 1987), which reviews the state of knowledge of aging voices at that time. The communication of age identity by the voice, however, is not simply about old voices but voices of any age. In this section, therefore, we cover the description and perception of voices linked to any age.

Hollien (1987) indicates that the literature concerned with perception of chronological age from voice suggests that listeners are able to judge speaker age to within 5 years at levels better than chance, but that there is a tendency to underestimate the age of older speakers. Pittam (1986) supports the latter point. There is also some earlier evidence (Hollien & Tolhurst, 1978; Shipp & Hollien, 1969) suggesting that accuracy of judging chronological age from voice is partly determined by the listener's age: one overestimates the age of speakers younger than self, accurately estimates the age of speakers who are of the same age, and underestimates the age of those older than self.

While we have some idea of the accuracy with which we perceive actual age, it is not yet clear what the acoustic and temporal correlates of perceived age are. Shipp, Qi, Huntley, and Hollien (1992) suggest that no single measure is sufficiently important of itself, but that multiple parameters may be involved, including interactions among those parameters. Their results suggest that speaking rate, mean fundamental frequency, and total time may be some of the more important cues used—a profile of features.

A number of vocal and temporal features change across the period of childhood. Walker, Archibald, Cherniak, and Fish (1992) found that speaking rate increased from ages 3 to 5. The most commonly measured acoustic correlate of children's voices, however, has been fundamental frequency (F0) (Glaze, Bless, Milenkovic, & Susser, 1988). In general, F0 decreases with age and with increasing size and structural changes of the larynx and vocal folds as children move from infancy to puberty. Glaze et al. measured the relationship between a number of acoustic correlates and children's age, gender, height, and weight. As with earlier studies, they found decreasing F0 with increasing age, but noted that girls retained higher frequencies than boys. The gender difference, particularly for those children under 10, is likely to be due not to differences in vocal fold length but to cartilaginous differences. It is also likely that parameters such as height and weight, which may be indicative of the child's maturation, may be more closely correlated to vocal measures than absolute chronological age.

At the other end of the age scale a number of acoustic and aerodynamic associates of aging voices have been measured. Fundamental frequency is again perceived to be an important measure, and once again it appears to interact with gender. Thus, F0 has been shown to increase with age in males (Shipp & Hollien, 1969), while the results for females seem less certain, with some studies suggesting F0 stays stable (McGlone & Hollien, 1963), others proposing a slight decrease (Benjamin, 1981), and still others, a decrease followed by an increase in extreme old age (Chevrie-Muller, Perbos, & Guilet, 1983). F0 variability has also been shown to be less in older females (Brown, Morris, & Michel, 1989). Intensity may also be implicated. Hollien (1987) reports studies that propose an increase in intensity for older people that may not be linked to hearing loss.

There is also a possibility of an increase of the use of the laryngeal setting of creaky voice (or vocal fry as it is sometimes called). The characteristics of this were discussed in Chapter 2. This may be linked to an increase in vocal tremor and roughness in advanced age and to differences in type and amplitude of vocal fold vibration, including greater aperiodicity and incomplete glottal closure (Biever & Bless, 1989). Associated with this is the suggestion that we hold stereotypes about older voices that include an increased incidence of creaky voice. Pittam (1986) found that perceptions of speakers' ages differed when they adopted different laryngeal settings. In particular, creaky voice resulted in the perception of the speakers as older.

Another voice quality that may characterize old age is breathiness, resulting from the loss of fine control of laryngeal muscles (Hollien,

1987). In addition, temporal factors such as a general slowing down in speech rate (Amerman & Parnell, 1992; Hartman, 1979; Ptacek, Sander, Manoley, & Jackson, 1966; Ryan & Burk, 1974) may be implicated. Hollien (1987) also reviews the literature on aerodynamic factors related to aging and concludes that although the evidence supports the notion that reductions occur in respiratory function in the aged, such as reduced vital capacity, air flow, and total lung capacity, it is not clear how or whether this actually affects the voice. For a fuller account of this and other matters relating to the aging voice, the reader is referred to the Hollien article.

In terms of vocal characteristics, while there may be high and positive correlations between particular changes in the voice and advancing chronological age, changes in body physiology that often accompany advanced age may be more important determiners of changes in voice (Ramig & Ringel, 1983). In other words, once again body physiology may be the key factor rather than chronological age per se.

The concept of age is complex. In particular, the fact that chronological age is often not the salient aspect of age identity in social interaction has led Rubin and Rubin (1986) to propose the idea of contextual age. This comprises a number of parameters related to physical health, mobility, life satisfaction, degree of social activity, economic security, and amount of interpersonal interaction. Such parameters are not necessarily orthogonal, of course, which may lessen the usefulness of the idea. Indeed, Giles and Mulac (personal communication, August 1993) did not find this concept useful as a significant correlate of perceived, actual, or psychological (the age one feels) age.

One aspect of aging not covered by contextual age is the degree with which individuals affiliate with particular age groups (although this may in part be incorporated into the life satisfaction parameter). Individuals differ in this: A person may affiliate with those of similar chronological ages or not. One reason for not affiliating with an older age group when one's chronological age is advanced may be the negative stereotypes often associated with older people. Such stereotypes may be triggered by the voice (Stewart & Ryan, 1982). Stewart and Ryan found that young judges downgraded old speakers relative to young speakers and that this downgrading was increased if the old person spoke slowly. Deal and Oyer (1991) showed that perceptions of pleasantness from the voice decreased as chronological age of their speakers increased. Such studies suggest that we have access to and often use vocal stereotypes about the elderly. If this is so, these stereotypes may be closely linked to the analogous language stereotypes. In other words, vocal stereotypes become part of the discourse of the elderly, particularly in Western communities (see Coupland, Coupland, & Giles [1991] for a discussion of the dimensions of the discourse of the elderly). Putting this another way, perceived age from voice alone may be an important socially diagnostic cue in interactions (Giles, Henwood, Coupland, Harriman, & Coupland, 1992).

Such stereotypes may also, in certain contexts, result in younger people using particular vocal patterns when talking to the elderly. Caporael (1981), for example, uses the term *baby talk* to describe the way some caregivers speak to the institutionalized elderly, pointing to higher perceived pitch and greater pitch variation. Ryan, Bourhis, and Knops (1991) reconceptualize such ideas into the communication accommodation theory framework (see Chapter 7 for a discussion of this theory). They examined the patronizing speech that may be used by nurses to elderly patients in nursing homes and indicated that patronizing speech was thought to be more shrill, louder, and produced with more exaggerated intonation. In an earlier study, Ryan and colleagues (Ryan, Giles, Bartolucci, & Henwood, 1986) pointed out that such vocal (and other speech) patterns may be mediated through stereotypes about the elderly and even used as a form of establishing social control. As such, they will be an important influence on the establishment of age identity through the voice.

The Communication of Gender

As we have seen, gender is often included as one of several independent variables in psychological studies of the voice. In this section we will review a number of studies for most of which gender is the primary variable under consideration. That is, the major focus of this section will be on possible differences between male and female voices. That there are vocal differences between females and males as a general rule is probably not contentious. One piece of evidence supporting the complexity of the difference may come from Lass, Trapp, Baldwin, Scherbick, and Wright (1982). They found that even when speakers attempted to sound like the opposite sex, judges could still accurately pick their actual sex. Unfortunately, Lass et al. give no indication of what their speakers were doing vocally or even if they were all doing the same thing, but the inability of all speakers to disguise their sex suggests the difference might be quite complex and multidimensional. The acoustic dimensions studied that have revealed gender differences support this: fundamental frequency, intensity, the glottal wave, and long-term articulatory settings.

In Chapter 3, mean F0 values for males and females were cited: 120 Hz for males and 225 Hz for females (Fry, 1979). Difference in perceived pitch is sometimes proposed as the most important perceptual vocal parameter distinguishing females and males as social groups (Smith, 1979). The values offered by Fry for females at least are somewhat higher than those proposed by other researchers. Saxman and Burk (1967) suggest a mean of 196 Hz (F0 range of 171-222 Hz for their subjects) for females in the 30- to 40-year-old range and 189 Hz (168-208 Hz range) for those aged 40 to 50 years. Michel, Hollien, and Moore (1966) suggest a mean of 207 Hz for females aged 15-17 years, while McGlone and Hollien suggest 200 Hz for females aged 70-85 years. In a study of both males and females, Monsen and Engebretson (1977) reported that F0 of their female subjects averaged one octave above the males, while Linke (1973) found only a one-third octave difference, although she commented than her female speakers generally spoke lower than they should for maximum effectiveness.

Other gender differences concern the glottal wave, intensity, and fundamental frequency variation. Monsen and Engebretson (1977) suggest that females have a more symmetrically shaped glottal waveform, although the energy tends to fall off more steeply. It will be remembered from the glossary of Chapter 3 that the glottal wave form is typically triangular in shape. The asymmetrical, somewhat humped, appearance of the male glottal wave they speculate may be due to slightly out-of-phase movements of the upper and lower parts of the vocal folds as they oscillate. They also found female voices less intense than male voices by approximately −4 to −6 dB; a result supported by Higgins and Saxman (1991). In addition, in general, the evidence suggests less fundamental frequency variation in females than in males (Linke, 1973).

There is a small amount of evidence showing that particular long-term articulatory settings may be characteristic of one sex rather than the other. Henton and Bladon (1985) found more breathiness in their female speakers than their male speakers. Klatt and Klatt (1990), in synthesizing male and female speakers, found that those perceived as female had higher levels of breathiness. Complementing these studies, Pittam (1987a) found that both male and female judges preferred breathiness in female voices to males. Scherer's (1979a) comment that passive, submissive, and relaxed speakers have rather lax voices (laxness is a major component of breathiness) may suggest that Pittam's judges were using a general stereotype related to female passivity and submissiveness. Some of his judges may also have been influenced by the possibility that a slightly breathy voice is associated with sexual arousal (Laver, 1968).

When we hear voices that we perceive as female or male, another set of attributions and inferences may be triggered. Berry (1990) found that as perceived attractiveness of male and female voices increased, so did judgments of different sets of personality characteristics. Personality characteristics will be dealt with in the second part of this chapter. This result, however, tells us more about stereotypic expectations of gender group identity than it does about individual identity. Male voices deemed attractive by Berry's subjects were also rated highly on assertiveness, invulnerability, and dominance, whereas female voices judged attractive were rated highly on warmth, honesty, and kindness. That we have expectations about male and female voices is also supported by the results of Wolfe, Ratusnik, Smith, and Northrop (1990). They found that male-to-female transsexuals categorized as having a female voice had higher F0 than those categorized as having a male voice.

Details of the context will also be important here (as they will for all interactions, of course). Montepare and Vega (1988) found that females' voices varied when speaking to intimate male friends from when they were speaking to casual male friends. With the former, their voices were higher pitched, relaxed, softer, and exhibited more pitch variation. They were also perceived as more pleasant and feminine, more submissive, approachable, and sincere—again, indicating that we hold stereotypic gender expectations related to voice. One of the clearest indications of this comes from Kramer (1977), who found that perceptions of male and female speech differed significantly. This study considered far more than the voice, but in terms of vocal characteristics males were thought to have more demanding, deep, loud, and dominating voices than females. Also supporting the concept of vocal stereotypes are the findings of Batstone and Tuomi (1981) who found that male and female perceptions of female voices could be described in terms of the dimensions of passive and active, with the latter being related to perceived sexiness by their subjects.

The Communication of Occupation

It has been suggested that in business a weak voice can significantly affect first impressions (Fanning, 1990). It is not only first impressions that are important in vocal communication and occupation, however, particularly when voice is a key part of the job concerned. Occupation types characterized by frequent public use of the speaking voice include actors, radio and television announcers, attorneys, politicians, educators, telephonists, and clergy. There are no doubt others. Interest in vocal production and occupation stems in part from the long-standing and ongoing interest in elocution, which itself, as has already been suggested, has traditional links to high status professions such as law and politics. The existence of occupations characterized by frequent use of voice, however, was sufficient in itself to create an early interest in the characteristics of the types of voices used and our expectations of them. It has been suggested, for example, that military drill sergeants typically have harsh voices (Laver, 1968), and that vocal stereotypes are held about a number of occupations including the preacher, the politician, and the actor (Fay & Middleton, 1939). Indeed, with the widespread interest in the theater and movies during the 1930s, one psychologist (Pear, 1931) predicted that types of voices would be created by actors to represent occupation types.

A more recent study (Cox & Cooper, 1981) indicated that stereotypes held about one type of social group (gender) can influence perceived suitability for another (occupation). In their study, however, the influence was not as expected. While both males and females were judged equally suitable to be a telephone receptionist, those female voices perceived as assertive were preferred, whereas male voices perceived as assertive were not. Similarly (and this was almost certainly linked to the perceptions of assertiveness by Cox and Cooper's subjects), female speakers using a fast rate were preferred, whereas slower speaking males were not.

Radio broadcasting is an occupation in which the voice to a large extent defines the task. Television broadcasting also requires its presenters to have a particular type of voice, but visual factors are also important. When broadcasting began in the early 20th century, decisions were needed on what constituted a good broadcast voice. Given that audience perception of the announcers' voices were as much a consideration as their effective transmission, such decisions were inevitably linked to perceived personality—another example of the interaction between group and personal identity. One of the early decisions faced by radio producers was whether to use male or female announcers. For the most part, women were excluded from this occupation, largely because it was believed that listeners preferred to hear a male voice speaking over the radio (Cantril & Allport, 1971). This is a legacy that still influences broadcasting. Cantril and Allport's study (which was first published in 1935) concluded that the major reason for preferring male voices was prejudice against females, and that there were no significant problems with transmitting female voices, even given the state of technology at that time. That said, listeners did seem to prefer voices of lower pitch, meaning that women with voices in the alto range would be preferred over those in the soprano range. Again, this still seems to influence choice of female radio and television announcers today.

The prejudice against women in early radio broadcasting did not result in their total exclusion, although they were few in number and assigned specific tasks, such as hosting the "homemaker" program on Detroit's WJR station. Cramer (1989) provides an historical account of women's roles in American radio. She points out that the first radio news team was created at CBS in 1933 and included one woman to report on "society" news. It was not until the 1940s, however, that women became established as announcers. Today there are many women announcers in both radio and television in roles not traditionally or stereotypically associated with being female. We have yet to see, however, male announcers taking on female-stereotyped roles.

Keith (1989) discusses a number of voice types suitable for different types of radio and television programs. Although a relatively recent publication, we still find the use of impressionistic terminology that is difficult to link to articulatory, physiological, or aerodynamic features, although Keith does include some useful terms. Thus, he suggests that the broadcast news voice should have a rich timbre and depth with no nasal tone; classical radio requires a resonant, mature voice; for pop radio, good overall tonal quality that is non-muddy is suggested, while for easy listening programs, a smooth medium-paced delivery is required. Similarly, Keith proposes a nice rich resonant voice for on-camera television work.

For occupations in which the voice is prominent, determination of what is a suitable voice is often given over to those with experience of the field. In itself, this is not a problem. Attempts to communicate the criteria used for determining a suitable voice, however, usually produce inadequate results such as those above. The position is somewhat similar for acting.

It was noted in Chapter 1 that this book is not a training manual for voice. There have been many such books written specifically for the actor from within the traditions of elocution and, more recently, actor training. The first is an outmoded tradition, while the second in general relies on the talents of gifted individuals. The transmission of their ideas, however, as noted above, is often inadequate (this is not necessarily their fault, of course). Despite this, acting, as a profession that makes considerable use of the voice, deserves mention with the other occupations.

As indicated in Chapter 1, interest in the voice for acting purposes can be traced back to classical Greece. It is a particularly important instrument for any actor no matter what the era or culture. Arlington (1966) makes an interesting observation connecting voice to Chinese actors' salaries—as an example of vocal function, possibly unique. Apparently, an actor's salary depended above all on voice, those with the loudest voice or, as Arlington notes, the "largest throat" getting the highest salary. It is not surprising, therefore, to learn that apprentice actors were to be seen at dawn walking the city walls of Beijing shouting, using the walls as a sounding board.

Anecdotes of this type, while interesting and amusing, tell us little about the actor's voice itself. Unfortunately, the advent in the 20th century of electronic measurement of the voice has not resulted in much additional (and objective) information becoming available on what constitutes an effective actor's voice. Very few researchers have attempted to quantify the major features of the actor's voice or to determine the acoustic and articulatory correlates.

Acker (1987) provides one of the few studies in this area, pointing out that one of the basic distinctions drawn between the actor's voice and the everyday speaker's voice is what some people have referred to as the ring of the actor's voice. Comparing a ringing voice to a constricted voice (unfortunately in a single subject only) Acker proposes, among other things, that a ringing voice was characterized by the larynx being held higher, the soft palate being held higher and the mouth opening being considerably larger. These articulatory settings produced the ringing tone associated with an effective (projected) actor's voice and gave the audible sensation of being louder.

A few aerodynamic and acoustic studies of actors' voices have also been conducted. Breathing technique is a key factor in producing an effective voice for the theater. Thus, Watson, Hixon, and Maher (1987) found a number of overall characteristics that included greater lung volume and greater rib cage and abdomen movement. These need to be coupled with prolonged periods of greater alveolar pressure as the voice is projected into the forward part of the oral cavity. In an acoustic study, Raphael and Scherer (1987) found that the ringing quality in two female and two male actors was characterized by differences in the long-term spectrum (LTS), a form of measurement discussed in Chapter 3. Lower energy was found in the spectral range between 700 and 1,000 Hz and higher energy was found in the 2,150-2,350 Hz range. Finally, Feudo, Harvey, and Aronson (1992) measured changes over time of actors undergoing voice training. A number of temporal and acoustic parameters responded significantly to the training. The changes included increased mean frequency and frequency range, decreased usage of the actors' established frequency range (i.e., they used frequencies outside their already established range more frequently), increased mean and peak intensity, and increased maximum phonation and exhalation times. These complement the notion of a ringing voice as characteristic of the professional actor, as well as indicating greater control of the voice source and airstream. In general, the area of actor voice training would benefit from more studies of these types being conducted.

The Communication of Accent and Language Group Differences

A number of studies indicate that long-term settings distinguish language groups and accent groups at both national and regional levels. The term *accent* is used here in the sense usually adopted within linguistics to refer to the sounds of speech that characterize a national, regional (or other) group. In this tradition, the term *dialect* is set in opposition to accent (unlike the general usage of the two terms in which they are often used interchangeably). Dialect refers to the lexical, syntactic, and semantic characteristics of national, regional (or other) groups. Accents may include vocal settings. Thus, for example, Laver (1980) points to the Liverpool-English accent being characterized by two long-term articulatory settings—velarization (an habitual placement of the tongue in the area of the velum, involving a retraction and raising of the tongue) and denasalization (a setting that minimizes the occurrence of audible nasality).

In societies with a well-defined and generally accepted social class system such as the United Kingdom, however, accent group seems to interact with social class in the use of voice. Thus, Trudgill (1974) reported that working-class speakers of Norwich English in the United Kingdom display a greater incidence of the habitual use of creaky voice and nasality and a higher degree of vocal tension than other class groups. Similarly, with speakers of Edinburgh English, Esling (1978) found that tense voice was associated with informants from a lower social class. His highest class informants displayed a greater incidence of breathy voice and nasality. These two regional accent groups, then, may be distinguished on how the different class groups use these settings.

The concept of social class is difficult to define. It may involve socioeconomic status, type of occupation, education levels of self and/or parents, and even residence, type of possessions, or access to cultural facilities. Few studies of voice have focused on class, although the above two examples suggest that it may be an important variable for future researchers to consider. Comments by Brown and Lambert (1976) would support this. They suggest that social status (defined in terms of the difference between blue-collar and white-collar workers) may be judged accurately from vocal qualities alone.

Even in countries with less well-defined social class systems, such as Australia, nationality and class may interact. Mackiewicz-Krassowska (1976) proposes that nasality is associated with the nonstandard form of Australian English known as Broad Australian (Mitchell & Delbridge, 1965). This form of Australian English is sometimes linked with working-class Australians, although this is confounded by its often being perceived as a marker of national identity that crosses class boundaries. Nasality, in one form or another, is a setting that has been associated with a number of other English speaking groups: some varieties of American English (Bullen, 1942) and the prestigious British English accent known as received pronunciation (R. P.) (Laver, 1980).

The links between class and language varieties have received considerable attention (see, e.g., Giles & Coupland, 1991a), although vocal features as such are often not specified. Much of this work falls within the language attitudes area. As Sebastian and Ryan (1985, p. 116) point out, "a speaker with an ethnic accent may be downgraded largely because of social class assumptions" (see also Giles & Powesland, 1975). Where relevant, this work will be discussed in the attitudes section of Chapter 5.

Early studies using the long-term spectrum (LTS) as an acoustic measure of long-term vocal effects suggested significant differences across language groups. As Pittam (1987b) points out, however, there may be problems with some of these studies in that insufficient control may have been taken with some variables. Considerable control is needed over the vocal stimuli recorded for study (see Chapter 6 for further discussion on this and other methodological points). Thus, studies concerned with language group differences need to take account of the inventory of speech sounds characterizing the languages studied for features that could confound long-term acoustic or perceptual measurement. As indicated in Chapter 2, long-term articulatory settings may operate at both the linguistic and longer term levels, sometimes simultaneously. If we are concerned with whether a particular long-term articulatory setting charac- terizes a language group, the possible effects of individual speech sounds in that language that also display this setting must be con- trolled for.

A hypothetical illustration of this would be a comparison between French speakers and those of the language Nimboran (see UPSID, 1981) in terms of whether the long-term articulatory setting of lip rounding distinguishes these two languages. French has 10 rounded vowels from a total of 16, whereas Nimboran has six vowels, all spread or neutral in terms of the lip configuration used when articu- lating the vowels. In such a comparison, the potential confounding effect of the French rounded vowels on the perception, or acoustic measurement, of the long-term setting of lip rounding needs to be controlled for.

Other early work attempting to show language group differences in the profile of the LTS appears to be confounded by gender. For example, Tarnóczy and Fant (1964) produced spectra for Hungarian speakers (10 females, 10 males), Swedish speakers (16 F, 16 M), and German speakers (16 F, 16 M). Significant differences were found in the 700-1,500 Hz range for males and in the 1,000-2,000 Hz range for females. For females, Hungarians showed the greatest amounts of energy in the 1,000-2,000 Hz range, followed by Swedish speakers and then German speakers. The males showed a different pattern, however, with the Swedish and German speakers reversed. The results, therefore, only partly support Tarnóczy and Fant's claim that the LTS may be used to distinguish language groups.

Both language and accent differences and our perception of them may be confounded by ethnicity and race. There is very little evidence suggesting we are able to perceive race differences in the voice, although Coleman (1976) found that ability to distinguish race was confounded by the listener's race: one distinguishes own-race speakers more accurately than others. It seems possible to say, however, that judges are able to identify accurately the ethnicity of speakers from the voice alone (Gallois & Callan, 1981, 1991; Gallois, Callan, & Johnstone, 1984), although our ability to do this may itself be particularly influenced by some vocal features rather than others. Mencel, Moon, and Leeper (1988), for example, indicate that the complexity of the utterance judged and the presence of voicing significantly affected their subjects' ability to identify accurately North American Indians.

What remains largely unclear, however, is just what dimensions of the voice carry these aspects of our identity. Long-term settings such as those noted above—nasality, creakiness, and tension—seem to provide part of the answer. Other parameters such as frequency and frequency variability, intensity and intensity variability, and aerodynamic/temporal factors such as phonation time may also be involved. A study by Hanley, Snidecor, and Ringel (1966) proposed all of these as important discriminating parameters for speakers of Spanish, Japanese, and American English. In general, this is one area where much additional work needs to be carried out.

Finally, there are a few studies that suggest we hold expectations about vocal behavior that may be related to our perceptions of language/cultural groups. Thus, for example, Gallois and Markel (1975) indicated that temporal aspects of speech may be linked to perceived self-identity of Cuban bilinguals as members of different language speaking groups (in this case, Spanish and English). Hall (1966) related vocal shifts in loudness to perceptions of appropriate behavior of language groups, and Barker (1993) suggested that perceived social rules about the use of vocal behavior in conversations may be more salient to ethnic Chinese (from South Asia) than to Anglo-Australians.

Age, gender, occupation, language, and accent groups, then, may all be reflected in the voice, and we may have expectations about the use of vocal behavior by such groups. As has been seen, however, the vocal communication of some aspects of our group identity has received considerably more attention than other aspects. The level of sophistication of the studies and degree of control over potentially confounding variables have also varied widely. The next section of the chapter considers areas that have also in part received much attention and whose methodological sophistication is also very mixed.

The Communication of Personal Identity

As indicated earlier, this section of the chapter covers two perspectives of the communication of personal identity: personality characteristics and the unique individual. Before moving on to these, however, an area related to both will be introduced briefly. This is the possible influence of our own vocal feedback on self-concept and feelings (making this brief account relevant to the vocal communication of emotion discussed in the next chapter). It is a somewhat contentious matter as to whether vocal feedback does operate in this or any other way; that it is similar to, for example, the claims made for facial feedback (e.g., Zajonc, Murphy, & Englehart, 1989). While some claims for facial feedback make intuitive sense (smile and you will feel happier), it is less clear that a similar statement could be made for the voice (speak faster, louder, and with more variability of fundamental frequency and you will feel happier).

Given that we are concerned in this section with the communication of personal identity, can raising such issues be justified? They can, because if vocal feedback does influence our feelings and our self-concept, this may have a direct influence on how we as individuals communicate. As it happens, there has been little work conducted in this area, although two lines of research may be usefully mentioned: one concerned with affect, the other concerned with vocal self-perception. Siegman (1987) has proposed that what we call "personality" may be in part a product of our nonverbal behavior, including vocal behavior. In interactions with others, our behavior may be interpreted as, for example, incompetent. This may then lead those others to behave toward us in a manner that reinforces that characteristic in us, which could itself set up a vicious cycle of events. A similar explanation could be offered that leads to a benign cycle.

This would seem to entail a monitoring of the interaction that is largely unconscious. We will return to this in Chapter 8 when the taxonomy of voice is developed. Siegman and his colleagues have also suggested that vocal feedback, particularly from such cues as loudness and speech rate, influences the experience of emotions such as anger (Siegman, Anderson, & Berger, 1990) and is linked to activity in the cardiovascular system. If Siegman is correct, our vocal behavior may be more important than we had realized not only to our ability to communicate but to our health also.

Haskell (1987) provides an overview of the small literature on vocal self-perception. He defines vocal self-perception as "the physical and psychological experience of one's own voice" (p. 172), and proposes two levels at which it operates: monitoring of sensory feedback and vocal self-identification. Our experience of our own voice differs from the experience of others when they hear our voice. We hear our own voice in part through bone conduction and in part through air conduction. There is a slight phase difference between the two, producing part of the perceived difference. In addition, Gauffin and Sundberg (1974) suggest that the higher notes of our voice tend to go straight out from the mouth, whereas lower notes tend to curl around the head to our ears. This can result in a self-perception of voice as lower in pitch than others perceive it. These differences in what we actually hear link up to Haskell's second level of vocal self-perception: self-identification covering learned behavior from cultural sources. Haskell (1991) has used the concept of vocal self-perception in the rehabilitation of adolescents with voice disorders.

If our affect states can be influenced directly by vocal feedback, and cycles of behavior set up within interactions as Siegman (1987) suggests, and if, again as seems intuitively the case, we have a vocal self-identification developed from a complex mix of learned cultural sources and how we hear and process our voice (Haskell, 1987), then vocal communication should be characterized as having both cognitive (internal) and social (external) sources. As will be shown in later chapters (particularly Chapters 5 and 7), Scherer and his colleagues (Scherer et al., 1980; Pittam & Scherer, 1993) have suggested the need to take account of both the push (internal) and pull (external) influences on the vocal communication of affect. Perhaps the same claim should be made of all aspects of vocal communication. We will see later that all the theoretical models introduced in Chapter 7 allow for such a combination.

The Communication of Personality Characteristics

There has been a long tradition of relating personality characteristics to voice and speech features, although for the most part this material has not been theorized in the way adopted in this chapter, which draws a distinction between intergroup and interpersonal communication. Brown and Bradshaw (1985) and Scherer (1979a) provide overviews of the personality area, and the reader is directed to those accounts for further and more detailed reading (although it should be noted that they include material that we would place in the earlier group identity section).

The communication of personality characteristics is an area that ranges from the measurement of "normal" personality types to the "abnormal," the neuroses. This section will concentrate on the former, as the majority of the work is in this area, although it is worth noting that Moses (1954) proposes that compulsives use many pauses in their speech particularly between sentences as they survey and coordinate their thoughts before speaking. He suggests also that neurotic anxiety may be reflected in the voice due to a pressure on the diaphragm and laryngeal pressure not being in synchronization. This results in a quavering vocal tone. In addition, the phonation type can range from breathy hoarseness to inspiratory whisper. Acoustically, both variability of intensity and frequency can be large. This is one area where personality and emotion overlap.

The structure that is often placed on personality and voice research is a useful one and will be followed here. This is to divide it into externalization studies, attribution (or inference) studies, and accuracy studies. As with other sections of this book, the idea is not to provide an exhaustive review of the literature, the earlier published overviews already provide that, but to introduce the reader to the main issues and problems, to indicate what the major findings have been, and to examine the role played by the voice. Where necessary, the material presented in the earlier overviews will be extended to cover more recent research. This will include the work on vocal attractiveness (Berry, 1992; Zuckerman, Hodgins, & Miyake, 1990). It should be noted that the personality and voice research overlaps to some extent with that concerned with attitudes, persuasion, and to a lesser extent with the communication of emotion. This section, then, can usefully be linked to the next chapter, and in particular to the second half on attitudes and voice, which includes a subsection on persuasion.

As Brown and Bradshaw (1985) note, apart from the early work conducted in the 1930s and 1940s, which was concerned with how accurately judges could identify personality types from voice, most research in the personality area has concentrated either on what have been called externalization studies, that is, the study of which vocal features are characteristic of which personality types usually demonstrated by showing significant correlations between the two, or attribution (or inference) studies, that is, how vocal variations affect judgments of speakers. Scherer and his colleagues (1978, 1979a, 1984b; Goldbeck et al., 1988) have adapted the so-called Brunswikian lens model to bring together these two perspectives and to explore the possibilities of validly measuring accuracy of listener judgments. As such, it is the only model of personality perception that tries to overcome some of the problems associated with each of the areas.

Scherer's (1978, 1979a, 1984b; Goldbeck et al., 1988) use of the Brunswikian lens model provides a theorized account of voice and personality that attempts to relate personality traits to precise measurement of acoustic and temporal vocal features, and relates both to the perception of these features and the personality inferences drawn from those perceptions. This model, which has also been used in the vocal communication of emotion area, will be introduced fully in Chapter 7 as one of the models needed for a theoretical framework of vocal communication.

The early accuracy studies (at least those that set out to measure aspects of personal identity, not those that measured group identity such as age or occupation, physical characteristics such as speaker height, or even political preference) concentrated on how accurately judges could identify concepts such as dominance, intelligence, and introversion from speakers' voices. In general, as Brown and Bradshaw (1985) point out, the results of these studies show listeners are unable to judge these concepts accurately but that inter-rater reliability is very high. Unlike earlier interpretations of these results, however, which have tended to propose that listeners use inaccurate but similar vocal stereotypes when making their judgments (Allport & Cantril, 1934), Brown and Bradshaw suggest that the problem lies more with the personality measures used. As they point out, it is questionable whether we can or should attempt to measure personality objectively, that the judgment of whether an individual is dominant, intelligent, or introverted is above all a social judgment on the part of the listener, a social perception of personality rather than a judgment of actual personality traits. This differs from our perceptions of group identity that, while they are also social perceptions, can actually be confirmed or disconfirmed by recourse to known facts (social class might be slightly problematic here). Brown and Bradshaw's interpretation does not preclude the possibility of vocal stereotypes being used, of course.

A small but related literature concerns the accuracy with which listeners can judge physical characteristics of individuals such as height and weight from the voice. Early work suggested listeners could not do this with any degree of accuracy. A series of studies by Lass and colleagues in the late 1970s (e.g., Lass, Beverly, Nicosia, & Simpson, 1978; Lass, Kelley, Cunningham, & Sheridan, 1980), however, suggested otherwise. This more recent work has been criticized on the grounds that the estimated weights and heights were compared to mean values of the speakers' actual weights and heights, thus effectively blurring the accuracy. Van Dommelen (1993b) reevaluates the results of the Lass et al. work and suggests that the early studies were correct—we cannot judge weight and height from voice alone—and proposes a similar thing to that noted above for personality perception: listeners use similar but inaccurate vocal stereotypes.

Externalization studies suffer from similar problems to the accuracy studies. Again, following Brown and Bradshaw (1985), we can point to the type of personality measurement and the correlative nature of the studies as the most significant areas of concern. Scherer (1979a) also comments on the lack of control and precision of the acoustic measurements used in many of these studies. Some of the best studies, such as Scherer (1978, 1979a), overcome the latter problem to a large extent. Fundamental frequency (F0) and intensity are the two most cited acoustic features that correlate significantly with personality variables, so that higher fundamental frequency may be equated with self-ratings of competence and dominance, while higher loudness is associated with dominance and extroversion.

It is the attribution studies that potentially at least provide the most compelling findings and the most interesting prospects for future research. Addington (1968) would rate as the classic study in the slightly earlier body of research. By experimentally manipulating speech rate, pitch, and a number of voice qualities, some of which admittedly are not described precisely phonetically, Addington was able to show the relationship of these variables to a number of perceived personality characteristics. Addington's and other early findings for speech rate (Smith, Brown, Strong, & Rencher, 1975; MacLachlan, 1979), for example, show a considerable degree of consistency, with a slower rate being related to perceptions of incompetence or lower intelligence. Brown and Bradshaw (1985) provide an interesting reanalysis of this work using more sophisticated statistical techniques. They show the inherent richness of Addington's multivariate data, clarifying and extending the findings. Thus they show that breathy voices were perceived as intelligent, polite, and artistic, whereas the same speakers' orotund voices (full, clear, rounded voices) were seen as mature, sophisticated, and proud.

More recent studies (Montepare & Vega, 1988; Montepare & Zebrowitz-McArthur, 1987) have linked perceived maturity of adults' voices to lower pitch, less tightness, and to some extent greater clarity of speaking. The reverse of these was shown to relate to perceived childlike voices. Montepare and Zebrowitz-McArthur, in a correlational analysis, went on to show that a composite of the childlike vocal qualities in adults related to perceptions of weakness, incompetence, and warmth.

Even more recent work has introduced the concept of a vocal attractiveness stereotype (Berry, 1990, 1992; Zuckerman & Driver, 1989; Zuckerman et al., 1990). Zuckerman and colleagues proposed that people hold vocal stereotypes, that they can agree on what is an attractive voice, and that this perception will influence personality ratings. Berry's work confirms this and links the concept of vocal attractiveness to vocal maturity, showing that perceived attractiveness and maturity go together to some extent. Her earlier work also indicated a link between attractiveness, personality characteristics, and gender of speaker. Thus, males' attractiveness rose as perceived strength, dominance, and assertiveness rose, whereas females' attractiveness rose as warmth, honesty, and kindness rose. This would suggest that any vocal stereotypes held may have more to do with perceived group identity than with perceived personality characteristics per se. At the very least, there is an interaction there.

Numbers of studies have indicated a link between voice, perceived personality, and group identity factors. Indeed, as indicated above, the overviews of this area have tended to include such work within the personality domain. While we will not do that here, it does indicate a need to be aware of the complexity of personality attribution and inference and the need to control for a greater range of social variables in our research. As well as those already mentioned, the potential influence of several other factors has been discussed in the literature (see Brown & Bradshaw, 1985). Thus, recent studies have indicated that where judges are presented with a context for the speaker, personality ratings of that speaker can change significantly. As indicated above, it has been shown that a speaker using a slow speech rate will be seen as incompetent or less intelligent. However, a slow talker may not be perceived so negatively if a reason is provided suggesting that the speaker is using a slower rate consciously for a specific purpose. Also, as Brown and Bradshaw point out, when constructing the stimulus tapes for perception experiments, if a slow rate is produced by the inclusion of pauses rather than slowing the actual speech down the personality judgments again may not be as negative.

Situational context, other social variables including aspects of group identity, emotion type, and level of arousal may all influence judgments of personality. The recognition of this and the use of the increasingly sophisticated technology for measuring voices as outlined in Chapter 3, particularly the potential usefulness of resynthesis techniques (see Chapter 6), will allow more precise and carefully controlled examination of the voice and our attributions and inferences made from it. This can only make the attribution studies in the personality area even more compelling.

The Communication of Uniqueness

The idea that we all have a unique voice has been current for many years. Science fiction writers (and many other writers of fiction) have made much use of such a concept. This fictional account presupposes that the voice can be measured, usually in some unspecified way, and that a print of the voice can then be produced. That print will supposedly be characterized by observable patterns; patterns unique to the individual. From such accounts, it is likely that the idea of a voiceprint, akin to a fingerprint, has gained popular acceptance in many Western communities. This section introduces the vocal communication of the unique individual, including mention of the idea of the voiceprint as well as the parallel development of speaker verification and identification. The term *speaker characterization* is often used these days to refer to the broader area of concern (i.e., not just identifying speakers but characterizing them). This parallel body of research has developed within the speech science and technology area. Associated with this, but often conducted within psychology rather than speech science, is the work on deception, which itself links to the communication of emotion through the examination of vocal stress (i.e., arousal levels rather than linguistic emphasis).

Such a concept as individual speaker identification has many practical applications, from security systems for banks or restricted access areas, through intelligence work, to the law and law enforcement. One major researcher in the area has used the umbrella term *forensic phonetics* (Hollien, 1990) to describe this body of work when applied to the law and law enforcement—detailed phonetic analysis is usually required in any attempt at identification. Earlier in the chapter we introduced the work of Hollien in the area of aging. Hollien has also worked for many years in the communication of individuality. The reader is referred to his 1990 book *The Acoustics of Crime: The New Science of Forensic Phonetics* for a closer examination of the methods, history, underlying assumptions, and social implications of this work.

In a legal setting, a voiceprint could prove very useful as an effective tool in a prosecutor's armory: the voice of a person charged with a crime could be compared to a recording of the voice of someone connected with the crime (a recording of a telephone message in a kidnapping case, for example) and an identification made (or not, of course) from the comparison. Over the past 40 years, one approach to making such a comparison (in the United States, at least) has been by using a voiceprint—an appropriation of the popular name for what is simply a spectrogram. The different types of spectrogram mentioned in the last chapter may both potentially be used as voiceprints in this sense of the word. The analysis involves a pattern matching procedure. Just which aspects of the spectrogram are matched seems to vary across the exponents of this process. They seem to include, however, matching the pattern of commonly used words by looking at the various contours and bars of energy that characterize spectrograms. The aim, as indicated above, is to find sufficient similarities in these patterns across two or more recordings. Pattern matching is sometimes supplemented by the examiners listening to the voices and making aural judgments of similarity.

Voiceprint analysis has been, and remains, a controversial technique, first because of the intrinsic problems in matching patterns of this sort, when it is possible to distort the spectrogram by altering the voice in some way; second by the subjective nature of certain aspects of the process; and third because of the social implications of making a mistake. Many other criticisms may be made. Hollien (1990, p. 230) presents a detailed critique of the process and sums up the situation as follows:

> There is little question but that confusion exists relative to the nature and merit of the "voiceprint/gram" technique of speaker identification. Among the major criticisms that can be leveled are that (1) it is an archaic procedure, (2) its validity is in question (due to insufficient and/or negative research), (3) it appears to permit decisions to be made only about a third of the time and (4) the training and competencies of its operators are largely a mystery.

It is almost certain that, if individual speakers are to be accurately identified from the voice alone, the more sophisticated machine recognition techniques being developed under the labels of speaker verification and speaker identification within speech science and technology will prove to have greater and lasting import.

Of these two areas of research, the more difficult is that of speaker identification—identifying an unknown person. Researchers are still a long way from achieving sufficient accuracy in this task. Even with the somewhat easier task of speaker verification, however, much work remains to be done. This process entails verifying a particular speaker's identity from a known subset of speakers. The applications for such a process are those in which an individual wishes to gain access to a restricted area or perhaps to get bank records, or those where there is a need to verify that someone talking over a telephone, radio, or intercom system really is the person claimed. Given these applications, samples of the speaker's voice can be kept on record for comparison by the computerized system. One important point that makes this task somewhat easier than speaker identification, as Hollien (1990) points out, is that unless the speaker is an imposter the individual concerned wants to be recognized.

The vocal parameters that may be used to make comparisons in speaker identification and verification tasks are ones that have been introduced before in this book: fundamental frequency (means, standard deviations, ranges); vowel formants (frequencies, bandwidths, transitions); temporal features, plus characteristics of complex measures such as the long-term spectrum. These may be used individually or together as a profile of features. Also, in practical applications of speaker verification, known social features of a speaker may be used in the profile: gender, age, nationality—even though this moves away from the concept of individuality per se. All of these features, then, may prove useful, although aspects of vowel features, in particular, seem to be sensitive to individuality (see Laver, Jack, & Gardiner, 1990). See also Furui (1991) for a discussion of recent advances in speaker characterization.

Most researchers consistently achieve results of well over 90% accuracy in their experiments. Numbers and type of speakers used, vocal parameters, and other key factors of the methodology adopted vary quite widely, however, often making comparison of results difficult. And although above 90% accuracy is encouraging, for most applications it is simply not good enough. Many factors can produce changes to the acoustic signal of a speaker's voice, making speaker identification and verification even more difficult. Extraneous noise can distort the recordings. Fatigue, stress, emotional state, particularly high arousal emotions, can all affect the voice. (There is a considerable body of research linking voice, stress, and the psychoses. This work will not be covered here as it moves into the medical arena, in particular, psychiatry.) For all this, some practical applications are currently operating successfully.

In addition to these factors potentially affecting the voice, people can set out to deceive their listeners. Most work in the deception area has been concerned with face and body, although some researchers have included speech disfluencies and hesitations. Pitch is the most frequently cited vocal cue in this literature. For a discussion of a general model of deception, covering language, voice, and other nonvocal behaviors, see Friedman and Tucker (1990), and for a recent account of an empirical study in the area, see Ekman, O'Sullivan, Friesen, and Scherer (1991).

Not all examples of deception are necessarily sinister, of course (Friedman & Tucker, 1990). Indeed, most societies require their members to hide their feelings or thoughts to some degree in many contexts—a point that affects not only the speaker but the listener, for listeners also comply with such social rules and "tune out" or ignore lapses in accepted codes of behavior. Minor deceptions of one sort or another take place every day in social interactions with few or no consequences and, in addition, some individuals are not as good at detecting deceit as others, meaning that much will pass unnoticed. Friedman and Tucker indicate that detection accuracy is often in the very modest 45% to 60% range. They also make the interesting observation that people take into social interactions naive (and often wrong) perceptions of what behaviors are associated with deception. Thus, in terms of voice and speech, high pitch, lower speech rate, and increased hesitations are popularly regarded as good indicators of deception. They go on to point out, however, that the vocal cues used will depend largely on the demands of a particular deception. Thus when a deception causes a speaker to become aroused, the salient cues will be ones affected by that arousal. These are likely to include pitch level and vocal tension. Ekman et al. (1991), in fact, show that pitch level is a good cue for accurately detecting deceit or honesty. This area will be introduced again in the next chapter when stress, which may be associated with lying, is discussed.

For many years we have known that some aspects of our behavior in social interactions are easier to control than others and that this will affect which cues may "leak" information about our deceptions to our listeners (Ekman & Friesen, 1974; Ekman, Friesen, & Scherer, 1976). Scherer, Feldstein, Bond, and Rosenthal (1985) suggest that vocal cues are centrally implicated in leakage information. Again, however, task demands may determine which cues we can control and which we cannot. The level of motivation to deceive, for example, can influence the level of arousal, which in turn can affect vocal control. It is possible, however, that vocal cues such as pitch and tension are generally harder to control than other verbal and facial cues.

Summary

For all the difficulty experienced at times in comparing studies concerned with the vocal communication of identity, it seems clear that several aspects of group identity, particularly in terms of social categorizations, can be communicated by the voice, and that perceptions of personality can and are made using the voice. The question of uniqueness is not as clear cut, however. In an articulatory sense, Laver's (1980) concept of voice quality provides the possibility of measuring aurally one aspect of the individual voice. Acoustically, however, we are far from being able to do this. While the speaker verification studies are encouraging, the idea of a physically measurable unique voice remains a science fiction writer's dream.

We have theorized this body of work rather differently than others have done, making a division between intergroup and interpersonal communication. That is not to say, however, that the group identity-personal identity continuum found within social identity theory and introduced at the start of this chapter has been supported. Indeed, it seems most likely that aspects of group and personal identity will always be present simultaneously, although one may be more salient than the other. Identity will not be seen as a continuum here. Rather, group and personal identity will be seen as independent but interacting concepts with perceptions of one often interpreted in terms of the other. That is, people may attribute things to a social group (e.g., ethnic group) based on characteristics of an individual's personality and vice versa. Indeed, the first is typical of the stereotyping process.

The range of work covered in this chapter is large. Throughout, we have pointed to areas where more research is needed. However, before closing this chapter it may be useful to summarize some of the major points for a future research agenda. Within the group identity area there is perhaps a need to extend the social categories that have been traditionally associated with voice. In particular, the ethnic/national/racial/language group differences should be teased out and their relationship to social class established. With all categories, a clearer link is needed between perceptual measures and their physical correlates. With age, a better indication of what role this category has in social interaction would help our understanding of stereotyped inferences based on perceived age. More is needed on just what constitutes a male voice and a female voice. With occupation, it seems less important these days to determine if particular jobs are associated with specific voice types than to learn in objective terms what aspects of voice are most effective for what jobs.

The main agenda for personal identity must be to link accuracy, inference, and externalization studies. This will require both theory and methodology to be developed. Scherer's (1978, 1979a, 1984b) modified lens model (see Chapter 7) seems the most useful approach to date. This should be developed to cover all aspects of vocal communication. Speaker identification and verification are major concerns within speech science and technology around the world. There is little doubt that this interest will result in advances in our ability to verify, and perhaps identify, individuals. One area that demands consideration, however, is the role played by vocal feedback in social interaction and the extent to which this is determined by external and internal sources.

CHAPTER FIVE

The Vocal Communication of Emotion and Attitude

The vocal communication of emotion and attitude are both placed firmly within the discipline of psychology, at least in the sense that they use psychological theory and methodology. Even those researchers working in communication studies adopt similar approaches. The communication of emotion is perhaps the one area that has received the most attention within the study of vocal communication generally. This will be reflected in the account given here. We will consider both general affective states and discrete emotions in order to cover those studies that have dealt with affective dimensions such as arousal or positivity/negativity rather than specific emotions such as anger or sadness. Details of these dimensions will be introduced later. Also included is a brief account of stress. In examining attitudes to others, some researchers have adopted a dimensional approach that echoes the emotion literature. This second set of dimensions evolved parallel with the affect set and has been used within the language attitudes area but also in studies of the voice. These will be introduced and the small literature in the area discussed. The chapter will end with a brief discussion of vocal persuasion.

The Vocal Communication of Emotion

Changes in emotional state result in changes to respiration, phonation, and articulation, which lead to changes in the acoustic signal. Listeners can then infer affective or emotional state from that signal.

Table 5.1 Major Types of Physical Measures Used in Studies of Emotion

1. F0:	mean
	range
	variability
	perturbation
	contour details
2. Intensity:	mean
	range
	variability
3. Formants:	means
	bandwidth
4. Temporal:	speech rate
	pausing
5. Fluency:	slurring of articulation
6. Spectral:	noise
	proportion of high frequency energy to
	low LTS contour and frequency range
	short-term spectral envelope measures

Unfortunately, as Pittam and Scherer (1993) point out, there is little systematic knowledge about the details of either the encoding or decoding process, although work has appeared in both areas over the last few years. By encoding, Pittam and Scherer were referring to the externalization of underlying psychophysiological states and the realization of culturally determined display characteristics. The decoding process refers particularly to the acoustic cues listeners use in inferring speaker state. Table 5.1 provides a list of the major physical measures that have been linked to emotion (for a more detailed account of these, see Scherer, 1986a). These measures have been discussed in more detail in Chapter 3.

The following section on the vocal communication of emotion covers both the communication of discrete emotions and the more general affective states. I am indebted to two publications (Pittam & Scherer, 1992, 1993) for providing points of departure for this section of the chapter. While it is reasonably clear that listeners can distinguish some specific emotions in the voice with some degree of accuracy (see Scherer, Banse, Wallbott, & Goldbeck [1991] for a recent account of accurate decoding of a number of discrete emotions), these tend to be basic or fundamental emotions such as anger, grief, or elation. Even children as young as 3 or 4 years seem able to distinguish with reasonable accuracy basic emotions such as anger, happiness, and sadness from intonation patterns (Baltaxe, 1991) and anger and happiness from vocal cues alone (Hortaçsu & Ekinci, 1992). It is less clear that listeners can distinguish accurately the more subtle or compound emotions such as relief and apprehension or, indeed, whether they are able to distinguish accurately even fundamental emotions from anything other than a relatively small subset of emotions. That is, listeners may not be able to distinguish even fundamental emotions from all possible emotions.

Inability to distinguish discrete emotions from the voice (or any nonverbal behavior) may not be of major concern to our understanding of social interaction, however. It may be that one need only to be aware that some nonneutral emotional state is being experienced. If it is then sufficiently important to pursue the matter, one can resort to asking. It is possible, then, that in the first instance levels of arousal and positivity/negativity (i.e., affective dimensions) tell us all we need to know about our interactant's emotional state.

The Discrete Emotions

A number of discrete emotions have been studied. Researchers have typically sought to establish what the physical correlates of particular emotions are. Apparent contradictions occur, however, on which physical correlates are important for which emotions and in which way. One possibility for this may be that different studies measure different types of emotion while using the same broad category label. Anger, for example, seems to cover a range of states from irritation to rage. Given the apparent contradictions, rather than present a lengthy review of the literature reporting the physical correlates of discrete emotions, a summary of the more consistent findings is presented for five broadly labeled emotions that have been regularly studied: anger, fear, sadness, joy, and disgust. This information is based on that in Pittam and Scherer (1993). For more detailed accounts of these studies and more comprehensive reviews of the literature generally, see Pittam and Scherer, and particularly Scherer (1985a, 1986a, 1989).

Anger. The frequency domain seems to be particularly important for the encoding of anger, although intensity also has been found to play a vital role. Whether it is cold or hot anger, this emotion seems to be characterized by an increase in mean fundamental frequency and mean intensity. Some studies, which may have been measuring hot anger, show increases in F0 variability and in the range of F0 across the utterances encoded. Other studies, however, have not found these characteristics, although they may have been measuring cold anger. Other anger effects include increases in high frequency energy and downward directed F0 contours. The rate of articulation usually goes up.

Fear. There is considerable agreement on the type of acoustic cue associated with fear. High arousal levels would be expected with this emotion, and this is supported by evidence showing increases in mean fundamental frequency, in F0 range, and high frequency energy. Rate of articulation is reported to be speeded up, while an increase in mean F0 has also been found for milder forms of the emotion such as worry or anxiety.

Sadness. As with fear, the findings converge across the studies that have included sadness. A decrease in mean fundamental frequency, F0 range, and mean intensity is usually found. There is also evidence for downward directed F0 contours. There is evidence that high frequency energy and the rate of articulation decreases. Most studies reported in the literature have studied the quieter, resigned forms of this emotion rather than the more highly aroused forms such as grief or desperation.

Joy. Joy is one of the very few positive emotions studied, most often in the form of elation rather than quieter forms such as enjoyment or happiness. Consistent with this high arousal level we find a strong convergence of findings on increases in mean fundamental frequency, F0 range, F0 variability, and mean intensity. There is some evidence for an increase in high frequency energy and rate of articulation.

Disgust. The results for disgust tend to be less consistent than the others across studies. The few that have included this emotion vary in their induction procedures from measuring disgust (or possibly displeasure) at unpleasant films to actor simulation of the emotion. The studies using the former found an increase in mean fundamental frequency, whereas those using the latter found the reverse—a lowering of mean F0. This inconsistency is echoed in the decoding literature.

Even from such a brief overview as this it becomes evident that where there is consistency in the findings for a particular emotion, it is usually related to the dimension of arousal and in particular the high arousal emotions such as anger, fear, and elation. Given the relationship between such emotions and the sympathetic nervous system, this is perhaps not too surprising. One should not assume from this, however, that discrete emotions are not differentiated by vocal cues.

The lack of evidence for vocal differentiation of specific emotions results from several factors. The number and type of acoustic cues used has generally been very limited. Other cues could be used, including the more complex measures derived from short-term and long-term spectra. Also, there is a need to differentiate emotions more precisely (Pittam & Scherer, 1993). This applies not only to discrete emotions, however, but to affective dimensions also.

The Dimensionality of Affective Space

To consider the functional measurement of voice (or any other communicative channel) is to be concerned with the measurement of meaning itself. One tradition concerned specifically with this stems from the well-known work of Osgood, Suci, and Tannenbaum (1957): the measurement of the underlying or latent dimensional structure of our perceptions and/or attributions made from those perceptions.

The early work by Osgood et al. (1957) produced the instrument known as the Semantic Differential. By scaling subjects' responses to stimuli using pairs of bipolar adjectives, such as good-bad or beautiful-ugly, Osgood and his colleagues were able to show both direction and intensity of each judgment made. Examples of questionnaires using these types of scales are given in Chapter 6. These scalar responses could then be factor analyzed to reveal underlying or latent dimensions that represented the semantic space. Three major factors or dimensions were revealed in the work. These were interpreted as dimensions of evaluation, potency, and activity. The reliability of these dimensions, which were seen by Osgood et al. as orthogonal, was established in a series of studies using different stimuli, which eventually included validating them cross-culturally (Osgood, May, & Miron, 1975). They were believed to represent, therefore, the major structural dimensions of meaning or semantic space.

This dimensional tradition of measurement has received considerable attention over the past three decades with several models being proposed that utilize different dimensions. Some of these have been used to measure the voice. The dimensional approach has been particularly central to the development of models of emotional experience and has been seen as providing useful descriptions of emotional response domains (Scherer, 1985a). It is in the latter sense that affect dimensions are potentially useful here: as descriptors of the communication of emotion.

Following Osgood et al. (1957), Mehrabian and Russell (1974) proposed three affect dimensions: pleasure, which in general ranged from positive to negative and is the equivalent of Osgood et al.'s dimension of evaluation; arousal, ranging from sleep to frantic excitement and is the equivalent of Osgood et al.'s activity; and control or power, which relates to degree of potency. The first two dimensions, pleasure and arousal, have proven to be the most robust and have been included in other more recent models such as Daly, Lancee, and Polivey's (1983) conical model for emotional experience, in which intensity was added as the vertical axis of the cone. Russell (1980) used the same two dimensions in his circumplex model to show that affect trait words lie in an approximate circle described by these dimensions. The circumplex model has more recently received cross-cultural validation (Russell, Lewicka, & Niit, 1989).

It has been suggested (Gallois, 1993) that, of Mehrabian and Russell's original three dimensions, pleasure and arousal appear to be useful across a number of different situations, whereas control or power seems to be more specific to interpersonal contexts. Arousal has been clearly linked to vocal cues (Burgoon, Kelley, Newton, & Keeley-Dyreson, 1989) and has tended to be the most studied of these dimensions in the vocal communication area—although see Pittam et al. (1990), who found evidence that all three dimensions were reflected differently in particular frequency ranges of the long-term spectrum (LTS). Thus they found that arousal and positivity were both reflected in the 2-2.5 kHz range but in different ways: as arousal levels rose, spectral energy increased, while the reverse was found for positivity. Control, on the other hand was prominently reflected in the 0-350 Hz range and above approximately 4 kHz.

Scherer (1986a; Scherer & Oshinsky, 1977) has also used this dimensional tradition to study affect and the voice. Scherer and Oshinsky used semantic differential ratings of synthesized tone sequences that had been manipulated on a number of parameters such as amplitude, frequency, and tempo. They were concerned with the use of such vocal cues in the attribution of affect. In the more recent work, Scherer predicted vocal outcomes to three "response dimensions," representing affective responses to incoming stimuli. These three dimensions, which Scherer labeled hedonic valence, activation, and power, correspond to the original Osgood et al. (1957) dimensions of evaluation, activation, and potency.

Latent dimensions, as a way of measuring meaning, are as useful to studies of the voice as they are to other communicative channels. They provide us with important insights into the judgments we make about an individual's personal and group identity. They also give us information about the strategies we adopt in interactive situations.

Issues and Research Problems

Pittam and Scherer (1992, 1993) have pointed to a number of research issues and problems related to the vocal communication of emotion. Some of these are dealt with here. Other methodological issues of a more general nature appear in Chapter 6. One major problem, shared with most research on the communication of emotion, vocal or otherwise, is the difficulty of studying not only real but strong emotions. Very few studies have used naturally occurring strong emotions. One of the best known is the spectrographic analysis of an American radio announcer's voice recorded at Lakeside, NJ, in 1937, when the German zeppelin *Hindenburg* burst into flames (Williams & Stevens, 1972). The distress, horror, and shock in the announcer's voice were reflected in heightened mean fundamental frequency and rapid changes in F0 variation. Another study (Popov, Simonov, Frolov, & Khachatur'yants, 1971) measured the voices of Russian cosmonauts during periods of high stress in space. They suggested that heightened emotional stress could be distinguished in the LTS. Such studies, however, are few.

Because of this dearth of data, researchers have either studied emotion portrayals by actors (see Scherer et al. [1991] for a detailed review of this type of approach) or have used induction techniques that are ethically acceptable. This issue is raised in more detail in Chapter 6 when methodological issues related to the construction of stimulus tapes are discussed. For the moment we can add that, as

Pittam and Scherer (1992, 1993) note, data utilizing these two approaches for studying emotional portrayal need to be systematically compared to determine how much of the acoustic variation may be due to these factors.

Two other concerns in the area of the vocal communication of emotion are the range of emotion categories studied and the meanings associated with the labels used for those categories. Too often, the range of categories studied is restricted to the basic emotions. More differentiation is needed (e.g., cold versus hot anger as well as compound emotions such as apprehension, which may be a combination of fear and surprise). In addition, there is a need to calibrate the labels used and to do so in terms of the important affect dimensions. That is, it would be very useful to interpret the labels used for discrete emotions by placing them into a multidimensional space consisting of the affect dimensions. This could also be used to compare the definitions adopted by different researchers for the same labels.

This book has separated out issues of identity and emotion. In social interactions, however, the two cannot so easily be kept apart. The importance of personal and group identity in emotion encoding and decoding is an area that only recently has attracted attention. Where apparent lack of replication in studies has occurred in the past, this may well be due to inadequate sampling based on the social identity of the subjects.

It is important to remember that voice is multifunctional. The vocal features used to encode emotion may also encode biological, linguistic, or other sociocultural factors. For example, intensity, fundamental frequency, and temporal features have all been shown to serve linguistic functions and to communicate personality characteristics in addition to emotion. There is also some evidence suggesting that linguistic phenomena and emotion are interrelated in the acoustic signal. Liberman (1978) has pointed to the slight variations in intonation that provide the listener with information about subtle shifts in affect and attitude, while Cahn (1990) has shown a relationship between linguistic stress (emphasis) and emotion. Evidence is beginning to emerge, however (Hermansky & Cox, 1991), that linguistic and speaker dependent information (which may include emotion) can be separated during speech analysis. If so, it would be a significant step forward in our understanding of vocal communication. It is likely that a number of factors will be important in trying to untangle biological, linguistic and sociocultural information.

Table 5.2   A Summary of Some Issues Needing Consideration in the Vocal Communication of Emotion

---

The relationship between acoustic features and perception
The range of acoustic features used
Greater differentiation of emotions and affective dimensions
The calibration of emotion labels and their definitions
A systematic comparison of emotion induction techniques
The influence of identity and contextual factors
Relationship between external (nurture) and internal (nature) effects
The multifunctionality of vocal features
The relationship between emotion and linguistic phenomena
Models incorporating both encoding and decoding of affect

It has been suggested (Pittam & Scherer, 1993; Scherer et al., 1980) that the vocal expression of emotion is jointly determined by an externalization of internal states and the requirements of species- or culture-specific normative models for affect displays—the push and pull effects noted in the previous chapter. This is one area needing further clarification. It is likely that more cross-cultural comparison studies are needed if we are to increase our understanding of this "nature/nurture" relationship.

It will be clear from what has already been said in this book that a large number of factors influence voice production and perception. Any theoretical bases adopted must reflect this complexity, including the relationship between encoding and decoding (as discussed by Scherer [1986a] for example; see also Chapter 7). Such an approach not only provides an overall analysis of the complete vocal emotion expression and communication process, it can also help disentangle the different factors that determine accuracy of recognition or lack of it.

Table 5.2 summarizes the issues raised in this section that need to be considered further by researchers in the area.

Stress and Fatigue

We indicated in the last chapter that the "abnormal" end of the personality continuum, the neuroses, overlapped to some extent with the emotion area. This is where neurosis and anxiety come together. Anxiety also links with stress and fatigue. It has been known for many years that fatigue may affect the voice (Laver, 1968).

Scherer et al. (1987) propose that the vocal symptoms of fatigue are hoarseness, huskiness, register breaks, loss of range, inability to use or maintain intended pitch, pitch breaks (presumably both of these may be linked to register breaks—see Chapter 2), unsteadiness of voice, lack of vocal carrying power resulting in a need to use greater effort. They speculate that changes in jitter may reflect vocal fatigue also.

The vocal communication of stress should be incorporated into a more general model of emotion and the voice. This is now accepted by major researchers in the area (Hollien, 1990; Scherer, 1989). For this reason it is included here. Major issues and concerns of this area are analogous to those discussed above for emotion—a need to define clearly the type of stress studied, problems with induction techniques, and the variety of stressors used—as well as the need to account for individual variation in the ability to cope with stress, the coping strategies adopted, and the subsequent encoding of stress in the voice (Scherer, 1986b). For all these reasons, then, it is once again difficult to compare results of different studies and, as Scherer (1986b) comments, they probably account for the inability to find predictable patterns in the use of vocal cues to encode stress. The cues proposed range over fundamental frequency, intensity, speech rate, and possibly some longer term voice qualities (Hollien, 1980).

Just as the possibility that we encode unique individuality in the voice has aroused interest in the area of crime detection (see Chapter 4), so the possibility of detecting vocal stress has resulted in a similar interest (Hollien, 1980, 1990) due mainly to the notion of lie detection. As Scherer (1989) points out, however, there is a need to differentiate between lying and being stressed: the former can occur with no stress experienced. As with the voiceprint area introduced in the last chapter, lie detection is outside the scope of the present book. In general, and where possible, the many commercially available instruments have been shown to be fallible, and Hollien (1990) warns of the social implications of using such instruments. To link lie detection with stress is probably a fatal flaw in the whole procedure. If lying is ever to be detected accurately from the voice, we need, as Hollien, following Lykken (1981), suggests, a valid lie response—a measurable event that always occurs when someone lies.

We know a considerable amount about emotion and the voice; it remains one of the most studied areas in the vocal communication literature (and this includes stress). Both methodologically and theoretically, however, many questions remain. We indicated in Chapter 1 that the different channels of communication could result in redundancy and/or confusing double messages, that in social interaction there is a close relationship between the verbal and nonverbal (see Cappella, 1989; Cappella & Palmer, 1989). This is particularly the case with the communication of emotion. In interactions, participants may use several channels both simultaneously and serially to determine which is carrying the relevant information (see Walker & Trimboli, 1989). In such a situation the verbal channel can influence perceptions of the vocal and vice versa. In the final instance, the voice, as a carrier of emotion, must be placed back into its communicative context.

The Vocal Communication of Attitude

Attitude formation and attitude change represent major areas of study not only within social psychology but psychology generally. The relationship between voice and attitude has never been developed fully in its own right, however, but has been studied across a number of different areas. As well as introducing the few studies that have considered the role of voice in the formation of attitude, in this section we will examine some of the work in the related area of language attitudes. Language attitudes developed from the study of attitudes toward specific languages to, more recently, the study of attitudes toward speakers who use a particular language or language variety. This work has relevance for the vocal communication of attitude. As we have seen, language varieties, be they geographic varieties, ethnic, class, or whatever, will often include salient vocal features. In addition, the vocal communication of attitude crosses over into personality and persuasion. In the present book, personality was covered in the previous chapter under personal identity. An introduction to persuasion and voice, including what is usually known as compliance, is presented as part of the present section.

As with the communication of emotion, a number of researchers working in the language attitudes area have tended to adopt a dimensional approach and, once again, this approach has its origins in Osgood et al.'s (1957) set of semantic differential adjective scales. One of the best known and arguably most influential of methods employing such a technique for the study of attitude, although not used specifically for the voice in its original form, is the Matched Guise Technique developed by Lambert, Hodgson, Gardner, and Fillenbaum (1960).

Using this technique, judges are presented with recordings of speakers containing two or more instances of the same speaker reading the same passage with one voice or speech feature varying each time. Judges are (supposedly) unaware that the same speaker is presented more than once. Lambert et al. (1960) used French and English guises produced by bilingual speakers. In other words, each speaker spoke the same passage twice, once in French and once in English. In that instance, judges' ratings of the two recordings could be said to be influenced by the language used.

When the Matched Guise Technique is used to obtain ratings of speakers' voices, the results obtained represent vocal stereotypes made up of a profile of traits for a particular group of speakers (Giles & Powesland, 1975). That profile depends on the details of the task judges are asked to do. For example, they may be asked to rate the speakers on a series of bipolar scales covering such concepts as whether the judges perceive the speaker to be friendly or not, dominant or not, beautiful, rich, and so on. Examples of this type of scale may be found in Chapter 6, as may comment on the neutrality or otherwise of standard reading passages.

The early work by Lambert et al. (1960) did not examine the underlying dimensional structure of the ratings collected. However, in the same year Brown and Gilman (1960) proposed the concepts of power and solidarity as providing revealing insights into pronoun use in several languages. Brown (1965) went on to propose status and solidarity as important dimensions of social interaction underlying language use generally. This led to the scales proposed by Lambert et al. being factor analyzed into latent dimensions such as status and solidarity.

Within the language attitudes area, status is usually thought of as incorporating perceived power, prestige, influence, and control, whereas solidarity covers perceived similarity (in group or individual terms), friendliness, and intimacy. Since that time these two dimensions have been proposed as underlying attitudes to a variety of languages and dialects or accents (e.g., Gallois et al., 1984; Genesee & Holobow, 1989; Lyczak, Fu, & Ho, 1976; Ryan & Carranza, 1975). The status dimension overlaps to some extent with the control or power dimension noted in the preceding section for the emotion literature, while solidarity has some similarity to pleasantness. Solidarity and status have also been used to study attitudes to vocal articulatory settings (Pittam, 1987a). As with the affect dimensions, different versions of the attitudinal dimensions have been developed. Lambert, Frankel, and Tucker (1966), for example, proposed a three-dimensional solution to the earlier work of Lambert et al. (1960): personal competence, personal integrity, and social attractiveness. As can be seen, these seem to be as much personality dimensions as ones concerned with attitude. Giles and Ryan (1982) also used these three dimensions. Effectively, the second and third of these dimensions cover similar ground to the solidarity dimension but account for a person-group orientation (Bradac, 1990). Others proposing a three-dimensional solution are Zahn and Hopper (1985) (superiority, attractiveness, and dynamism), which to some extent breaks down the status dimension into superiority and dynamism; and Mulac and colleagues, who suggested something very similar a decade earlier: socio-intellectual status, aesthetic quality, and dynamism, as part of the Speech Dialect Attitudinal Scale (SDAS) (Mulac, 1976; Mulac, Hanley, & Prigge, 1974; see also Mulac, Incontro, & James, 1985). In all cases, these proposals include a form of attractiveness dimension that appears to have something in common with the equivalent affect dimension (Osgood et al.'s [1957] "evaluation" or Mehrabian and Russell's [1974] "pleasure"). Indeed, in each case the three dimensions appear to be somewhat similar to the original set of affect dimensions suggested by Osgood et al. and described in the previous section. The concept of social attractiveness used in these studies seems to be different from the concept of vocal attractiveness introduced in the last chapter. There, the concept seemed to be linked to personality characteristics rather than social factors per se.

The most consistent finding in the language attitudes area is that speakers of perceived nonstandard or perceived foreign accents are downgraded relative to those with perceived standard or nonforeign accents. This basic principle was originally proposed by Giles (1970) and has remained the basis of all other studies. As might be expected, since that time researchers have refined this principle largely by proposing a range of additional factors that influence attitude formation. In most studies, however, it is the gestalt term *accent* that has been used rather than specific characteristics of the accent concerned.

It is possible, then, that voice (or more likely some aspect of it) will have been one channel influencing the results obtained. For general accounts and reviews of the language attitudes area, the reader is referred to Giles, Robinson, and Smith (1979), and Ryan and Giles (1982).

Giles (1970) indicated that aspects of both speaker and listener identity influenced his results: age, sex, class, and regional group membership. These and other factors have been proposed as influencing attitude formation since that time including perceived speaker age (Giles et al., 1992; Stewart & Ryan, 1982), perceived social desirability of speaker characteristics (Aboud, Clément, & Taylor, 1974), level of ethnic "accentedness" (Brennan & Brennan, 1981; Ryan & Carranza, 1975; Ryan, Carranza, & Moffie, 1977), social class of speaker (Ryan & Bulik, 1982; Ryan & Sebastian, 1980), context (Ryan & Giles, 1982), language choice (Genesee & Bourhis, 1982), and salient self-categorization of listener (Abrams & Hogg, 1987). Others could be added. Street (1985), for example, comments that speech evaluation should take into account whether listeners (in experimental studies) are participants in the interaction or simply observers.

It is quite clear that attitude formation and change are complex issues dependent on a large range of social factors. The notion of salience introduced by Abrams and Hogg is likely to be a key point. In all of the above studies the variable under consideration was made salient by its very presence in the study. The fact that voice may carry information about all such social factors (see Chapter 4) suggests that potentially it will be an important element in attitude formation and change.

As indicated, few studies have emphasized the voice in this role. Pittam and Gallois (1987), however, in a two-stage path analysis, showed that values associated with the LTS significantly predicted expert ratings of four voice qualities: creaky voice, tense voice, breathy voice, and whispery voice. The first two were shown to be negatively correlated with perceived status. In addition, Pittam (1987a) found that levels of both perceived status and solidarity vary when the same (and other) voice qualities vary. Thus, as reported elsewhere, nasal voice was perceived to be low in status but somewhat higher in solidarity. Further, tense voice was accorded high status when used by males, whereas high solidarity was accorded females who used breathy voice. The role of gender can be further illustrated by another anecdote from the Chinese drama (Arlington, 1966; see also Chapter 4). This is concerned with audience reaction to a performance. Arlington comments that audiences at the Chinese drama expressed their liking or otherwise for an actor differently depending on whether the actor was male or female (a practice that may be echoed in other cultures). The word *hao* (meaning "good") was used as the carrier of the feeling with the vocal tone being differentiated. When acclaiming male actors, the word was pronounced "loud and sharp," for female actors, however, the word was "prolonged into a soft slur" (p. 60).

Within the language attitudes area itself, few researchers have acknowledged the importance of voice. Giles (1970), however, did so by controlling for a number of his speakers' vocal features when producing the stimulus recordings: speech rate, vocal intensity, and pitch (the need for control of extraneous factors in stimulus recordings has been mentioned before and will be introduced again in the next chapter when we consider methodological issues in the study of voice). Gallois and Callan (1986) included the vocal channel in their study of Anglo-Australian attitudes to other ethnic groups in Australia. They found their Anglo-Australian subjects were less accurate in decoding affect in Italian-accented English speakers when the voice was made salient (they compared the results obtained when presenting subjects with audio and video recordings), and that this could be attributed to negative attitudes held by the subjects for such speakers. In other words, the accent became a distracter to their subjects.

Vocal Persuasion

As indicated above, the literature on attitude formation overlaps to some extent with that of persuasion. Once again, we need to state from the outset the potential for persuasion to interact with other social and personal variables. Many things can prove to be effective when trying to persuade another person. Given the appropriate context, emotion, aspects of group identity such as social class, ethnicity, gender, age, occupation, personality characteristics, and personal relationships may all persuade or help to persuade the listener. Even so, speakers may adopt a particular set of vocal characteristics when trying to persuade another person in the belief or hope that the vocal profile adopted will prove to be successful. Persuasion, however, requires both someone to persuade and someone to be persuaded. Successful persuasion may depend as much on (or more than) the ability of the decoder than the encoder. Hall (1980b) found that persuader's ability to send persuasive messages vocally did not relate significantly to their success, but that decoder's ability did. The better decoders were those most likely to be persuaded. Decoders may also influence level of persuasion in at least one other way. Buller and Burgoon (1986), for example, suggest that people hold expectations about the vocal (and other nonverbal) behavior of others and that when these expectations are violated the level of compliance may vary.

There is no clearly defined area of vocal persuasion in the literature, although a few studies have indicated a link between vocal cues (and other nonverbal behaviors) and persuasion as well as other factors such as competence and sociability (Burgoon, Birk, & Pfau, 1990). Although a few studies such as this have directly measured persuasibility of particular vocal features, others have been more related to attitude or even personality characteristics. Similarly, it is not clear exactly what is covered by the term *persuasion*. A better term might be simply *influence*. This might allow the inclusion of such comments as those by Burgoon, Buller, and Woodall (1989) who propose the use of a harsh voice quality to threaten and the use of cold and angry tones for negative reinforcement. It would also include the literature on compliance, some of which has included vocal features (Buller & Aune, 1988; Buller & Burgoon, 1986).

In one of the few studies directly measuring vocal features and persuasion, Pittam (1990), in a study involving white American and white Anglo-Australian listeners, found that for both groups perceived pitch variability correlated positively and significantly with perceived persuasiveness. The reverse was true for the long-term setting of nasality. Few researchers have considered the persuasiveness of nasality. Scherer (1979b) included it in his study of perceived influence on simulated juries but found no significant correlation between this vocal feature and perceived influence, although the levels of nasality present in his speakers' voices may have been low.

Several other vocal characteristics have been related to persuasion in the literature. As indicated, however, some of these studies are as much related to attitude and personality as persuasion. Pearce and Brommel (1971) reported that a conversational style of speech, characterized in part by less volume, was rated as more trustworthy than a dynamic delivery. Trustworthiness may be one element determining levels of persuasion. Set against this finding is that of Scherer (1979b), who reported that louder voices were perceived as more influential. The link between perceived pitch variation and persuasion may follow a similar pattern. The more variation perceived in the voice, the more influential the speaker (Scherer, 1979b) and confident (Hall, 1980a). Also, one finding for pitch and persuasion relates to a point made in Chapter 4 about lower pitched voices being deemed more suitable for broadcasting: lower pitched speakers are perceived as more truthful and potent (Apple, Streeter, & Krauss, 1979).

The findings for speech rate are a little more ambiguous in terms of perceived persuasiveness. Woodall and Burgoon (1984) found that faster speakers were thought to be more dominant (and may, therefore, be more persuasive) but less socially attractive (and less persuasive). Other studies support Woodall and Burgoon's findings. Speakers who speak faster have been perceived as more competent (Machlachlan, 1979; Smith et al., 1975), confident and competent (Scherer, London, & Wolff, 1973), and as having enhanced credibility (Miller, Maruyama, Beaber, & Valone, 1976). Similarity of speaker rate and (pretested) listener rate can also raise social attractiveness (Buller, LePoire, Aune, & Elroy, 1992) and increase chances of compliance.

Once again we begin to see the complexity of the influences on the variable studied. This has been acknowledged by a number of researchers examining speech rate, some of whom have indicated a need to take account of other factors. Woodall and Burgoon (1984) suggest that using faster speech as a strategy to enhance credibility may result in higher ratings on perceived extroversion and dynamism but lower ratings on such scales as trustworthiness and honesty. Also relevant here are the findings of Bond, Feldstein, and Simpson (1988). In a series of studies they found that perceived rate was influenced by two other voice features: fundamental frequency and intensity. This may provide support for the comment made earlier in Chapter 1 about the need to include the appropriate combination of vocal features in our studies.

Summary

If nothing else, the last two chapters should have shown that vocal communication is a complex, multifunctional affair. Aspects of group identity, personal identity, emotion, attitude, and persuasion interact in confusing ways that are not easy to isolate in experimental studies or empirical studies generally. This chapter, like Chapter 4, has simplified the situation somewhat to allow discussion on these major aspects of communication. The vocal communication of emotion probably constitutes the most comprehensively studied of these areas. Even here, however, as we have seen, many problems remain. We still have little systematic knowledge of either the encoding or decoding process as far as voice is concerned. In the section on issues and research problems we tried to indicate the extent of these problems, many of which are methodological and/or determined by lack of communication among researchers working in the area. Most in need of consideration is the systematic understanding of the relationship between acoustic features and our perception of emotional state; the need to study a greater range of real emotional states; and working out the relationship between the vocal communication of emotion and linguistic phenomena.

Within the attitudes area much more work is needed. Little is known of the effect of vocal features on attitude formation or how this links to aspects of group or personal identity. The whole area of expectancy violations needs to be brought to bear on vocal communication, also. The few studies that have included voice features have indicated this is likely to be a fruitful area of study; that we do have expectations about the voice in social interactions and that violation of these expectations will have an important effect on the interaction, particularly in terms of attitude formation and/or compliance.

Consistent and appropriate methodology (or lack of it) has been cited on several occasions throughout Chapters 4 and 5 as being crucial to the validity and reliability of the results obtained. Studies of voice are no different from any others in this respect. Having reviewed the multidisciplinary literatures concerning voice, we now turn to some points of methodology specific to the study of voice.

CHAPTER SIX

Methodological Issues
in the Study of Voice

Studies of voice nearly always involve an audio recording. This recording may be analyzed to determine its acoustic properties, or it may be played to listeners who then judge the recordings on the tape in some way. Some studies may use both types of analysis and try to relate the two. Occasionally, audio tapes will not be used. Instead, trained speakers interact with a number of different unknowing individuals, modifying their voices in prearranged ways, thus allowing the researchers to observe the differences in the interactant's behavior following each type of vocal presentation. In all cases, however, one of the underlying (often unstated) aims of these studies is to better understand the way different voice types function communicatively. Sometimes voice is only one of the nonverbal channels studied. In studies such as these, video tapes may also be used and subjects asked to comment on visual channels as well as voice. Sometimes written transcripts or video tapes without sound are presented to subjects in an attempt to determine which channel is most useful in communicating the variable under study.

The study of voice, like many other fields, requires careful planning. Unfortunately, there are usually no guidelines available to help with the appropriate methodology. This chapter is designed to provide such information. It will not cover basic issues of experimental design, but only those issues specifically relevant to voice. For those interested in methodological issues relating to nonverbal behavior generally, see Harper, Wiens, and Matarazo (1978) and Scherer and Ekman (1982). Three areas will be considered: issues relating to the recording of voices; the construction of the stimulus tapes played to listeners in perceptual studies and the types of control that need to be placed on them; and finally the form and types of judgments listeners may make.

Audio Recordings

Acoustic analysis of the voice requires high quality recordings. This means, if possible, recording in a sound dampened studio. Extraneous noises can be found in the most unlikely places, including fluorescent lights and air conditioning. Once such noises have been recorded along with the speaker's voice it is almost impossible to remove them. It is not intended to go into detail here about speech enhancement techniques (i.e., the cleaning up of tapes to remove extraneous noises and to enhance the speech signal). Suffice it to say that even the state-of-the-art techniques are not guaranteed to produce a signal completely free of unwanted noises. Neither will they result in a speech signal that is identical to one recorded without the noise. If we remove noises from an audio tape, we remove also the parts of the speech signal that were underneath them. Only in recent years have researchers in this area begun to understand how we might put back the parts of the speech signal that are removed (for recent accounts of such techniques see Bregman [1990] and Cooke and Brown [1993]). If at all possible, then, high quality recordings free of extraneous noise should be used in the first place.

Microphones and recorders should have a high fidelity over the range of human hearing. This is estimated to be at best 20 Hz to 20,000 Hz (although 16 Hz to 18,000 Hz is also cited). Below this we may not hear the signal but we will probably feel it. The frequency range important for speech is about 100-5,000 Hz, although there are several studies suggesting that higher frequencies may be also important for voice (see Pittam et al. [1990] for a review of these). For this reason it is important to use recording equipment that can retain high fidelity over the hearing range. High quality analogue cassette recorders are usually used these days, although digital cassette recorders are better. The recording capability of the machine is the important thing rather than its playback facilities. In the studio, playback will usually be achieved through an independent amplifier and loudspeakers or headphones. In the field (i.e., not in the recording studio) one only needs to be able to check that recording is taking place. High quality playback facilities on a working speech and voice recorder are not needed.

When recording it is better to use a unidirectional rather than multidirectional microphone as the latter will pick up sounds from around the room as well as the speaker's voice. This will be determined in part, however, by the number of speakers and availability of microphones. The ratio between the sounds wanted (the signal) and the extraneous ones (the noise) should be as high as possible (i.e., more signal, less noise). Even dubbing from one tape to another can produce a hum that will lower the signal-to-noise ratio. The lower this ratio, the less useful the signal will be for acoustic analysis.

Where possible, the distance from the speaker's mouth to the microphone should be kept constant. This is to remove one of the many sources of variation of sound intensity in speech signals. Similarly, the gain controls on the recorder should be kept constant throughout a recording and across all recordings made, if at all possible. Unless such controls are placed on all the recordings made for a study, measurement of voice intensity or perceptual measures of loudness across speakers become meaningless. It will not be possible to tell whether the variation in intensity comes from the speaker or some aspect of the recording conditions. If it is necessary to the study to have all the recordings of similar intensity, the speaker may need to repeat the piece being recorded, rather than the researcher trying to adjust the recording intensity levels by shifting the gain control.

Duration of each recording should suit the needs of the study. As indicated in Chapter 3, if the intention is to conduct long-term spectral analyses such as the LTS, at least 30 seconds of continuous speech from each speaker and preferably closer to 60 seconds will be needed. What the speakers actually say will again depend on the needs of the study (see the next section of this chapter for types of material used as stimuli). In special cases, such as the study of the vocal communication of emotion, the type of signal recorded will need to be very carefully prepared. To obtain recordings of discrete emotions such as anger or grief is not easy. It is not ethically acceptable to induce strong examples of such emotions in subjects. Because of this, as indicated in Chapter 5, there is a dearth of data of naturally occurring strong emotions. Researchers have either studied emotion portrayals by actors (see Scherer et al. [1991] for a detailed review of this type of approach) or have used induction techniques that are ethically acceptable. The latter tends to result in relatively weak affect states of the subjects studied. Whichever approach is used, there are both advantages and disadvantages. While emotion states portrayed by actors in the studio are generally of sufficient intensity and clearly differentiated, it is possible that the actors portray socially shared expression prototypes (Pittam & Scherer, 1993) or learned theatrical stereotypes. Induction techniques using nonactors as subjects run the risk of not eliciting the same emotion in each subject. Ascertaining whether this is so or not is both methodologically and practically difficult, especially if the intensity is low.

If the recordings have to be made in the field, poorer quality recordings will inevitably result; extraneous noise is ever present. One example of an actual incident that happened to the author may illustrate the frustration that can result from not being sufficiently aware of noise in the recording environment. The author was involved with a colleague in recording conversations with Vietnamese refugees that had been brought to Australia as part of the Australian Federal Government's Family Reunion Program. This involved recording in the refugees' homes. One hot evening in summer we were recording in the home of one of the subjects when our host asked if we wanted a cold drink. We accepted gratefully. This should have been the moment we switched off the recorder. Instead we kept recording. When we came to analyze this tape acoustically, we were surprised to see sharp spikes of energy right through a very interesting section of the recording. It was only later that we remembered the cold drinks. The spikes were the sound of ice cubes being dropped into the drinking glasses, a sound we had not been aware of at the time. Microphones do not have the capability to select only the important sounds and "tune out" the unimportant ones as the human auditory system does.

Recording in the field will always produce problems. It is impossible to remove all the extraneous noises. One must be constantly aware of them, however, and ask the speaker to repeat when necessary. If it is important to understand the actual words the speaker uses, and the speaker slurs the words or distorts them in some other way, the researchers should always ask if they have heard correctly. In general, however, the longer the stretch of speech obtained without interruption, the better. Other more practical problems can be overcome by ensuring that the equipment used is working well before leaving the studio, that spares of everything are taken including the recorder, tapes, microphones, microphone batteries if necessary, extension power leads, and assistants to take care of other interested parties, including the overfriendly family dog. An earlier account of the problems of audio recordings may be found in Scherer (1984a). While technology has advanced considerably since that piece was published, many of the practical issues discussed remain relevant to the researcher.

Constructing the Stimulus Tape

Stimulus tapes used in perceptual studies will usually (although not always) be produced in the recording studio. In presenting stimulus voices to judges, researchers have a number of decisions to make concerned with the construction of the stimulus tape itself (or, if "live" voices are to be used, with the specific modifications the trained speakers will make). In other words, decisions need to be made on what it is the subjects will actually hear. These represent controls over and above the ones noted in the previous section for general audio recording.

The comments that follow are concerned particularly with audio tapes. The points made, however, may be applied to any type of stimulus used for subjects to judge voices. Depending on the particular research aims, subjects in perceptual studies may be played an audio tape containing a number of different speakers, the same speaker repeated several times, or a combination of the two. The task is a comparative one, therefore. Given that the voice is a package of behaviors over and above the words being spoken, it follows that considerable control is needed over the recordings if we are to manipulate the voices successfully such that our judges hear what we want them to hear. Thus, for example, if we are interested in studying the relationship between speaking rate and the social category of age, we must ensure that other vocal parameters such as mean fundamental frequency, F0 range, mean amplitude, amplitude range, plus the various articulatory settings remain constant (or as constant as we can get them) across all the recordings made. At the same time, we must manipulate the variable under study (speaking rate) in a controlled way. In doing this, we can be reasonably sure that when the subjects listen to the recordings and make their judgments of age, it is the variation in speaking rate that is influencing the variation in judgments made.

So far in this chapter we have considered only the recording of real speakers. It is also possible, however, to construct a tape that modifies those voices in various ways electronically or even uses synthesized voices rather than "natural" ones. With the availability of more sophisticated electronic analysis equipment, relatively easy acoustic manipulation of the speech signal has become possible. This has been an important development for the construction of stimulus tapes in voice and speech studies. Thus we find the use of electronically synthesized voices as stimuli (Scherer, 1982). The more sophisticated voice and speech synthesis systems allow the researcher to select specific values for key acoustic features such as fundamental frequency, duration of various parts of the signal, amplitude, and so forth. This type of micro-acoustic control, while useful for the degree of control it gives over the stimulus (not to mention dispensing with the problems of live recording), nonetheless has problems of its own. Few synthesis systems that give this level of control, even today, sound "natural." The resulting stimulus, from a decoder's perspective, may be very odd and influence any judgments made about it.

Another, more recent, technique that may overcome this is what has been called resynthesis (Scherer, 1987). This technique takes a recording of a real speaker and digitally encodes and stores the recording on computer, allowing the researcher then to analyze the digitized signal and modify selected key features. Again, these tend to be features such as fundamental frequency and intensity, but many micro-acoustic details may be modified. The technique utilizes spectral analysis such as linear predictive coding (LPC). This is a popular technique for extracting frequency information from the signal, although its primary use is to provide information about the configuration of the vocal tract (O'Shaughnessy, 1987). Resynthesis potentially offers the most useful digital signal processing technique to date for the construction of stimulus tapes, even though the problems associated with recording remain.

Most tapes used in perceptual studies use "natural" voices that need controlling in the ways suggested above. The controls we place on those recordings, however, need to cover more than the practical problems discussed in the previous section and the physical vocal features noted above. There are other factors that need controlling, including the words and sentences the speakers say. In other words, the semantic and syntactic content of the recordings we make also require our attention.

Neutralizing Semantic and Syntactic Content

One of the central concerns facing the researcher in the voice perception and attribution/inference area is the semantic and syntactic content of the passage recorded for subjects to judge. The researcher may wish to provide subjects with stimulus recordings that are content free, in that the semantic and syntactic content of the utterances used in the recordings is somehow neutralized. The point to be made here is that the subjects' attention should be focused on the voice only—the channel we are interested in—and not influenced by what the speakers are saying. A number of ways of isolating voice from the linguistic channel were developed quite early. These included playing speech backwards to the listeners (Sherman, 1954) thus effectively removing the content; using a language not understood by the judges (Kramer, 1964) and recording meaningless content such as the alphabet (Davitz & Davitz, 1959), both of which have a similar result. Starkweather (1956) provides a review of the early work.

Somewhat more recently other means of isolating voice were developed. The main ones were randomized splicing (Scherer, 1971) and content filtering (Rogers, Scherer, & Rosenthal, 1971). For reviews of these methods, see Johnson, Emde, Scherer, and Klinnert (1986) and Scherer et al. (1985). Originally, with randomized splicing, the audio tape itself was cut into small pieces which were then spliced together again supposedly in a random order—hence the name randomized splicing. These days it is effected digitally, the signal being divided into short segments of about 250 milliseconds and then randomly reordered. The new signal is then restored into analogue form. The effect of this technique, it is claimed, is to remove, or at least partially distort, all temporal sequencing cues from the speech signal, leaving long-term effects such as voice quality, amplitude, and fundamental frequency present in the signal. Van Bezooijen and Boves (1986), however, suggest that some information relating to articulatory and dynamic features also remains.

Distortion or deletion of sequencing cues from the signal may be a problem. If one is interested in collecting attitudinal or affect ratings of the voice, for example, the naive judges may still need to make use of sequencing cues. As Noller (1984) points out, to understand, say, the discrete emotion of anger, one may need the gradual crescendo of amplitude that can be associated with this emotion. While this inevitably raises questions about the effectiveness of randomized splicing for this type of study, some success has been claimed for it in studies of the perception of affect (Johnson et al., 1986) and deception (Scherer et al., 1985). When compared to other masking methods, it has proven to be at least equally successful to backwards speech and content filtering in the recognition of sadness, anger, and fear (Johnson et al., 1986).

With content filtering, the semantic and syntactic content is masked by removing or attenuating relevant frequency ranges. These would usually be all frequencies above about 400 Hz or possibly lower. The effect is that of a muffled voice; the words are not clear. The most significant objection to this method is that, depending upon the frequency range filtered, sequencing cues such as pausing, rhythm, patterns of emphasis, and intonation contours remain relatively unaffected (Harper et al., 1978). These will all give clues to the semantic and syntactic content, and may lead to recognition of the content by subjects listening to the tape after repeated exposure unless the frequency cut-off point is very low. Apart from loudness, all dynamic features remain unchanged, and while some voice quality features may also remain (van Bezooijen & Boves, 1986), others are thought to be totally masked or even distorted.

Rogers et al. (1971) detail a simple but quite flexible content filtering system. Some researchers have claimed success with this method, showing that naive judges could differentiate emotions (Alpert, Kurtzberg, & Friedhoff, 1963), personality characteristics (Milmoe, 1965, cited in Scherer, 1971), affect such as warmth and hostility (Blanck & Rosenthal, 1984), and assertiveness (Kimble, Yoshikawa, & Zehr, 1981). Krauss, Apple, Morency, Wenzel, and Winton (1981), however, found filtering less effective for judgments of affect than other types of presentation such as written transcripts and the full speech signal.

One of the major problems with any method of content masking is the oddity of the resulting stimuli. This itself may affect the judgments made. Also, as was indicated in the above paragraphs, the retention or otherwise of sequencing cues can prove problematic depending on the type of study. Randomized splicing removes or distorts many sequencing cues, content filtering often does not. The researcher must take this into consideration when selecting an appropriate means of isolating voice from linguistic cues.

A further method of neutralizing content that does not rely on distortion of the acoustic speech signal or manipulating it in any way is the use of standard reading passages. Such passages as the Rainbow Passage (Fairbanks, 1940) have been available for many years. All speakers in studies using these passages read (or speak) the same passage, thus ensuring that semantic and syntactic content remains constant across speakers and, presumably, therefore, is neutralized. Whatever variable the researcher is manipulating may be changed while holding semantic and syntactic content constant. The Matched Guise Technique developed by Lambert et al. (1960), and discussed in Chapter 5, uses such a method. As was noted in that chapter, the variable under study in Lambert et al.'s study was the language itself—French or English. The passage and speaker remained the same, only the language changed.

Standard passages, while free of the problems confounding content masking, are at a fundamental level problematic. They can never really be neutral, even though semantic and syntactic content remains the same. As Giles and Coupland (1991b) indicate, when a subject listens to a series of recordings using such a passage, responses will be made based on preexisting social schemata. Experimental conditions cannot remove all social influence on the subjects' responses. Indeed, as they point out, the more contextual specificity that is removed from the stimulus, the more variable and inventive will the listeners become in creating a context for that stimulus. A different but more specific problem can appear in a guise study of different accents. If the strict controls advocated above are not adopted when recordings are made, recordings may vary on features extraneous to the accents involved.

One potential problem relating to studies that examine the longer term tones of voice or voice qualities can be the presence of segments in the spoken passage that utilize the same settings under study. It was noted in Chapter 2 that articulatory settings can operate at the segmental level as well as in a longer time frame. If segments characterized by the setting being examined are present in too large numbers in the reading passage used, they may influence judgments made. An example where the latter problem was overcome may be found in Pittam (1987a). In this study a Matched Guise Technique was adopted. Judges were asked to rate recordings of speakers who were using different articulatory settings. One of the settings examined was nasality. In English, the language used in this study, there are three nasal consonants. To overcome the potential influence of this linguistic nasality on judges' ratings of the long-term setting of nasality—the variable under study—a standard passage was devised containing no nasal consonants.

The points made in this section have been concerned specifically with the making and playing of stimulus tapes to listeners. As indicated at the start of the chapter, however, sometimes studies will be designed that use "live" speakers. Given the problems outlined in maintaining maximum control of the vocal signal presented to listeners, it will be appreciated that such studies are fraught with difficulty. Whatever the type of study, control of the vocal stimulus is essential if we are to make meaningful predictions about how particular vocal parameters function in social interaction.

Naive Judgments and Questionnaire Design

Many studies of voice are perception studies concerned with naive subjects (i.e., untrained, inexperienced, and unknowing subjects) listening to recordings of speakers, recordings that have been controlled in particular ways. The subjects may then judge the speakers on certain parameters, such as indicating what they believe the age, gender, or ethnic group of the speaker to be; or they may comment on what they perceive the personality characteristics of the speaker to be, or even comment on the voice itself: the speaker has a high pitched voice, a loud voice, or the speaker speaks slowly, and so on. The studies are often not simply perceptual, then, but attributional and inferential. Questionnaires are usually used for the subjects to record these judgments, often utilizing scalar measurement. Sometimes psychological studies statistically relate these judgments to physical measurements of the voice in attempts to determine which aspects of the voice may be linked to identity, the communication of affect, attitude, and so forth.

This final, and brief, section presents examples of types of questionnaire that have been adopted in perceptual studies of voice. The two basic forms of questionnaires used have tended to be the Likert scale and the semantic differential scale. Table 6.1 gives an example

Table 6.1 An Example of a Likert Scale

After you have listened to each speaker, please indicate the extent to which you agree or disagree with each of the following statements about that speaker.

1. The speaker has a friendly voice.

1	2	3	4	5	6
Strongly disagree	Somewhat disagree	Slightly disagree	Slightly agree	Somewhat agree	Strongly agree

of the former. With the Likert scale, the researcher presents a set of statements to the judges who are asked whether, and to what extent, they agree or disagree with the statement. Usually, instructions are given to the judges at the head of the list of scales.

In the example shown in Table 6.1, both numbers and descriptive labels are used. Sometimes the labels only are used. At other times a numerical scale with labels at the end points may be used. Such scales may be used for eliciting attitudes to a speaker. As can be seen, the scale shown has 6 scalar degrees. It is a matter of some controversy how many points should be used. There are two issues to consider here. First, the researcher must decide whether the subjects can reasonably be expected to distinguish, in this case, 6 levels of agreement. Six is probably an acceptable number. It is a moot point whether a scale with as many as, say, 9 points is still as reasonable, and that the divisions between two points on the scale have any meaning at all. The second issue is whether to use an odd or even number of points. An odd number allows the subject to "sit on the fence" and select the central point; an even number means the subject is forced to choose one side or the other, to agree or disagree. There is no right or wrong answer to this; the researcher must decide these issues on the merits of each case.

The second type of scale is one based on the semantic differential—introduced in Chapter 5. Table 6.2 gives an example. The researcher usually uses a set of adjectives drawn from the standard set of semantic differential scales, although others may be used if appropriate. With this type of scale, labels are placed at the end points only.

As can be seen, the type of scale presented in Table 6.2 may ask the subject to rate the speaker on scales that contain a single concept—such as pleasantness—or scales that seem to have different concepts at each end. In each case, however, this type of scale assumes that

Table 6.2   An Example of a Semantic Differential Scale

For each of the following list of adjectives, circle the number that best corresponds to your feelings about the speaker.

I feel the speaker is

1	2	3	4	5	6
Good					Bad
1	2	3	4	5	6
Strong					Weak
1	2	3	4	5	6
Pleasant					Unpleasant
1	2	3	4	5	6
Powerful					Powerless

each scale contains a single idea. Thus, to be good is to be not-bad, and to be strong is to be not-weak. These are all examples of what was referred to in earlier chapters as bipolar scales. In addition, it is assumed that the scale is a continuum and an interval scale; that is, it is comprised of perceptually equal intervals.

Finally, judges can be asked to comment on the vocal features themselves. Usually, as indicated above, judges in these studies are naive, in the sense of being nonexpert, not trained in the task. The researcher is limited, then, in what can be asked of such judges about vocal features. Naive judges will not know what an articulatory setting is, for example. We can ask about such features as pitch, loudness, and speech rate, possibly also about fluency of a speaker. The concern here is similar to one raised earlier: all the judges must have the same idea in their heads about the feature being rated. This type of questionnaire might present judges with a scale of the type shown in Table 6.3.

Summary

This chapter has presented only an introduction to some methodological issues relating to the study of voice. Voice studies, like all

Table 6.3 An Example of a Vocal Feature Scale

For each speaker, decide how high or low pitched their voice is, how loudly or softly they are speaking, how fast or slow and so forth. Circle one number of each of the following scales for each speaker.

1	2	3	4	5	6
Very High Pitch					Very Low Pitch
1	2	3	4	5	6
Very Loud					Very Soft
1	2	3	4	5	6
Very Fast					Very Slow

empirical work, are subject to fundamental rules of experimental design. The points raised here should be seen as additional to such rules. The examples of scales presented in the final section are not the only possibilities. As indicated at the start of the chapter, we may be concerned not only with attitudes or perception of vocal features, we may also be interested in affective judgments, which, as was indicated in Chapter 5, may also be elicited using the same techniques. In addition, sex, age, or ethnicity of speaker, in other words, aspects of their social identity, or personality characteristics may be of interest.

Questionnaire studies are used in many areas of social scientific research. The types of questionnaires represented here may be familiar, therefore, although perhaps not in this form. No detail has been given on what the researcher does with the ratings once collected. This is simply because, just as this is not a book on experimental design, neither is it a book on statistics. Ratings of the type described in Tables 6.1 and 6.2 would usually be analyzed statistically. The most common form of analysis of this type of material is factor analysis or principal components analysis to examine the underlying dimensional structure. This refers to the dimensions discussed in Chapter 5: status and solidarity, for example, or the affect dimensions of arousal, pleasure, and control. The ratings of the vocal features in

Table 6.3 would usually be considered individually. The concepts dealt with (pitch, loudness, etc.), are sufficiently different that one would not expect them collectively to display an underlying dimensional structure.

The material in the first two sections of this chapter is less likely to be familiar. By providing such guidelines and information it is hoped the study of voice will be seen as within the reach of more researchers. That said, control over the recordings and construction of stimulus tapes must remain a major concern for all researchers.

CHAPTER SEVEN

A Theoretical Framework for Vocal Function: Models of Communication

No theoretical models have been developed solely to explain the functioning of voice within social interactions. There are, however, a number of existing models of nonverbal behavior and communication that may provide appropriate explanations for vocal communication. In determining which of these should be discussed, the principles that underlie this book have been used as a guide. The principles have all been stated elsewhere but may be summarized as follows:

1. Voice is a communicative channel comprising a package of nonverbal (specifically, vocal) behaviors.
2. Like other nonverbal channels, voice may be used in social interactions to communicate group and personal identity, affect, attitude, and so forth.
3. Voice is used with speech in most interactions; it underlies all speech.
4. Voice can be described using the same types of articulatory and acoustic parameters as those used for speech.

It will be argued in this chapter that a single theory of the functional communication of voice in social interactions is unlikely to be developed. The multidisciplinary nature of vocal communication, the multifunctionality of voice, the complexity of verbal and nonverbal communication (of which voice is itself a complex package of behaviors), and the simultaneous compound functioning of particular vocal behaviors all mitigate against the development of such a "super theory." In the light of this and the four principles listed above, and the fact that we are concerned particularly with the *functions* of voice, a number of theories will be proposed in this chapter, each theory providing specific insights into vocal communication within social interactions and operating on independent but interacting planes or dimensions. These will then become part of the proposed theoretical framework discussed in this chapter and in Chapter 8.

Three theoretical models will be introduced in this chapter: Patterson's (1983, 1990) sequential functional model of nonverbal exchange, communication accommodation theory (CAT) (Giles & Coupland, 1991a), and Scherer's (1978; Goldbeck et al., 1988) modified Brunswikian lens model. The first focuses on the functions of nonverbal behavior within interactions and is a model of social exchange; it does not consider the voice in any comprehensive way, however. The second model (CAT) in some respects combines the other two. It too is a model of social exchange that examines communicative expression, perception, and subsequent behavior change, is mainly concerned with speech but may cover all types of nonverbal behavior. Unlike the other two, however, CAT is seen as an intergroup model of interpersonal behavior (as will be noted below, it may be possible to classify Scherer's model in these terms also). The last model to be discussed was designed specifically for the voice, but is not a model of social exchange, examining instead the externalization of speaker characteristics and the perceptions and inferences of the listener. In discussing this model, another theoretical perspective proposed by Scherer (1988) will be introduced briefly for the insights it too can bring to the vocal communication of emotion.

These models form three major theoretical approaches appropriate to a study of vocal function. They will be introduced and their strengths and weaknesses for explaining vocal function discussed. As indicated, the way they might be integrated into a theoretical framework of vocal function will be outlined in this chapter. It is worth noting at the outset, however, that Patterson's model and CAT will be seen as having certain elements in common, whereas Scherer's model is of a different type with different aims and assumptions. As a way of leading into the three theories, a number of other concepts will be introduced that also have relevance to a functional account of voice. These are mostly taken from somewhat older functional models of language and speech (e.g., Bühler, 1934; Jakobson, 1960) and other functional models of nonverbal communication (e.g., Argyle,

1988; Hall, 1966) and provide a theoretical context for the framework to be proposed. Following the presentation of the three major theories the concept of communication itself will be examined.

Functional Models of Language and Speech

This section introduces examples of earlier functional models of language and speech. They show that a number of key concepts relating to communication have been discussed for many years and provide the context for more recent theory. In some instances they have had a direct influence on the work of such researchers as Scherer and Laver—the latter's work was discussed in Chapter 2.

In the area of the communication of affect, Scherer (1988) argues for vocalizations functioning symbolically. In doing so, he follows the early functional model of speech developed by Bühler (1934), who proposed the tripartite scheme of speech functioning as, (a) a symptom—representing the state of the speaker, (b) a symbol—the representation of the object, event, and so forth, spoken about, and (c) a signal—representing the attempt to elicit a response from the listener. This model is entirely linear in terms of its ability to account for a relationship between interactants, being firmly oriented toward the speaker.

Scherer (1988) uses this early model to isolate questions concerning the functions of vocal affect expressions. While concentrating on the voice as symbol, he presents reviews of studies that deal with the voice as symptom and signal—the least developed of Bühler's three speech functions as far as voice is concerned. Voice will usually be multifunctional in social interactions, and Scherer's use of Bühler's model provides a relatively straightforward account of this, although it is a little difficult to know how to separate the symptomatic use of vocal affect expression from the symbolic, given that the object represented by the voice (symbol) is a state of the speaker (symptom).

Another early functional model of language is that of Jakobson (1960). Jakobson proposed a set of six functions: referential, emotive, conative, phatic, metalingual, and poetic. The first three constitute Bühler's set of symbol, symptom, and signal, respectively. Jakobson extended this, however, to include the other three functions. The last two of these are less useful to the present work: metalingual serves primarily to check whether a common code is held by both speaker and listener, while the poetic function focuses on the message for its own sake. The phatic function, however, is a very useful addition as far as voice is concerned. It serves primarily to establish, prolong, or discontinue communication; to check whether the channel works; and to attract attention. It seems to have been first used by Malinowski (1923). Laver (1975a, 1981b) has also commented on this concept. In what Coupland, Coupland, and Robinson (1992) call the "richest post-Malinowski treatment of phatic communion" (p. 211), Laver uses the concept to analyze opening and closing phases of conversations from a relational or interactional point of view. Later in the chapter and again in Chapter 8 we will expand on the need to regulate interactions and the role voice may play in this.

Even though the conative, metalingual and phatic functions in Jakobson's model take a listener into account, they still do so from the perspective of the speaker. Jakobson was intent on developing a functional model of language and was not concerned with social interaction as such. From a linguistic point of view, then, the six functions can usefully be seen as separate but interdependent. From a social interactive point of view, however, the three functions of conative, metalingual, and phatic overlap to some extent in that they all take the listener into account. While this is so, however, neither Jakobson's model nor Bühler's is oriented toward the listener as such, or indeed to the interaction as a whole. They may be seen, however, as early precursors of Scherer's work and, while focusing on language, tell us something about how voice functions, showing that, like phonetic descriptions of speech and voice, similarities exist between these two communicative channels at the level of function also.

Symbolic or Indexical?

Scherer is not the only figure central to vocal communication who touches on the functionality of voice. As noted in Chapter 2, Laver also referred to the voice functioning in certain ways. In his earliest work, Laver (1968) categorized voice quality as indexical (remembering that in Laver's terms voice quality covers only the long-term, quasi-permanent biological, psychological, and social attributes). By 1974, however, Laver was using the term *indexical* to cover, in addition, the shorter term aspects of psychological states in the communication of mood or attitude. In other words, he was now including some of the paralinguistic (in Laver's terms) uses of articulatory settings to communicate affect and attitude.

At one level, both Laver and Scherer are saying the same thing: voice stands for something other than itself, but we need to ask whether, in using the different terminology of symbol and index, they are making different claims about how the voice functions. Scherer appears to be saying no more than we have already noted, that the voice stands for something other than itself. This is not the case with Laver, however. Laver is careful to note that he is following Abercrombie (1967) in the way he uses *indexical*. On two occasions (1974, 1976) Laver links his use of the term back to the second trichotomy of communicative signs developed by Peirce (Hartshorne & Weiss, 1960). For Peirce, indexicality was one of three ways that a sign could stand for its object, the other two being iconically—having a resemblance to its object, and symbolically—related to its object by convention only. It is unclear whether Scherer (1988) is using symbol in this sense.

The index is in many ways the most difficult of Peirce's types of sign to understand. His clearest statement is when he notes that indices are different from the other types of sign in three ways: by having no significant resemblance to their object; by referring to individuals, single units, single collections of units, or single continua; and by directing attention to their objects by blind compulsion (Hartshorne & Weiss, 1960).

The first of these distinguishes indices from icons, while the third effectively distinguishes them from symbols. This third characteristic is deictic; that is, indices direct attention to the objects they represent. One example that is often given is that smoke is an index of fire. Laver indicates that he is not using indexical in this deictic sense. Rather, he is using it in Abercrombie's (1967) sense of evidential (Laver, 1976), and to mean that it "reveals personal characteristics of the . . . speaker" (Laver, 1974, p. 63). These seem to refer to the second of Peirce's distinguishing characteristics listed above. Laver is saying, then, that he is not using indexical in the third sense—the deictic use of the word—but in the sense covered by the second of the above characteristics, which seems to cover Abercrombie's sense of evidential.

Peirce also comments that "psychologically, the action of indices depends upon association by contiguity" (Hartshorne & Weiss, 1960, p. 172). This contiguity potentially may be achieved by both the deictic and evidential nature of the sign. The position adopted in the present book is that voice does function deictically. The voice is psychologically contiguous with the individual and does direct attention to the individual as a whole, or at least to that characteristic of the individual that we associate with the particular voice type being used. Thus, for example, certain features of the voice will lead us to infer that the speaker is male or female. The voice is, therefore, indexical, and in the full Peircian sense. It can also function symbolically, however (again, in the Peircian sense). That is, it can stand for its object in a conventional way. The use of falsetto as an honorific in the language Tzeltal (Brown & Levinson, 1978) would be an example. There is no intrinsic reason why falsetto should function this way. It does so purely by convention and so functions symbolically.

Scherer (1988) argues for the symbolic functioning of vocal affect expression. He is clearly correct in this, at the very least in a general sense. Vocal features can indeed stand for levels of affect, but as we have seen in Chapter 5 this may not involve a specific discrete emotion but something more general, such as levels of arousal or pleasure. Voice does stand for characteristics of the individual (not simply affect), and can do so both symbolically (by convention) and indexically (by contiguity and directing attention), and while the first will not always operate, the second will.

Functional Models of Nonverbal Behavior

A number of general models of nonverbal behavior, while not dealing solely with vocal behavior, can nonetheless provide important insights into the way we communicate and, consequently, into the way voice may function in social interactions. In this section, theories proposed by Hall (1959, 1966, 1974, 1981) and Argyle (1988) will be considered for the relevance they have to vocal communication, both in terms of underlying principles and how they may add to what we have already discussed about vocal function.

Although Hall (1966) was concerned with personal space and crowding (proxemics), he included a vocal loudness scale in the nonverbal behaviors considered important to personal space. Some years previous to this, in association with Trager, he had proposed eight distances (of speaker to listener), each of which involved a vocal the channels we use to provide feedback is voice. We noted earlier the need to regulate interactions. Here, it is seen as a social skill needing to be learned.

Social interactions are, then, dynamic, and we monitor the changing situation in part through our observation of back-channel or feedback signals, which then allows us to regulate our own behavior and guide the interaction as a whole. One consequence of this may be the coordination of behaviors between interactants. Voice is one of the communicative channels on which the temporal patterning of interactions may occur. This is at the level of vocal synchrony or coordination of acoustic and temporal behaviors. It has been shown that rhythmic and well-coordinated exchanges are perceived as more pleasant (Buder, 1992). The relationship between vocal activity and silence has perhaps been the most popular area of study in this tradition, although Buder's study of the fundamental frequency characteristics of dyadic conversations revealed synchrony in this acoustic variable also. The presence of temporal patterning does not mean that conversations are solely reactive, however, a point made by Patterson (1983, 1990), whose work is discussed below.

The earlier models of language and speech, as well as the more general models of nonverbal behavior, provide a context for the three theoretical models to be discussed below. They also show direct links with some of the work on vocal communication and provide a number of potentially useful functions in their own right. These will be reintroduced in Chapter 8, when the taxonomy of vocal function is developed.

Patterson's Sequential Functional Model of Nonverbal Exchange

Patterson's is the first of the three models to be discussed in detail in this chapter. It, too, is a model of nonverbal communication but one that is particularly important to the discussion here. In large part this is because it is one of the most comprehensive functional models of nonverbal behavior developed to date. It is discussed most fully in Patterson (1983, 1990).

This is a model of nonverbal exchange, focusing to a large extent on the interaction itself. Patterson's (1990) model is represented in Figure 7.1. As can be seen, there are three phases external to the

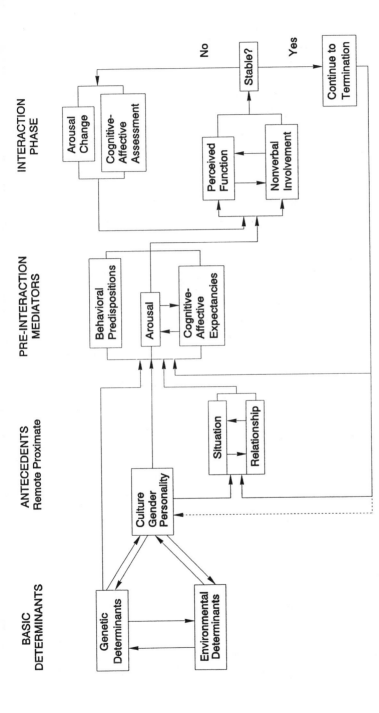

Figure 7.1. A sequential functional model of nonverbal exchange (from Patterson, 1990).

SOURCE: "Functions of Non-Verbal Behavior in Social Interaction," by M. L. Patterson, in *Handbook of Language and Social Psychology*, edited by H. Giles & W. P. Robinson, copyright © 1990 by John Wiley & Sons. Reprinted by permission of John Wiley & Sons, Ltd.

131

interaction: basic determinants, antecedents, and pre-interaction mediators. These are related to genetic, cultural, social, and individual influences on the interaction. Within the interaction itself the model is concerned above all with intensity of arousal and the perceived function of nonverbal behaviors.

From the outset, Patterson opposed a reactive account of nonverbal behavior; that is, an account in which our nonverbal behavior in social interactions is dependent only or largely on our interactant's previous behavior. Patterson also set out to show that the relationship between affect and nonverbal behavior is not necessarily consistent, in the sense that the behavior need not accurately reflect the emotion felt. In the present book we, like many others, will argue that there are multiple influences acting upon behavior in interactions, including social and cultural factors from outside the interaction itself, resulting in ongoing behavior that is not simply reactive.

Central to the model is a belief in the importance of an individual's perception of the purpose or function of an interaction. Individual factors such as emotional state and goals are seen as influencing both the pre-interaction phase and, through assessment of affective state and perceived function of nonverbal behavior, the course of the interaction. This model proposes two major factors that determine the course of the exchange from within the interaction: the relative intensity of each person's nonverbal involvement or attachment and the degree of correspondence between the functions he or she perceives the nonverbal behavior as having (Patterson, 1983, 1990). If the intensity of involvement of each of the interactants is not too disparate, and if there is a high degree of correspondence in the functions each perceives the nonverbal behavior to have then the exchange is likely to be stable. When disparities arise, however, the exchange is likely to be unstable and result in changes occurring to the arousal levels of at least one of the interactants and that person's cognitive-affective assessment of the situation, that is, any form of evaluative response (Patterson, 1983). These changes may themselves result in changes to the level of nonverbal involvement by that person and the function he or she perceives the nonverbal behavior as having. Patterson suggests that this type of loop may continue until a stable exchange is reached and/or the exchange is terminated. As was noted in Chapter 5, arousal is one of the most robust of the affect dimensions. In choosing this dimension for his model, Patterson is not only expanding on an earlier theoretical model—the arousal model of interpersonal intimacy (1976)—but is nominating nonverbal behavior (including the voice) as a major carrier of arousal. The level of intensity of nonverbal involvement, if high or even extreme, can produce negative affect in the interactant and result in changes occurring as described above. Each person has a preferred level of involvement that will be influenced by one's personal and group identity, previous relationship (if any) with the interactant, knowledge of the topic, the type of exchange, and so forth. Similar to this, where a disparity exists between the functional expectations of the interactants, an unstable exchange is also likely to occur. But, as Patterson (1983) points out, there are some types of exchange (such as a power struggle, for example), in which the functional expectancies will presumably be very similar—some form of social control—and yet the exchange is still likely to be unstable. In this model of nonverbal exchange, Patterson concentrates on stability/instability and the interactants' evaluations and shifts in arousal level to achieve stability. Essentially, then, this model seems to have most explanatory force when dealing with potentially conflictual situations.

An important characteristic from the point of view of the present book is that the model deals *directly* with perceived function. In his model, Patterson (1983, 1990) proposes a set of functions for nonverbal behavior. In the 1983 version of the model, he labels these functions information, regulating interaction, intimacy, social control, and service-task. They are seen as falling on two orthogonal dimensions. Information and regulating interaction belong to a dimension he calls molecular, in that they identify isolated patterns of behavior. The other three functions belong to the molar dimension. These three describe the theme or motive underlying the interaction. As the two dimensions are orthogonal, a behavior might be either informative or one regulating interaction (or both), while at the same time functioning to describe intimacy, social control, or service-task. In the 1990 version, Patterson adds two other functions: presenting identities and images and affect management.

Without wishing to do an injustice to what is an extremely complex and carefully developed theory, some indication of the meaning Patterson (1983, 1990) attaches to the functions is necessary. The informative function represents an individual's characteristic relationship to others or reactions to various objects or topics, whereas regulating interaction relates to behaviors serving to control the development of the interaction. As such, the former is concerned with the meaning of a behavior pattern, while the latter stresses the structure of the interaction.

The three molar functions relate to longer term dispositions (longer term in the sense that they act as underlying themes to the interaction). Intimacy was developed from the proposals of Argyle and Dean (1965). It covers the relatively spontaneous "manifestation of an affectively based reaction toward another person" (Patterson, 1983, p. 96). This may change as the relationship changes within the interaction. Social control involves a primarily interpersonal "motive for attempting to influence or change the behavior of another person" (p. 101). We noted in Chapter 5 the need to expand the notion of persuasion using the voice, proposing *influence* instead. Using *social control* as a generic term, Patterson isolates several types: power and dominance; persuasion; feedback and reinforcement; deception; and impression management. Finally, the service-task function, which is independent of interpersonal relationship, may be divided into the two subfunctions. Service represents a relationship between individuals based on one requiring service of the other, such as a doctor-patient interaction. Task is similar but concerns a relationship based on a specific task such as a construction job.

The additional functions in the 1990 version of the model are presenting identities and images and affect management. The first covers the establishing of an identity at the individual or relational level. This is not for the benefit of the interactant but for third-party observers of the interaction. The interactant is still the focus of the behavior, however. Thus a speaker may wish to appear to be a loving spouse (Patterson's example). The other spouse (who is the interactant) becomes the focus of whatever behavior is used to achieve this end, but the purpose is to communicate the image or identity of the speaker as "loving spouse" to third-party observers. This is an interesting development, recognizing that communicative behaviors are sometimes aimed beyond the immediate interaction. One might want to add that, at such times, multiple interactions are taking place and that different channels can be used for different interactions simultaneously. The final function of affect management covers the adjustment in interactive behavior to regulate strong emotional arousal and the potential consequences of emotional expression. For a much more comprehensive account of these functions, including the difference between focused and unfocused interactions, the reader is referred to Patterson (1983, 1990).

In terms of the functions that may be useful to vocal communication, then, Patterson's (1983, 1990) model highlights the need to take account of a speaker's relationship to all aspects of the context in which the interaction takes place, both in terms of short-term spontaneous behaviors and longer term dispositions. Regulation of the interaction has been mentioned by many writers and must be included in any taxonomy of vocal function, as should the regulation of affect—we have noted that vocal features have been proposed as major carriers of affect. Patterson's model is also important for expanding the concept of social control. These are all strengths of this model.

A further strength is the inclusion of the service-task function. This highlights the importance of role to particular interactions. As noted above, both the service and the task subfunctions relate to role. In connection with this, however, it would be useful to draw a distinction between the process of an interaction and its content. All interactions have multiple goals. One form of goal will be concerned with the content or subject matter or task of the interaction; another form of goal will be concerned with the process, including the establishment and maintenance of role. The service-task function does not really allow us to make this distinction.

In general, however, the set of proposed functions plus the link made between these and arousal—one of the major dimensions of nonverbal communication—make this an important model for vocal communication. In addition, while it is essentially cognitive, the model allows for links with the social context in which interactions take place. In other words, it at least acknowledges that interactions are *social* events. The inclusion of the pre-interaction mediators, antecedents, and basic determinants, while not developed sufficiently from a social perspective, provide a starting point for such a development. That said, the whole area of social context needs to be developed and, while acknowledging the importance of Patterson's (1983, 1990) model, there are a number of points such as this that need attention.

Giles and Street (1985) provide a critical review of the model as an explanation of social exchange. As we are here concerned with the functioning of voice, not all their criticisms will be addressed. A couple of points, however, can usefully be mentioned. They too note that Patterson's model does not allow for social influences on interactants in a sufficiently comprehensive way, commenting that Patterson's interactants seem to be cognitive-physiological automata. As we have already indicated, with the emphasis in the present book on social interaction, this must be seen as a weakness in Patterson's model. Social factors both before the interaction (the pre-interaction phase) and during the interaction will be influences on how an individual behaves and the type of function(s) voice is likely to perform in any given situation. Thus we need to allow for such influences acting on the interaction throughout its duration. The loop shown in Figure 7.1 back to the situation/relationship box and possibly also to the gender/culture/personality box may be an acknowledgment of this need but appears to allow only for the outcome of the interaction to feed back into the situation/relationship for future interactions.

We have also noted the multifunctionality of voice. This does not necessarily fit well into a model such as Patterson's, which emphasizes sequential processing (although, as Giles & Street [1985] point out, some recognition is given to multiple functions operating simultaneously). It may be, as Giles and Street suggest, that parallel rather than sequential processing needs to be incorporated into the model. Perhaps we should say that both parallel and sequential processing need to be taken into account. A second criticism made by Giles and Street is that there is a presumed isomorphism between actual and perceived message variables in the model. This is not necessarily the case in social interaction. Scherer's (1978) modified Brunswikian lens model, discussed below, may provide some of the balances needed to account for the lack of isomorphism that is usually found between actual and perceived message variables. Despite these weaknesses, however, Patterson's (1983, 1990) sequential functional model of nonverbal behavior remains an important development in our understanding of interactions.

Communication Accommodation Theory

The second theoretical model to be discussed is communication accommodation theory (CAT). This has one thing at least in common with the model just discussed: it too is a model of social exchange. CAT, however, does not highlight arousal levels or perceived function per se but rather emphasizes the strategies we can adopt in interactions. One of the most recent accounts of CAT is in Giles and Coupland (1991a). This provides not only an historical background to the model and an examination of the theory, but also information on the areas to which CAT has been applied.

CAT is concerned with the verbal and nonverbal strategies adopted by individuals in social interactions, particularly those strategies that explain the behaviors we use to show convergence toward or divergence from another individual or group member. The model also covers strategies relating to role, interaction management and those focused on the perceived competence of interactants. As Giles and Coupland (1991a) point out, accommodation is "a multiply-organized and contextually complex set of alternatives, regularly available to communicators in face-to-face talk" (pp. 60-61).

The model was developed originally (Giles, 1973; Giles & Powesland, 1975) at least in part as a response to certain sociolinguistic accounts of the variable use of different speech styles (e.g., Labov, 1966); accounts that were rather situationally deterministic. Giles and his colleagues believed that particular speech styles may be adopted by a speaker not simply because of such factors as the formality or informality of the situation, but that interpersonal factors may also be a significant influence. A speaker may adopt a particular style, for example, in an attempt to converge with, to be more similar to, the speech of another individual or group member.

The basic model that came to be developed postulates that, within the interaction itself, a number of individual factors such as emotional state, interpersonal goals, and psychological orientation are the initial influences on the speech styles used during the course of the interaction. These individual factors, combined with a focus on one's addressee, are thought to lead causally to certain interactional strategies being adopted by the speaker; strategies that are manifested in behavioral changes to various aspects of speech style. Thus one might shift features of accent, or speak at a different rate or for longer (Street, 1982), and so on. The style used by the speaker is then decoded by the listener, giving rise to such processes as labeling the speaker in certain ways, or attributing intentions or personality characteristics to the speaker. These perceived changes of speech style on the one hand, and the attributions on the other, then feed back into the ongoing interaction, providing the opportunity for both interactants to continue modifying their speech, voice, and nonvocal behavior. In addition to this causally sequential process occurring within the interaction, the influence of a number of situational factors and the initial orientation of the interactants, in so far as this is determined by social and personal identity, are allowed for in the model. As in earlier chapters, then, we find a process being proposed that requires consistent, and probably constant, monitoring of the interaction, although this may not be consciously achieved.

Figure 7.2 shows the CAT model as developed by Gallois et al. (1988) and illustrates the processes just described. Although Gallois et al. were intent on applying CAT to intercultural communication, their model is perhaps more generally applicable to a range of social situations than other versions. Other recent accounts of the model may be found in Coupland et al. (1988) (on which the Gallois et al. figure was modeled) and Williams, Giles, Coupland, Dalby, and Manasse (1990). Both are applications of the model to the area of health and aging.

One very important distinction within CAT that has been developed is that of subjective and objective accommodation. This is the distinction between our perception of speech styles or voice types, both our own and those of others, and independently measured behaviors, respectively. In many ways, it is our perception of the speech styles of our interactants and the shifts they make that is more important both to the course of the interaction and its outcome.

From its earliest days, when it was called speech accommodation theory (Giles, 1973; Giles & Powesland, 1975), the model placed emphasis on a cognitive approach to communication. Giles and Coupland (1991a) state quite explicitly "it [CAT] originated in order to elucidate the cognitive and affective processes underlying speech convergence and divergence" (p. 63). In some ways this has been a limiting influence, although some of the more recent developments, such as Gallois et al. (1988) and Williams et al. (1990), have expanded the more socially oriented areas. One of the clearest ways that CAT reveals itself as a cognitive model is in the discussion of accommodative motives, particularly those underlying the interactional strategies of convergence and divergence. Convergence is the one area that has received the most attention over the past two decades. It is a strategy essentially concerned with making one's speech and voice (and other nonverbal behaviors) more similar to that of another person or group, or at least more similar to what one perceives as characteristic of that person or group. Divergence, then, refers to the opposite of this—making one's behavior less similar.

(often non-conscious) for social integration or identification with another" (pp. 71-72). This would lead us to predict that the greater the need to gain social approval, the greater the convergence is likely to be. If convergence does indeed result in social approval, we might expect this to be manifested in the speaker being perceived as more attractive, intelligible, supportive, or even as showing more interpersonal involvement (Giles, Mulac, Bradac, & Johnson, 1987).

Related to a perceived need to converge (or diverge) is the perceived power and/or status differentials between individuals or the groups they are believed to represent. One may converge toward the behavior of the more statusful group, for example, or diverge away from that of a subordinate group. This is only one set of possibilities. One may wish to show solidarity with one's in-group regardless of perceived power and status differentials, and one may wish to converge to a less powerful or statusful group (see, e.g., the "covert prestige" proposed by Trudgill, 1972).

In a discussion of causal attributions, awareness, and intentions and their relationship to CAT, Giles and Coupland (1991a) indicate that shifts in speech and voice behavior may occur without the full awareness of either encoder or decoder, as may the subsequent attributions, and that "speech adjustments cannot uniformly be taken as indicative of wholly intentional orientations" (p. 78). The use of the word *strategy* to refer to the different types of accommodation (such as convergence or divergence), however, may seem to imply that all accommodative behavior is in the conscious awareness of the encoder. The above quotation suggests that Giles and his colleagues do not believe this to be the case. The CAT model is acknowledging that both conscious and unconscious use of language and nonverbal behaviors can be strategic. Many uses of language and voice occur without the conscious awareness of the interactants. When functioning to manage interactions, for example, voice will usually not be consciously used. Argyle (1988) tells us that such behavior is learned. It is part of the body of commonsense knowledge and understanding that exists in the culture and that is used without really thinking, but it is still social knowledge that has to be learned. By using it we implicitly acknowledge its importance in helping to achieve our goals. It is, in other words, strategic, consciously used or not. Of course, there will be times when we do consciously plan out our interactions and there will be times when interactants perceive that some form of social advantage may be gained by adopting strategies such as convergence and divergence. The dynamic nature of the interaction, however, will ensure that even our best laid plans will almost certainly have to be changed at the time.

Convergence and divergence are only two of the proposed strategies in the CAT model. Coupland et al. (1988) provide the fullest description of the strategies to date. A number of the others have relevance for a model of communication concerned primarily with the voice; for example, the discourse management strategies. We have noted on several occasions the important role voice can have in managing interactions; this will be dealt with more fully in Chapter 8.

One other set of strategies can usefully be mentioned. Interpretability strategies focus on the addressee's interpretive competence. This is very often evaluated through social group memberships such as gender, ethnic group, or age. Indeed, it is by applying CAT to the general area of aging and health that Coupland et al. (1988) develop the idea of interpretability. Our perception of the other's ability to interpret our message can lead to modifications in our speech and vocal behavior. If, for example, when communicating with the elderly, we perceive their level of competence to understand us as low, we may well slow our speech, raise our voices, adopt particular intonation patterns and tones of voice, as well as limit the topics of conversation, and so forth. This may be the result of our perception of the addressee as handicapped in some way; or may be based on negative stereotypes of the competence of elderly people, and in particular that they are heavily dependent on us. One study (Ryan et al., 1991) utilizing the CAT framework examined the patronizing speech that may be used by nurses to elderly patients in nursing homes. They indicate that patronizing speech was thought to be more shrill, louder, and produced with more exaggerated intonation.

In general, the CAT strategies have been described as a means of cooperation, as ways of enhancing conversational effectiveness (Giles & Coupland, 1991a). It is recognized, however, that this need not be the case, that they can be used for the reverse effect. From our perspective, CAT has several strengths. It is an intergroup theory of interpersonal communication, although the interpersonal aspects have not yet been examined in detail by those working in the area. The importance of adopting such an intergroup theory for the framework proposed here comes from the emphasis the theory places on group identity, which itself stems from the traditional link CAT has to Social Identity Theory (discussed briefly in Chapter 4). This link manifests itself in the way the model allows us to relate speech and nonverbal behavior to strategies that tell us something about our personal and group identity and the relationship between this and that of our interactants. The intergroup nature of CAT has also been shown by a number of the variables that have been studied. Thus, for example, accent or lexical items are institutionalized sociocultural markers related to power, status, and solidarity. CAT is also a theory of communication and as such has developed from an interdisciplinary perspective, drawing on psychology, linguistics, and to a lesser extent, sociology. This should give it the potential to account for more aspects of the interaction than a theory developed within a single discipline.

To date, like Patterson's (1983, 1990) model, CAT has not incorporated to any great extent the social influences acting upon the interaction. Figure 7.2 shows that CAT includes a loop within the interaction to allow its dynamic nature to continue to influence the individual's goals and sociopsychological orientation as well as the addressee focus. Only the outcome of the interaction is allowed to influence the initial orientation, however, and situational factors seem to play no part once the interaction is under way. Both models need to allow for the outcome and the changes occurring during the interaction to feed back through the longer term social factors influencing social interactions. This is something we will take up again in the next chapter. Finally, CAT is a process model, taking little account of the content of an interaction. Being basically sequential, like Patterson's model, it does not account for multiple goals particularly well.

As discussed below, the theoretical framework proposed here consists of a series of interacting dimensions, one of which is that of social exchange. To account for the functions of voice within social interaction we need to allow for the dynamic nature of interactions. The two models discussed so far provide this. One critical area for vocal function that neither model covers, however, is the relationship between the expression and physical measurement of the voice, our perceptions of it, and between both of these and the inferences and attributions we make about the speaker based on those perceptions. This takes us to a different dimension within the theoretical framework and it is Scherer's (1978) modified Brunswikian lens model that represents this.

Scherer's Functional Model of Vocal Communication

We saw in Chapter 6 that Scherer has been centrally involved in the development of content free techniques for studying the voice (1982). Scherer works mainly in the area of affect (Scherer, 1988; Scherer & Oshinsky, 1977), and to a lesser extent, personality characteristics (Scherer, 1978) and vocal disorders (Scherer, 1985b). His work can be traced back to that of Rosenthal and colleagues, who later developed the PONS test (Profile of Nonverbal Sensitivity), in which randomized spliced voice and content filtered voice were included as two nonverbal channels in their own right (Rosenthal, Hall, DiMatteo, Rogers, & Archer, 1979). In the past two decades Scherer has developed a functional model of communication used exclusively for the voice. As the one researcher who has developed such a model, his work demands particular attention here.

As well as providing an understanding of how voice is perceived, Scherer's work makes two important links. First, it relates perceptual measures of voice to acoustic measures. Second, it links the effects of innate mechanisms to social learning. The latter relationship can be seen most clearly in the concepts of push and pull (Scherer et al., 1980). As has already been noted, Scherer et al. propose that vocal cues can be governed by internal personality characteristics and affective states (push) and social norms and expectations (pull).

Scherer has, in fact, developed two theoretical models, both concerned with the communication of emotion. Both have some importance to the study of voice. The more recent (Leventhal & Scherer, 1987; Scherer, 1988) is the component patterning model of verbal affect expression. As the less central to an account of voice, it will be dealt with briefly here. The component patterning model proposes a sequence of checks made by the individual when confronted with an incoming stimulus. The checks proposed by Scherer and a summary of their meanings are presented in Table 7.1.

By going through the sequence of checks, the emotion is evoked in the individual in response to the stimulus, and an expressive response is produced. Like the early models considered in the first part of this chapter, this too is a functional model oriented toward the speaker. Scherer (1986a) predicts a number of voice types that may be associated with the checks or stages in the model. Thus, for

Table 7.1 Proposed Checks on Incoming Stimulus

---

1. Novelty Check
   Determines whether the stimulus is as expected or is novel.
2. Intrinsic Pleasantness Check
   Determines whether the stimulus is pleasant or not.
3. Goal/Need Significance Check
   Determines whether the stimulus is relevant to important goals and needs.
4. Coping Potential Check
   Determines the causation of the stimulus, the coping potential available, and
   the potential to change or avoid the outcome.
5. Norm/Self-Compatibility Check
   Determines whether the stimulus conforms to social norms and conventions
   expected by self and any significant others.

SOURCE: Adapted from Leventhal & Scherer, 1987.

example, if the outcome of the second check, the intrinsic pleasantness check, is that the incoming stimulus is pleasant rather than unpleasant, the predicted voice type is wide voice, which Scherer then links to articulatory and acoustic features. There are predicted voice types for most of the stages of the model. Table 7.2 provides a summary of these showing the predicted voice type and some of the associated vocal features. For a full account of this see Scherer (1986a).

The component patterning model sets out to explain the link between incoming stimuli, physiological response, and expressive behavior in the vocal communication of affect. As such, it tries to relate precisely vocal features to internalized states under the influence of external stimuli. These links are characteristic of Scherer's work in this area: precise measurement of vocal behavior and the way this relates to internal and external stimuli. It is Scherer's earlier theoretical model that has the wider application, however, in that potentially it has explanatory power beyond the communication of affect. This is his modified Brunswikian lens model (1978, 1979a; Goldbeck et al., 1988) based on the earlier model by Brunswik (1956). The model as used by Scherer is illustrated in Figure 7.3, which shows a hypothetical account of how an internalized personality trait, in this case extroversion, is manifested through certain vocal features—the distal cues—which are perceived by a listener—the proximal cues—and a subsequent attribution made about the speaker. This is explained in more detail below. The last part of the lens model is

Table 7.2 Predictions of Voice Types Following Stimulus Check

Outcome	Voice Type	Vocal Features
novel	no name	interruption of phonation silence sudden inhalation with ingressive sound and glottal stop
not novel	no change	no change
pleasant	wide voice	relaxation and expansion of vocal tract vocal tract shortened by corners of mouth raised more low frequency energy frequency of formant 1 falls increase in nasality in velar/pharyngeal areas
unpleasant	narrow voice	tensing and constriction of vocal tract vocal tract shortened by corners of mouth lowered more high frequency energy frequency of formant 1 rises, formants 2 & 3 fall increase in nasality in pharyngeal/laryngeal areas
relevant	relaxed voice	relaxation of vocal apparatus F0 at lower end of range low to moderate amplitude slight decrease in high frequency energy
irrelevant	tense voice	tensing of vocal apparatus F0 and amplitude increase presence of jitter and shimmer increase of high frequency energy pronounced formant frequency differences
control	tense voice	as above
no control	lax voice	hypotension of vocal apparatus low F0 and restricted F0 range very low frequency energy neutral setting of formant frequencies
power	full voice	deep forceful respiration low F0 high amplitude strong energy in entire frequency range
no power	thin voice	rapid shallow respiration raised F0 relatively low energy
conforms	wide + full voice	see above
does not conform	narrow + thin voice	see above

SOURCE: Adapted from Scherer, 1986a.

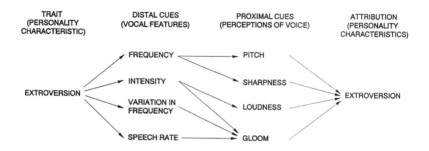

Figure 7.3. Hypothetical example using the modified Brunswikian lens model for the trait of extroversion.

analogous to part of the CAT model. While the lens model explains this process somewhat more precisely in the sense of matching a single label to a particular vocal behavior, the CAT model has considered the process in considerably more detail. Scherer's model, then, combines externalization, attribution and accuracy approaches (see Chapter 4) to the study of personality and affect.

Brunswik (1956) pointed out that one of the most important features of functional models of communication is the relationship between utilization and the ecological validity of the external cues. Ideally, one utilizes (i.e., perceives and makes inferences about) only those cues that are ecologically valid (i.e., those cues that really do stand for the things we take them to represent). The measurement of ecological validity is represented in the model by the correlation coefficient between the trait and the external cue. We have already noted (Chapter 4) some of the problems associated with this type of accuracy measurement. At the very least, we must acknowledge that inferences can also be made from cues that are invalid ecologically, giving rise to misinterpretation of the speaker's state, which may then have an important effect on the ongoing interaction or on the future relationship of the interactants.

In the hypothetical example shown in Figure 7.3 (which does not reproduce any published findings) extroversion is shown to be correlated to four vocal features—frequency, intensity, variation in frequency, and speech rate (these are shown by the arrows in the figure). The four vocal features are perceived by the listener as pitch, loudness, sharpness, and gloom (the latter two proximal cues are ones used by Scherer), and from these the listener infers that the speaker is extroverted. When using this model the researcher hopes to find significant correlations between pairs of concepts. As indicated, in Figure 7.3 these are shown by the arrows. Thus, for example, a significant correlation is shown between extroversion and frequency; between frequency and two of the proximal cues—pitch and sharpness; and between both of these and the attribution. Such linkages enable the researcher to isolate the specific vocal features that communicate the trait. To avoid presenting a confusing figure, only a few arrows have been shown between the distal and proximal cues in Figure 7.3. In practice there are likely to be other significant correlations.

As indicated in Chapter 4, prior to Scherer's use of Brunswik's (1956) model no studies had combined personality dispositions with vocal cues and combined both with attributions. Scherer (1978) points out that he introduced the model to account for the variance in personality attributions and the degree of accuracy between vocal cues and the attribution (i.e., to take into account ecological validity). The latter, of course, depends on the existence of a stable relationship between voice and personality characteristics in the first place, as well as our ability to isolate relevant vocal cues. Given this, Scherer suggests, accuracy of judgment also depends on a large degree of correspondence between actual and inferred voice-personality correlations. As indicated in Chapter 4, determining the accuracy with which people can perceive concepts such as extroversion from the voice is somewhat controversial. The use of the lens model is in part an attempt by Scherer to overcome some of the problems associated with earlier accuracy studies.

Scherer has used the lens model to examine the expression of personality characteristics in the voice (1978, 1979a) as well as emotion (Goldbeck et al., 1988). It seems clear, however, that any aspect of group or personal identity communicated by the voice could be studied using this model (as, indeed, could other nonverbal channels). In other words, while developed as a model of interpersonal communication, it is potentially useful as a model of intergroup communication. As such, it remains potentially one of the most useful models in vocal communication. For all that, few studies (even by Scherer) have utilized it.

Unlike Patterson's (1983, 1990) model or CAT, Scherer's proposal is not an exchange model; it cannot account for changes across time. Its importance lies in the predictive power it brings to the externalization of speaker characteristics and listener perceptions and inferences.

Scherer's lens model is also unlike the early models we have considered in that it tends to be oriented toward the listener, not the speaker. The terms *distal* and *proximal* show this to be the case. As Figure 7.3 reveals, both the distal and proximal cues are seen from the perspective of the listener, who then makes inferences based on that observation. In using the model, Scherer accepts behaviors that are both intentional communicatively and unintentional. Once again, this appears to be taking a listener's perspective, although the check of ecological validity of the distal cues shows the model to be concerned to some extent at least with speaker orientation also.

Overall the strengths of Scherer's model lie in its predictive nature, in the detailed relationships it reveals between speaker characteristics and how these can be manifested in nonverbal expression; the relationships it reveals between both of these and interactants' perceptions; and between all of these and the inferences and attributions made by interactants about speakers. It is not an exchange model and consequently cannot deal with the dynamism of an interaction, neither does it really explain an interaction in its social context. These should not be seen as weaknesses, however. As indicated at the beginning of this section, Scherer's model represents a different dimension of the theoretical framework from the social exchange models: the precise link between expression, its physical measurement, and attribution.

Communication: Intention and Conscious Awareness

The acceptance of unintentional behavior into communicative models such as Scherer's (1978, 1979a) and CAT (Giles & Coupland, 1991a) needs further consideration. By including such behavior, they enter the long-standing debate conducted within several disciplines— linguistics, psychology, and philosophy, to name three—on whether intention and conscious awareness should be included in a definition of communication.

Traditionally there are three approaches to the definition of communication, each of which takes a different standpoint on this question. The first argues for all behavior to be seen as communicative, as long as another person is present to perceive and interpret it (Watzlawick et al., 1968). This perspective tends to focus on the interaction, with its many cultural and personal influences, rather than the interactants, and as a result notions of intention and conscious awareness are irrelevant. While the focus on the interaction and the devaluing of intention can be seen as advantages of such a system, de-emphasizing the roles of speaker and listener and allowing anything to be deemed communicative must be viewed as weaknesses.

A version of the second tradition can be found within linguistics. Lyons (1977) draws a distinction between communicative and informative. Only signals of the former type are intentional. As such, they are speaker oriented. Informative signals, on the other hand, do not necessarily involve intention, being listener oriented. This second tradition requires that all communicative behavior be intentional (Ekman & Friesen, 1969). A third tradition (Weiner, Devoe, Rubinow, & Geller, 1972), while demanding the use of a shared code and an encoder and decoder to use the code, rejects intention on the grounds that it cannot be operationally defined.

Both Weiner et al. (1972) and Burgoon, Buller, and Woodall (1989) point out that reliance on intention and conscious awareness to determine what is or is not communicative is problematic. For example, the point at which a person is no longer consciously aware of a behavior is difficult to establish. A case in point is the nonverbal function that Burgoon, Buller, and Woodward call "regulation of interaction." (Earlier the term *phatic* was used and the example of feedback or back-channeling given. Nolan [1983] uses the term *interaction management* for the same function.) A vocal example would be the use of creaky voice with frequency lowering to indicate the end of a conversational turn. It is not entirely clear whether such uses of voice features are in the conscious awareness of the participants or not, and it seems unlikely they would be intended as such. Such behaviors, indeed, are so well learned they require little or no conscious awareness to be performed. Burgoon, Buller, and Woodward point out that we do not have to remind ourselves to smile and make eye contact when we greet a friend. Neither do we have to remind ourselves to lower our voices or use whisper once we have decided to be confidential with someone in a public place.

Several writers working within media and cultural studies have pointed out that intention is something to which we can never really gain access, even if we ask the individual who has sent the message (e.g., see Fiske, 1987). Such writers are concerned primarily with media or literary texts, that is, texts that are physically separated from their originators and/or are difficult to tie back to any one person working as an independent individual. In such cases authorial intention is indeed problematic. In spoken interaction, however, we would want to qualify such a position. While speakers may not be *fully* aware of what they intend, they will usually be consciously aware of *some* intentions even if this is at a very general level (e.g., the desire to please). As has already been said, speakers may have many goals in social interactions, including trying to make an impression on third-party observers—included in Patterson's (1983, 1990) model.

The voice, along with other channels, once used, produces a text for observers to interpret. Those interpretations may not accord with what the speaker intended, assuming that the speaker knew what that was, but they will influence the response. It is not only conceivable but likely that entire conversations take place with no participants understanding the full intention of any of the speakers. This should not necessarily be seen as a problem. A listener will interpret many vocal behaviors according to a set of codes. Some of these codes will be shared by the interactants allowing a conventional use of nonverbal behavior. Other codes may be used in the belief they are shared, possibly leading to misinterpretation from the speaker's perspective.

Burgoon et al. (1989) propose a "message"-oriented definition of communication, which, rather like the Watzlawick et al. (1968) system, does not focus on either speaker or hearer but rather on the shared codes of a particular community. As such, they too avoid the problem of focusing on intention or conscious awareness. If we are concerned with exploring social interactions and the use of specific channels, nonverbal or otherwise, we must orient our theoretical models toward the needs of the interaction, not simply concentrate on speaker or listener, or for that matter on social codes. We should not make intention or conscious awareness the key issues in determining when a vocal behavior is communicative, then, but we do need to allow for the possibility of both. While not trying to define communication as such, any communicative model based on social interaction must take into account speaker intention and conscious awareness, as well as unintention and unawareness, listener perception, and the dynamic influence all of these may have over the course of the interaction. This means taking into account speaker and listener as personal and social beings, the social context, the message itself, and time.

Summary

Earlier chapters proposed a range of functions for the voice. In discussing the three theoretical models in the present chapter, as well as the early theoretical positions discussed at the beginning of the chapter, several more functions have been suggested. These will be brought together in the next chapter to form the basis of the taxonomy of vocal function. The chapter started with the comment that there is no single theory that covers the functions of voice within social interactions. Voice functions in many different ways; we cannot expect to handle this in a single theoretical model. "Super theories" that try to explain too much are prone to foundering. In addition, as has been acknowledged from the outset, voice is a package of behaviors that itself is part of a larger package of channels of communication. A theory of vocal function is a theory of communication, which must by definition include all communicative channels. A theory developed specifically for vocal communication may not be capable of taking this into account.

What is needed is a theoretical framework comprising a series of interacting dimensions. The aims and assumptions of the theoretical perspectives that represent each dimension will be sufficiently different not to warrant collapsing them down into a single entity. At one level we need a phonetic model that centers on the individual's voice. Laver's (1980) model provides this. It is worth noting, however, that by linking articulatory settings to acoustic measures of the sound wave, Laver is moving away from the individual as such to a physical phenomenon that others can perceive. This links it to the next dimension: one relating precisely the physical measurement of voice to others' perceptions. Scherer's (1978) modified Brunswikian lens model provides such a theory, and just as Laver provided a link with the second dimension, so Scherer moves beyond perception to inferences and attributions, linking this dimension to the third one.

At the third level we need models that show us how events such as social interactions develop and proceed. This introduces the models of social exchange. CAT (Giles & Coupland, 1991a) and Patterson's (1983, 1990) sequential functional model of nonverbal behavior belong in this category. Finally, we need a broader perspective on the whole situation showing that social interactions are not just about individuals communicating, but are social events influenced by the institutional and generally sociostructural nature of society. Once again, the two social exchange models provide a link to this fourth dimension by allowing for social influences on the interaction.

The proposed framework, then, starts with the individual and, by a series of theoretical dimensions, places that individual into contact with others and the society of which he or she is a part. The links between the dimensions provide one way of bringing this all together. Another way, and one that highlights the relevance to vocal communication of the material covered in this and earlier chapters, is to develop a taxonomy of vocal function based on that material. This, along with some consideration of the fourth dimension, is presented in the next and final chapter.

CHAPTER EIGHT

A Theoretical Framework for Vocal Function: Taxonomy and Final Thoughts

The proposed theoretical framework was described at the end of the last chapter. As indicated there, three dimensions of the framework have so far been covered: the phonetic descriptive dimension, the predictive perceptual dimension, and the social exchange dimension. In discussing that material and in exploring the communication of identity, affect, and attitude, as was done in Chapters 4 and 5, an extensive set of possible vocal functions were introduced. In this final chapter a taxonomy of vocal function will be developed. This represents one way of bringing the wealth of material together in a form that highlights its relevance to vocal communication. A taxonomy, however, can also show the nature of the functions of voice and the relationships among them.

Following the development of the taxonomy, some discussion relating to the fourth and final dimension of the theoretical framework will be presented. This considers the relationship between the individual, the social interaction, and the hierarchical institutional structures of society.

A Taxonomy of Vocal Function

Robinson (1972) has pointed out that language, as a system developed by humans to serve a range of functions, can usefully be analyzed in functional terms. The same argument can be made here.

Robinson, in fact, has developed a functional taxonomy for language (1972, 1978, 1985). Where relevant we will relate the functions proposed here to his. Taxonomies will by their very nature be less than totally adequate. As Robinson (1972) suggests, language is subject to change, making a taxonomy almost obsolescent from the start. We could extend this to cover any human communicative system. In addition, the level of generality attempted will result in some contrasts being missed. Despite this, taxonomies do have their uses as indicated above and in the previous chapter. Before embarking on the details of the functions proposed here, however, a number of points concerning the scope of the present taxonomy need to be made.

In developing the taxonomy it is not meant to imply that all (or any) of the functions proposed are associated with the voice alone. Verbal as well as nonvocal behaviors are involved in social interactions. Within the package of communicative behaviors voice will play a greater or lesser role depending on a range of factors. Which channel of communication may be emphasized or made salient in the communicative process will depend on such things as speaker intention, the type of interaction, intensity of feeling expressed, and aspects of the social identity of both speaker and listener, such as gender and age.

In a similar way, the taxonomy does not imply that the proposed functions are independent of one another or that they necessarily operate in isolation. Multifunctionality in the voice will be the norm. We have already noted that more than one voice quality as well as dynamic features can work together seemingly simultaneously in the speech signal. We have also noted the possibility for the same articulatory setting or dynamic feature to function in more than one way simultaneously. Vocal parameters can function serially or in parallel. The possibilities for ambiguity multiply in such a situation. In social interactions it is likely that we consider a number of possible interpretations for the acoustic signal we are hearing, particularly the nonverbal elements. If the speaker has made one particular channel salient we may well focus on that channel in interpreting the signal. If the speaker has not, then we may choose from among the channels available to us and decide that voice, for example, is functioning in a particular way, one that fits with what we perceive as the most salient aspects of the interaction at that moment in time. Another possibility is that we make no judgment at all, either because of lack of perceived salience of nonverbal features at that time or the presence of ambiguity.

In addition, the way the voice (and other channels) functions throughout the duration of the interaction may well change. In monitoring the ongoing situation we need to update our interpretation and modify our behavior accordingly. This is to say that vocal function in social interaction is dynamic and complex, requiring constant monitoring and shifts in usage and interpretation on the part of all participants. We will return to this later in the chapter.

The proposed taxonomy is illustrated in Figure 8.1 and is discussed in greater detail below. We can note, however, that the functions presented in boxes, which are the end nodes of each taxonomic line, are not meant to be exhaustive lists. They represent prominent functions taken from the literature and discussed in earlier chapters. Others will no doubt be added in the future. In addition, concepts that have been taken from a specific theory, such as those discussed in the previous chapter, have not necessarily been retained as a set. Each concept has been placed into the taxonomy in a way that seems valid for the underlying principles of the taxonomy and thus for the theoretical framework developed here. For example, the functions taken from Patterson's (1983, 1990) sequential functional model of nonverbal exchange appear in a number of different places within the model shown in Figure 8.1. The informative function, for example, would be covered here under affect, attitude, and possibly relationship maintenance. It will be remembered from Chapter 7 that the informative function represents the individual's relationship to others. The relationship between the speaker, significant others, and objects may take several forms, however. The taxonomy tries to show this.

Immediately below the initial node is the distinction: "within the interaction" and "beyond the interaction." This distinguishes those individuals with whom we are interacting and those who are observers of the interaction but classed in some way as salient others to the whole or part of the interaction. This takes account of Patterson's (1990) function of presenting identities and images, introduced in the last chapter. All the functions included in the present taxonomy, however, could be aimed at salient others outside the interaction. As a result, Patterson's function is included at this early stage relating to all aspects of the interaction.

The third level of Figure 8.1 represents potential underlying themes of an interaction: roles, goals, attitudes, affect, identity, and phatic.

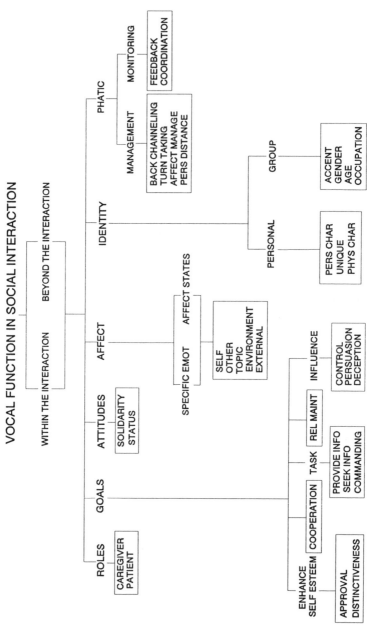

Figure 8.1. A taxonomy of vocal function in social interaction.

As ongoing themes they may relate to large portions of the interaction and possibly all of it. They are more abstract concepts than those at lower order nodes, the latter being more likely to be manifested as isolated patterns of behavior. Thus while the concept of goal may be an underlying theme, more than one goal may underlie an interaction, and any specific goal such as "control" or "seek information" will not necessarily be present for the full extent of the interaction but may appear only as isolated patterns of behavior. The further down the taxonomic line we go, then, the less abstract and more specific the functions become.

No attempt has been made to show the relationships between the third level functions—the underlying themes—with either themselves or lower order functions, except those immediately below each one. This is simply to avoid presenting a very confusing figure. It is likely, however, that most if not all functions in the taxonomy may, given the right context, be related to one another. Thus emotional state may be related to the way we attempt to influence another person or the level of cooperation we try to achieve. Similarly, if we have a role such as a group facilitator we may well pay particular attention to monitoring and managing the interaction, functions that may also be affected by our goals for that interaction; and if our intention is to deceive, this may be linked to affective states such as arousal. This situation reflects the point made on several previous occasions, the voice is multifunctional and more than one function may be operative simultaneously.

The way the body of work presented in previous chapters was structured reflects to some extent the interests of those working in the voice area. The taxonomy will not simply follow this measure of interest. Some aspects of identity, for example, have received considerable coverage in the literature, and identity as an important theoretical concept in its own right was given a chapter to itself in this book. A similar situation exists with emotion. Other, equally important aspects of vocal communication have received far less attention in the literature (e.g., roles, attitudes, or goals). All will be seen as important underlying themes to interactions in the taxonomy developed here.

When describing the various functions in Figure 8.1, for convenience a dyadic interaction has been assumed. We have already noted the need to allow not only for multiple interactants but for others outside the interaction who may nevertheless witness the interaction and at some level be a party to it. For purposes of this exposition, however, one speaker and one listener will be assumed. This will avoid the constant use of clumsy phrases such as "interactant(s) and other observers."

The Functions of Voice

In interactions, the voice may function in a number of ways relating to the roles we undertake; our goals; the attitudes we hold about the other person and the particular relationship we have with that person; the feelings or affect we have about a number of different aspects of the interaction; our identity; and the phatic relationship between speaker, hearer, and all aspects of the interaction in terms of the way we manage and monitor that interaction. These are the six proposed functions for the voice that potentially relate to all interactions and constitute the underlying themes of interactions. They will henceforth be referred to as thematic functions.

The first thematic function noted in Figure 8.1 is that related to roles. Both Patterson's (1983, 1990) model and communication accommodation theory (CAT) (Giles & Coupland, 1991a) include role as a potential influence on the dynamics of the interaction, although in the former model it is subsumed within the service-task function. Roles are often institutionalized, being related to the workplace. Thus Patterson suggests the doctor-patient interaction as one example. Other roles may relate to social institutions such as the family. Still others may not be institutionalized at all but be idiosyncratic or a function of a specific relationship. It is this range of roles and the fact that we each perform many different roles, even across a single day, that makes "role" different from, say, "occupational identity." In addition, roles emphasize the relational elements of interactions in a way that social categorization does not. Robinson (1985) includes role relationships in his taxonomy, also emphasizing the relational elements and separating this from identity as we do here. In the vocal communication literature, two of the few roles to have been studied are those found in the caregiver-elderly interaction. As it happens, these do relate to aspects of group identity—occupation and age—but it is the relational elements that are salient here. "Caregiver" and "patient" have been placed at the end node of this function, therefore, as examples of roles.

The second thematic function is that of goals. Both CAT (Giles & Coupland, 1991a) and Patterson's model (1983, 1990) include goals as major underlying themes. Many researchers (Argyle, 1988; Kellermann, 1987, for example) have shown that the attainment of goals is an integral part of interactions. Under the heading of goals in the taxonomy presented in Figure 8.1, five other functions are proposed: the enhancement of self-esteem, cooperation, a specific task orientation (noted as "task" in the figure), relationship maintenance (rel maint), and influence of various types. Three of these group together a number of more specific goals.

The desire and attempt to enhance self-esteem are well-established social phenomena (see, e.g., Hogg & Abrams [1988] and Taylor & McKirnan [1984] for discussions of this). The types of function that could appear in the box at the final node of this line have been represented by *approval* and *distinctiveness*. These are widely used concepts within psychology. Of more importance to this taxonomy, however, is that they represent two of the goals within the CAT model (Coupland et al., 1988) and are centrally related to the CAT strategies of convergence and divergence. They also link to social identity theory (Hogg & Abrams, 1988). The latter is manifested in the concepts of social mobility and social change. Where the boundaries between social groups are perceived by an individual as "soft" or permeable, social mobility may be seen as an option. This is the belief that individuals can move between groups to provide a more positive image for the self. Social mobility incorporates the seeking of social approval. Fostering the belief in social mobility can ensure the survival of dominant groups and their value systems. As Hogg and Abrams (1988) indicate, this can lessen the chances of conflict by weakening the cohesiveness of subordinate groups, while at the same time effectively ensuring that the dominant value system remains intact.

Often, however, mobility is not seen as an option. On such occasions as these, social change becomes a possibility. Hogg and Abrams (1988) propose two types of change: social competition and social creativity. The former concerns direct competition between subordinate and dominant groups, based on the idea that the relative status of the two groups should and can be changed. This will occur on dimensions that are valued by both groups. Social creativity, on the other hand, may involve finding new dimensions for comparison, the redefinition of values, or even finding new out-groups for comparison. Both types of social change incorporate the promotion of distinctiveness.

We commented in the last chapter that Patterson's (1983, 1990) model seemed to be most explanatory of conflictual situations. We also noted in Chapter 4 that social identity theory was essentially concerned with conflict. The five "goals" functions in the present taxonomy represent both conflictual and nonconflictual aspects of social interaction, reflecting that goals need not be only of the former type. Thus, while the enhancement of self-esteem is essentially a conflictual concept, cooperation is not (see Argyle [1991] for an account of cooperation in social interactions). No other specific goals are included under cooperation, although it is possible that the CAT goal of communicative efficiency (Coupland et al., 1988) could fit here. The remaining three functions under the goals node may reflect both conflict and its reverse.

Task and relationship have long been seen as basic to all group communication and as primary goals of all interactions (see Bales, 1950; Forsyth, 1990; Shaw, 1981). The specific task function in the taxonomy covers the providing of information (provide info) as well as seeking information (seek info), neither seen as conflictual, but includes also commanding, which may be conflictual. The task function differs from Patterson's (1983) function of the same name, in that "role" is not assumed to be an integral part of the task function. In Patterson's model it is included to allow for the completion of tasks that involve working together, such as a construction job. Here the function is broken down into three possible communicative tasks that may apply to any situation. Others could no doubt be included. Role, as noted, is provided as a separate third-level function, an underlying theme of the interaction. Once again, CAT's communicative efficiency may belong under this function. Relationship maintenance (rel maint) is to some extent self-explanatory. It too may relate to maintaining a conflictual situation or its reverse. The fact that it is a maintenance function means that it may relate to earlier interactions. It does not generalize to all interactions but rather concerns the maintenance of the relationship at the time of the specific interaction.

Finally, influence, while being basically oriented to conflict, including as it does the attempt to control the other person, nevertheless includes also persuasion, which may have as its driving force a positive, nonconflictual intention. The term *influence* was chosen to avoid the negative connotations of such alternatives as *manipulation* and to allow both conflictual and nonconflictual forms of influence. The influence function covers any goal aimed at bringing about a change in the interactant, whether that be a change of attitude, emotion, or belief, or a change in the state or situation of the interactant, such as would happen when that person is placed under another's control. Robinson (1985) uses the term *regulation of others* to cover *control;* Coupland et al. (1988) include interpersonal control strategies in their version of CAT, and Patterson (1983, 1990) uses *social control* as a cover term for a variety of types of influence including control, deception, persuasion, and power. All but *power* have been included in the taxonomy under the influence node. Deception is seen as a way to influence others by providing false or misleading information. The concept of power, however, may not necessarily be used to influence others—the important underlying principle of the influence function as it is used here. Power, in the present taxonomy, is not a function as such but is a concept that may be related to several functions, including the status function under attitude, the roles we might take in an interaction, and various aspects of our identity.

Goals are motivational, will often be intentional, and are usually cognitive. We should not forget, however, the social forces acting upon them. The positions we adopt toward a person, issue, and so forth, that may define our entry point into an interaction, including our goals, are socially derived. Having known goals for a particular interaction means that voice, language, and other communicative channels may be used strategically.

Just as the goals that underlie our interactions may be socially derived, so may the attitudes we hold toward our interactant. In Figure 8.1 two types of focus for these attitudes have been proposed. These are the degree of solidarity we believe we have with our interactant and the status we accord that person (Brown, 1965). The communication of status differences in the voice can be highly conventionalized, such as the example given in earlier chapters of the use of falsetto as an honorific to mark polite or formal interchanges in the language Tzeltal (Brown & Levinson, 1978). Some of the other attitudinal dimensions introduced in Chapter 5 that seemed to be specifically attitudinal rather than related to personality could also be included here: social attractiveness or superiority, for example. Attitude, as was noted in both Chapters 4 and 5, links to personality and to persuasion. It is not simply an aspect of an attempt to influence someone, however, neither is it simply related to personality, but may also be socially derived. Its importance as a separate function, therefore, is reflected in the taxonomy by being classed as a thematic function.

As was also indicated in Chapter 5, the vocal communication of emotion probably represents the largest body of work in the voice area. And as in Chapter 5, the affect function in the taxonomy takes into account both the specific emotions (specific emot) we might be feeling and the more generalized affective states (affect states) such as arousal and pleasure (Mehrabian & Russell, 1974). As the taxonomy is set up, both may function simultaneously. Some affective states in particular may need to be accounted for at the same time as a specific emotion: the level of arousal associated with the emotion felt in an interaction, for example. These functions will also incorporate stress and fatigue. Both may be seen as linked to affective states. Scherer's models (Goldbeck et al., 1988; Scherer, 1988) have specifically explored the vocal communication of emotion and as such are of particular relevance here. In Robinson's (1985) taxonomy, the communication of affect is covered separately for the verbal and nonverbal channels. In the latter case, it is a subfunction of what he calls "marking of emitter," which includes in other subfunctions the marking of identity. The affect subfunction, however, also covers linguistic communication at the phonological level.

The way we feel in an interaction may be directed toward any aspect of the entire situation. Here, five affective focuses have been suggested. The first two represent the participants (including significant others outside the interaction): the self and the other person. In addition, the topic of conversation may also attract affect such as excitement, interest, dislike, or embarrassment. Such a response to the topic of conversation may not be simply affective but could reflect social influences where the topic is taboo for one or other of the interactants. The environment in which the interaction takes place, too, may be the focus. The speaker may express dislike for a noisy environment, for example. Even here we may find social influences on the use of voice. The dislike expressed may stem from the fact that the environment is one associated with a different social class to that of the speaker. Finally, the external function shown under this node in Figure 8.1 accounts for the affect related to some event external to the specific interaction but which would not necessarily extend across more than the one interaction. Thus, if the speaker had very recently been involved in a road accident or was about to go into a very important exam, the affect felt relating to that event may be communicated by the voice at the time of the interaction, but would not relate to the interaction per se. Closeness in time of the event to the interaction seems to be an important factor here. It needs to be sufficiently close in time such that the emotion is detectable in the voice. Many of these affect functions may also be manifested as stress and fatigue in the voice.

Some earlier attempts to explain the communicative ability of the voice have collapsed the affective functions into a single focus. Nolan (1983), for example, possibly following Jakobson (1960), uses the cover term *affective* to embrace not only the feelings but the attitudes a speaker may wish to convey. This fails to capture many of the important communicative distinctions we bring to an interaction, even for models such as Jakobson's and Nolan's that are essentially linguistic.

The next thematic function in Figure 8.1 is identity. All three major theories discussed in Chapter 7 have relevance here but particularly CAT (Giles & Coupland, 1991a) and Scherer (1978, 1979). The former is an intergroup model of interpersonal processes, and the latter has specifically measured personality characteristics. We have seen in Chapter 4 that both group and personal identity must be accounted for. Robinson (1985) covers both as subfunctions of "marking of emitter." The term *group* is preferred here to *social* mainly because the personal identity of an individual is itself constructed partly by social forces giving rise, as indicated in Chapter 4, to the argument that "social identity" is really the more general term with "group" and "personal" being two types of social identity. The functions in the boxes at the end nodes of this taxonomic line could very easily be extended. Only some of those introduced in Chapter 4 have been included to provide an understanding of what is intended to be dealt with here. Under personal identity the three functions of personality characteristics (pers char), the unique individual (unique), and physical characteristics (phys char) have been included. The first refers both to our actual personality characteristics and the attributions our interactants make about us based on, in this case, the voice. Many types of personality characteristics were noted in Chapter 4: competence, extroversion, maturity, dominance, perceived intelligence, artistic ability, sophistication, pride, weakness, warmth. These and many others could take their place at the end node of this taxonomic line. We could also add those attitudinal dimensions that seem to be more related to personal identity (e.g., personal integrity, see Giles &

Ryan, 1982). The unique individual allows for the possibility that the voice may function in this way. As we have seen, articulatory parameters of voice quality (Laver, 1980) allow for this possibility, although the automatic acoustic measurement of uniqueness may be a long way off. Finally, physical characteristics cover such things as weight and height. As with many aspects of identity, we seem to hold vocal stereotypes about physical characteristics even if those stereotypes have little or no ecological validity. Stereotyping as such is not included in the taxonomy. It is a process that may be related to many functions including the identity functions and attitude. The group identity functions included are the major ones that have been studied in the vocal communication literature and which were introduced in Chapter 4. They are language and accent group (accent) (Esling, 1978), gender (Smith, 1979), age (Addington, 1968), and occupation (Fay & Middleton, 1939).

Finally, at the thematic level, we have the function of phatic. Interest in the monitoring and organization of conversations, as noted in the last chapter, stems back at least to Malinowski's (1923) introduction of the term *phatic*. The organization of many different aspects of conversations has since attracted researchers working in this area (e.g., Argyle, 1988; Argyle & Dean, 1965; Jakobson, 1960; Patterson, 1983). Schegloff and colleagues, for example, looked for sequencing rules in conversational openings (Schegloff, 1968) and turn taking (Sacks, Schegloff, & Jefferson, 1974), two areas of interest in early conversation analysis. Zimmerman and West (1975) suggest that the patterning of interactions may reflect power and dominance relationships between women and men. For an early model of such temporal patterning see Jaffe and Feldstein (1970).

Verbal, vocal, and nonvocal behaviors have all been cited as functioning in such ways as these. The term *phatic* (Jakobson, 1960; Laver, 1975a, 1981b) has been used in the taxonomy as a thematic function to account for both the (often unconscious) management and monitoring of interactions. The management of interactions has been called many things: interaction management (Nolan, 1983); regulation of interaction (Burgoon, Buller, & Woodall, 1989); organization (Kendon, Harris, & Key, 1975; Sacks, Schegloff, & Jefferson, 1974). It covers the control and structuring of the interaction. One vocal example would be the use of creaky voice and lowered fundamental frequency to indicate the end of a conversational turn. As can be seen from Figure 8.1, under the management function are included such things as turn taking and back-channeling, as well as the concept of affect management (affect manage) (Patterson, 1983, 1990), which recognizes that affect too may need to be regulated (an idea also included in Robinson's, 1985, taxonomy) and the proxemic parameter of personal distance (pers distance). As Hall (1963) noted, this will be linked to loudness and, as was indicated in Chapter 1, we might want to add pitch and speech rate as the cues most likely to be affected here. Vocally, the distance between interactants may need to be controlled. It is likely that aspects of initiating and ending interactions are effected vocally and could also be included here (Robinson, 1985). We can note that CAT (Coupland et al., 1988) includes strategies of discourse management that could fit here.

The term *back-channeling* is being used here to cover any vocal interjections we may use to facilitate the interaction by providing the speaker with "encouraging noises" indicating we are listening and taking note of the speaker, perhaps even agreeing with the speaker, and wanting the speaker to continue. In the taxonomy this is distinguished from feedback that has been placed under monitoring. The latter refers to the constant monitoring of the situation that interactants engage in resulting in the largely unconscious and usually very subtle changes in behavior that may be noted by our interactant. These may then be interpreted (whether or not they were intended to convey anything or were ecologically valid in the sense of accurately reflecting a feeling, attitude, etc.) and our interactant's behavior modified accordingly. It is this activity that is covered by feedback in this taxonomy. If the vicious and benign cycles (Siegman, 1987) mentioned in Chapter 4 have any validity, they would stem from the monitoring function of feedback. These uses of the terms *feedback* and *back-channeling* may not accord precisely with earlier uses. The way the taxonomy is structured, however, two terms were required. These were the most appropriate.

Also included under monitoring is coordination (Buder, 1992). This is the synchronous behavior two people may engage in as the interaction progresses and seems to arise from the monitoring process. Woodall and Burgoon (1981) suggest that, as long as other nonverbal behaviors do not interfere, it is possible that this rhythmic vocal patterning of an interaction is sufficient to assist information processing, while Gregory, Webster, and Huang (1993) propose that the convergence of amplitude and frequency patterns by interview partners may function as a marker of group membership—in this case, the membership of the interaction. It is possible that interactions that display synchrony or coordination on nonverbal parameters may be perceived as more satisfying or pleasant, and that when vocal and other channels are coordinated this may function as a marker of interpersonal attraction (Crown, 1991).

Any classification scheme such as this taxonomy will inevitably fall short of the ideal if for no other reason than it can never be exhaustive. It provides not simply a list of possible functions, however, but also a way of relating those functions to one another. In particular, it highlights longer term thematic functions and the more transient forms in which they may be manifested. As such it acknowledges the dynamic nature of interactions. It also incorporates other important concepts underlying social interaction such as the need to account for conflictual and nonconflictual goals and the multifunctional nature of vocal communication, thus allowing for both serial and parallel processing. In addition, the taxonomy has not simply followed the major interests found in the literature but has tried to emphasize the needs of social interactions. It is hoped that this will provide a spur for future research in areas that have hitherto found little support.

The Fourth Dimension:
Directions for Future Research and Conclusions

The fourth dimension in the theoretical framework will be somewhat speculative. Throughout the book the social elements of interactions have been stressed where possible. In the theoretical framework, however, the relationship between the interaction, its participants, and the socio-structural influences on both have received short shrift. It has already been suggested that the two models introduced in the last chapter as representative of the first dimension, the level of social exchange, have not been sufficiently developed on this front, although both provide a dynamic structure that has the potential to link back to these social influences. In this final section of the book, some ideas will be discussed that relate to the interaction as a *social* event. We will suggest that the major institutional forces that constitute any society will inevitably play a role in shaping the way individuals, as members of that society, interact. Such concerns have not really been dealt with in vocal communication research, although the link made by Spender (1985) between pitch level and social influences (see Chapter 1) moves in this direction.

Essentially, three points will be made that provide links to models of social exchange such as those discussed in Chapter 7, showing that the third and fourth dimensions are also closely linked. It will be argued that we should take account not just of the initial orientation of the interactants as they enter an interaction, but of the time from which they are aware that an interaction is to take place, and that this period or phase should be seen as fundamentally linked to the long-term orientation of each interactant to his or her society. In addition, there is a need to relate the individual, and the interactions that individual has with others, more closely to the society of which he or she is a part—to the values, structures, and practices of that society. To this end the concepts of positioning, hegemony, and the access individuals have to their own and their society's sociohistorical background will be introduced. Finally, it will also be emphasized that in interacting with others there is much individual variation in the way we position ourselves relative to society's values, structures, and practices.

In thinking of the social context in which the interaction takes place we can isolate two important domains, each of which will provide insights into the social influences acting upon that interaction. These are the long-term orientation of the interactants to the general social and cultural context, and the shorter term transitional phase that leads up to the interaction. The two theoretical models of social exchange introduced in Chapter 7 both allow for social influences on the interaction. The reader will remember that Patterson's (1983, 1990) sequential functional model of nonverbal exchange allows for pre-interaction mediators, environmental determinants, and antecedents, which include cultural influences. Communication accommodation theory (CAT) (Gallois et al., 1988) provides for an initial orientation of the interactants, which includes details about social identity, plus situational factors. Gallois et al. define situational factors in terms of attitudes, social norms, threat, and status-stressing situations.

Other versions of the CAT model (Giles & Coupland, 1991a; Williams, et al., 1990) use the term *(transacting) contextual systems* in place of situational factors. As Giles and Coupland indicate, this follows the work of Albrecht and Adelman (1987) on communication network systems and Bronfenbrenner's (1979) contextual model of networks as transacting systems. Such approaches highlight the fact that there are occasions when our relationships with society are akin to transactions and that many social contexts have a systematic structure that may be linked to social institutions. A further set of ideas will be introduced here to extend these approaches. As will be indicated below, however, the individual's relationship to society is not necessarily transactional and may be seen as only partially systematic. Nonetheless, Giles and Coupland's comment that contexts evolve and undergo constant change is very similar to the position adopted here.

We can see in the environmental determinants, antecedents, and situational factors of these theoretical models an acknowledgment of what is being called here the long-term orientation. This term is preferred to emphasize first that we are concerned with taking the interactant's perspective, and second the fact that an individual's relationship to society is active and interactive, not passive. Such phrases as *environmental determinants* and to a lesser extent *situational factors* seem to remove the individual from the process (the term *transacting* does not, of course).

The pre-interaction phase proposed here extends across time, allowing for relevant changes that may occur leading up to the interaction. It is important to bear in mind a number of things about this phase: it is transitional, dynamic, and starts once we become aware that an interaction is to take place. It is recognized that many pre-interaction phases will be of relatively short duration; other interactions, however, will be set up well in advance (a job interview, for example). In addition, we have the ability to be in multiple pre-interactional phases simultaneously that may interact and influence one another. The important point is that we are aware that the interaction is to take place.

CAT's initial orientation, while not extending through time in quite this way, nonetheless has implicit links to the history of individual and group relations (Giles & Coupland, 1991a). Similarly in the Patterson (1983, 1990) model there are analogous links with the pre-interaction mediators, although these are shown to be more explicit (see Figure 7.1). Both allow the outcomes of interactions to influence these parts of the models, thus linking interactions with the future. What neither model does with any clarity is to theorize the interaction in terms of societal relations.

In the proposal here, the long-term orientation of each of the interactants is fundamentally linked to the pre-interaction phase. The thing that distinguishes these two is that the second is focused on a specific interaction. This will make some things salient and others not. How we position ourselves relative to any issue, person, event, or set of values we perceive as salient to the upcoming interaction will essentially define our point of entry into the pre-interaction phase. Once entered, however (and therefore once the salience of these things become known), we may change our position vis-à-vis any of these throughout the duration of the phase, this being one of the sources of the dynamism of the phase. In other words, the long-term orientation will continue to influence the pre-interaction phase. Such changes will depend to some extent on how long the pre-interaction phase lasts. If it is very short there will be little time for changes to occur. If it lasts for days, weeks, or months many changes may occur in the way we position ourselves relative to such things as salient issues, or rather to what we perceive as salient.

The concept of positioning oneself relative to a set of values, a person, an issue, event, or society's structures and practices is important not only to the pre-interaction phase, but is one of the key characteristics of the long-term orientation of the interactants. It comes from the idea of subject positioning and has its origins in a number of areas: early structural linguistics, semiotics, and Freudian psychoanalysis (Silverman, 1983). The last of these in particular, and its development by Lacan (1968), has stressed the linguistic and social dimensions of subjectivity. Our role as subject, and our subjectivity, are not only the means of describing our unique individuality and our unique point of view, but are themselves products of our social relations (Fiske, 1987). This interpretation of "subject," then, emphasizes the similarity among individuals, stressing the elements of social identity we all have in common.

The concept of positioning proposed here, however, incorporates not only this commonality but the variation in the way individuals position themselves. Our social identity may be defined not only in terms of the social categorizations noted in the last chapter and in Chapter 4 in regard to social identity theory, but the multiple positionings that we take up relative to all society's values, structures and practices (in fact, the two—categorization and positioning—will be mutually influential and therefore mutually defining). The positions we adopt will be manifested on a daily basis as habits, prejudices, beliefs, knowledge, expectations, and so forth. In interactions we position ourselves in these ways as much as others position us. To the extent that the interactants position themselves similarly, the interaction will appear to be nonproblematic.

One of the underlying principles constituting many societies and that directly influences the interactive nature of each individual's long-term relationship with society and thus the idea of positioning, is hegemony. As such, hegemony is presented here as one useful way of relating individuals to the society of which they are members. It is not the only possible way, but has the advantage of emphasizing the interactive nature of this relationship. It is used here as proposed by Gramsci (Hoare & Nowell-Smith, 1971), and refers to the hierarchical power structure within most societies; a structure manifested mainly through the major institutions such as law, education, government, bureaucracy, as well as the media and family. The important point, however, is that the hierarchical power structure exists with the consent of the bulk of society. That is, despite the grumblings about details of the power structure and individuals in power, there is an underlying consensus that the unequal power structure itself is a normal, obvious, commonsensical structure that one does not seriously question. Indeed, at some levels of society, support is actively sought by the powerful (and would-be powerful) from the less powerful and the disempowered to maintain the structure (through national and state elections, for example). Hegemony will not usually be total in most of society's institutions, however (total, that is, in the sense that a single individual or group maintains power and allows no change in the hierarchical power structure). There will usually be sufficient dynamism in the society to ensure some degree of change occurs regularly, and that different individuals gain power. That said, members of some social groups, particularly minority groups, do not get to hold power in the major institutions of our societies all that frequently; also there are some institutional structures that change very slowly if at all, and the basic notion of an unequal power structure usually remains.

It is the presence of a hierarchical hegemonic structure in many societies that allows such ideas as social mobility to exist. To some extent the dynamism just noted is determined by the perception that some social boundaries are permeable for some people. Our ways of understanding society, then, and our position in it, our social self-concept, will be determined in large part by the hegemonic order and the degree to which we accept this as normal and natural. Consequently, this will be one of the major influences on the way we position ourselves, the way we are positioned by the hegemonic order, and how we interact with other individuals. The idea of positioning and the way this relates to such major social forces as hegemony, suggest that our relationship to social contexts is not always (or only) transactional.

As we have said, the social forces that constitute society are usually dynamic in the sense that they can and do change to some extent. The positionings we adopt and the way we are positioned change; values and expectations, beliefs and prejudices, all may change. It is important, then, that all interactions be placed in their sociohistorical context. To the extent that individuals have access to their (and their society's) past, that past may influence the way they interact with others in the present. The importance of taking a sociohistorical perspective in attempting to understand the current situation has been shown by Dubé-Simard (1983) and St. Clair (1982) in the area of language attitude formation. What is being suggested here is an extension of this to include not just attitude but the way we position ourselves relative to all aspects of social interactions. This, plus the ideas of positioning and hegemony, are ways of looking at societal relations.

The final point to be emphasized here is the similarity and difference in the way we as individuals interact with society. The first of these will depend in part on the hegemonic structures and practices of society, the norms, conventions, and so forth, positioning us in certain ways, thus ensuring that the way we interact with others will be similar to the way others interact with us. At the same time, however, there will be many differences depending in part on our individual reaction to society's structures and practices, on our positioning of self, and our access to the past. In any interaction, then, we encounter much variation of this type, but also much similarity with other interactions. It is in particular the ability to change position and the differences we find in specific encounters that ensure our relationship to any social context will be only part systematic.

If we are to include such ideas as these into models of social exchange, we need first to allow for our long-term orientation toward society to feed into the pre-interaction phase. The way we position ourselves once we enter this phase and particular issues become salient, plus the dynamic nature of this phase, are all centrally related to our long-term orientation. The interaction too is dynamic, of course, so a loop needs to be incorporated into the model allowing change to occur during the interaction. Both CAT and Patterson's model include this. However, our long-term orientation may also change as a result of events occurring within the interaction, and things may be made salient that were not perceived as salient in the pre-interaction phase. Both need to be accounted for. We must have access to our long-term orientation throughout the interaction both to allow this to be updated and so we can draw additional material from it. The loop in the model must allow for this also. The interaction is a pattern of behavior throughout which, and out of which, possible changes to our positioning may occur. As social events, interactions must have access to social forces mediated through the interactants' long-term orientation to society.

Throughout this book we have drawn on theoretical, methodological, and empirical research from many disciplines. In presenting these ideas relevant to the fourth dimension of the theoretical framework we have continued this practice. We have argued for a dynamic pre-interaction phase linked to the long-term orientation, and the need to link the individual more closely to societal values, structures, and practices. To this end, the concepts of positioning, hegemony, and access to past positioning have been introduced. In addition, we have emphasized the need to account for similarity and difference in the way individuals relate to one another and to society. One of the areas of greatest need in communication studies (not just vocal communication) is to bring together the social with the cognitive, to develop the interaction as a truly social as well as cognitive event. It is hoped that the ideas expressed here will help facilitate such a union.

Concluding Remarks

In terms of future research agendas, this book has argued for a number of things. At an early point in the research process, greater care and control in recording and construction of stimulus tapes is needed. Also, voice should be seen as a communication package of independently measurable behaviors in its own right. A coherent set of features (see Chapter 1) should be selected for study whether the concern is for the voice alone or voice in conjunction with other nonverbal and verbal channels. Even more fundamental, however, is for researchers from all disciplines to use a standardized terminology for describing the voice. It was stressed from the outset that the description of voice is necessarily phonetic. The use of a common set of terms that can be linked back to articulatory, aerodynamic, and physiological mechanisms, such as those proposed by Laver (1980), would facilitate research across disciplines enormously.

It will have become clear that much work needs to be done within the whole area of vocal communication: theoretical, methodological, and empirical. The framework presented in Chapters 7 and 8 provides the basis for the development of such theoretical models. A framework of theory (rather than a single theory) will almost certainly always be needed for the reasons expressed in the last chapter. The three models introduced in that chapter are all powerful models in their own right, and go a long way to providing us with the explanatory framework needed. As indicated, however, from a vocal communication perspective some development is still needed. We can summarize this by saying that the models we select to represent the dimension of social exchange need to allow for both serial and parallel processing as well as taking into account the content of the message; to account for a lack of isomorphism between actual and perceived message variables; and to allow for interactants having multiple goals in any one interaction. The model representing the predictive perceptual dimension—Scherer's (1978) modified Brunswikian lens model—needs to continue to explore the difficult area of ecological validity. Although this model is a linear one in the sense that it examines the relationships between aspects of the speakers's identity and voice, the listener's perceptions of this and the attributions made, the effect this process can have on the ongoing nature of the interaction may be profound. And, finally, above all, the models need to develop the way they account for the relationship between interactants, the interaction and society.

The social interaction should be seen as an essentially human enterprise. To emphasize the social is not to deny the affective and cognitive. Voice, as a carrier of emotion, attitude, and identity, is one of the major channels marking the humanistic nature of interactions. This book has not denied the cognitive and affective, then, but highlighted the fact that much of the research to date has emphasized these and has often not taken sufficient account of the social.

There is growing evidence in the vocal communication literature (and this accords with work in other areas) that perception of others is determined in large part by perception of self. Certainly a number of accuracy studies suggest that the closer one is socially to the other person the more accurate one's perception of that person is likely to be. Underpinning our research into vocal communication by concepts of social identity, as has been done here, seems likely, then, to prove fruitful.

Future research needs to consider more than the underlying theory, however. Methodological issues and empirical work also need our attention. Chapter 6 in particular raised a number of concerns about the former. Much of this will come from a better understanding of the function of voice in social interaction as a complex package of behaviors in its own right. In Chapters 5 and 6 we highlighted a number of methodological issues specifically concerned with the work on the vocal communication of emotion. As was pointed out, by the very nature of this area of study particular problems can be isolated. However, many of the points raised about this research apply to all aspects of vocal function. To start with, the linguistic functions of voice need to be clearly separated from all others. In addition, the distinction between encoding and decoding must be clear and, related to this, the internal push and external pull influences on the voice need examining more closely. And finally the different acoustic features, the combinations of acoustic features and what aspects of those features are used for which function all need clarifying. This leads us to the third area of need—more empirical work. No area introduced in this book has been adequately covered. Even those areas that have received considerable attention, such as emotion and group identity, need much additional work. Chapters 4 and 5 in particular indicated proposed research agendas in the empirical domain.

It has not been the intention to provide a review of the vast literature relevant to vocal communication but to provide a way of interpreting vocal communication. To provide yet another literature review when excellent recent ones exist for specific aspects of vocal communication would be to waste the readers' time when they could be reading those other reviews. The book set out to bring together the different disciplinary approaches, to break down disciplinary boundaries and provide a comprehensive account of voice; to enable researchers from any discipline to learn about the work in other areas and to understand that work. Above all it is hoped that this book will help promote interest in voice research and to some small degree provide the knowledge and understanding to do that.

The book started from a brief discussion of the use writers of fiction make of the voice. As a voracious reader, I am frequently delighted by the creative ways in which good writers can use the voice to describe their characters and the way those characters communicate. Long may it continue. As a researcher, however, I have the hope that one day we will know enough about the communicative nature of the voice to understand exactly what a writer of fiction such as P. G. Wodehouse (1938, p. 9) means when he says:

> He spoke with a certain what-is-it in his voice, and I could see that, if not actually disgruntled, he was far from being gruntled.

References

Abercrombie, D. (1967). *Elements of general phonetics*. Edinburgh: Edinburgh University Press.

Aboud, F. E., Clément, R., & Taylor, D. M. (1974). Evaluative reactions to discrepancies between social class and language. *Sociometry, 37*, 239-250.

Abrams, D., & Hogg, M. A. (1987). Language attitudes, frames of references and social identity: A Scottish dimension. *Journal of Language and Social Psychology, 6*, 201-213.

Abrams, D., & Hogg, M. A. (1990). *Social identity theory*. London: Harvester Wheatsheaf.

Acker, B. F. (1987). Vocal tract adjustments for the projected voice. *Journal of Voice, 1*, 77-82.

Addington, D. W. (1968). The relationship of selected vocal characteristics to personality perception. *Speech Monographs, 35*, 492-503.

Albrecht, T. L., & Adelman, M. B. (Eds.). (1987). *Communicating social support*. Newbury Park, CA: Sage.

Allport, G. W., & Cantril, H. (1934). Judging personality from voice. *Journal of Social Psychology, 5*, 37-54.

Alpert, M., Kurtzberg, R. L., & Friedhoff, A. F. (1963). Transient voice changes associated with emotional stimuli. *General Psychiatry, 8*, 362-365.

Alston, R. C. (Ed.). (1967a). *Noah Webster: Dissertations on the English language 1789*. Menston, UK: Scolar Press.

Alston, R. C. (Ed.). (1967b). *Roger Ascham: The scholemaster 1570*. Menston, UK: Scolar Press.

Alston, R. C. (Ed.). (1968a). *John Mason: An essay on elocution and pronunciation 1748*. Menston, UK: Scolar Press.

Alston, R. C. (Ed.). (1968b). *Thomas Sheridan: A course of lectures on elocution 1762*. Menston, UK: Scolar Press.

Alston, R. C. (Ed.). (1969). *Thomas Sheridan: A rhetorical grammar of the English language 1781*. Menston, UK: Scolar Press.

Amerman, J. D., & Parnell, M. M. (1992). Speech timing strategies in elderly adults. *Journal of Phonetics, 20*, 65-76.

Apple, W., Streeter, L. A., & Krauss, R. M. (1979). Effects of pitch and speech rate on personal attributions. *Journal of Personality and Social Psychology, 37*, 715-727.

Argyle, M. (1983). *The psychology of interpersonal behaviour* (3rd ed.). Harmondsworth: Penguin.

Argyle, M. (1988). *Bodily communication* (2nd ed.). London: Methuen.

Argyle, M. (1991). *Cooperation: The basis of sociability*. London: Routledge & Kegan Paul.

Argyle, M., & Dean, J. (1965). Eye contact, distance and affiliation. *Sociometry, 28,* 289-304.

Arlington, L. C. (1966). *The Chinese drama: From the earliest times until today*. New York: Benjamin Blom.

Bales, R. F. (1950). *Interaction process analysis: A method for the study of small groups*. Cambridge, MA: Addison-Wesley.

Baltaxe, C. A. (1991). Vocal communication of affect and its perception in three to four year old children. *Perceptual and Motor Skills, 72,* 1187-1202.

Barker, M. C. (1993). *Perceptions of social rules in intercultural and intracultural encounters: A study of Australian and ethnic Chinese university students*. Unpublished doctoral dissertation, The University of Queensland, Brisbane.

Batstone, S., & Tuomi, S. P. (1981). Perceptual characteristics of female voices. *Language and Speech, 24,* 111-123.

Benjamin, B. J. (1981). Frequency variability in the aged voice. *Journal of Gerontology, 36,* 722-726.

Berry, D. S. (1990). Vocal attractiveness and vocal babyishness: Effects on stranger, self, and friend impressions. *Journal of Nonverbal Behavior, 14,* 141-153.

Berry, D. S. (1992). Vocal types and stereotypes: Joint effects of vocal attractiveness and vocal maturity on person perception. *Journal of Nonverbal Behavior, 16,* 41-54.

Berry, F. (1962). *Poetry and the physical voice*. London: Routledge & Kegan Paul.

Biever, D. M., & Bless, D. M. (1989). Vibratory characteristics of the vocal folds in young adults and geriatric women. *Journal of Voice, 3,* 120-131.

Birdwhistell, R. L. (1952). *Introduction to kinesics*. Washington, DC: Foreign Service Institute.

Blanck, P. D., & Rosenthal, R. (1984). Mediation of interpersonal expectancy effects: Counselor's tone of voice. *Journal of Educational Psychology, 3,* 418-426.

Bond, R. N., Feldstein, S., & Simpson, S. (1988). Relative and absolute judgements of speech rate from masked and content-standard stimuli: The influence of vocal frequency and intensity. *Human Communication Research, 14,* 548-568.

Bradac, J. J. (1990). Language attitudes and impression formation. In H. Giles & W. P. Robinson (Eds.), *Handbook of language and social psychology* (pp. 387-412). Chichester: John Wiley.

Bregman, A. S. (1990). *Auditory scene analysis*. London: MIT Press.

Brennan, E. M., & Brennan, J. S. (1981). Accent scaling and language attitudes: Reactions to Mexican American English speech. *Language and Speech, 24,* 207-221.

Bronfenbrenner, U. (1979). *The ecology of human development: Experiments by nature and design*. Cambridge, MA: Harvard University Press.

Brown, B. L., & Bradshaw, J. M. (1985). Toward a social psychology of voice variations. In H. Giles & R. N. St. Clair (Eds.), *Recent advances in language communication and social psychology* (pp. 144-181). London: Lawrence Erlbaum.

Brown, B. L., & Lambert, W. E. (1976). A cross-cultural study of social status markers in speech. *Canadian Journal of Behavioural Science, 8,* 39-55.

Brown, P., & Levinson, S. (1978). Universals in language usage: Politeness phenomena. In E. N. Goody (Ed.), *Questions and politeness: Strategies in social interaction* (pp. 56-289). Cambridge: Cambridge University Press.

Brown R. (1965). *Social psychology*. New York: Free Press.

Brown, R., & Gilman, A. (1960). The pronouns of power and solidarity. In T. A. Sebeok (Ed.), *Style in language* (pp. 253-276). Cambridge: MIT Press.

Brown, W. S., Jr., Morris, R. J., & Michel, J. F. (1989). Vocal jitter in young adult and aged female voices. *Journal of Voice, 3,* 113-119.

Brunswik, E. (1956). *Perception and the representative design of psychological experiments.* Berkeley: University of California Press.

Buder, E. H. (1992, May). *Vocal synchrony in conversations between strangers: A gender effect.* Paper presented at the International Communication Association Conference, Miami, FL.

Bühler, K. (1934). *Sprachtheorie.* Jena: Fischer.

Bullen, A. (1942). Nasality: Cause and remedy of our American blight. *Quarterly Journal of Speech, 28,* 83-84.

Buller, D. B., & Aune, R. K. (1988). The effects of vocalics and nonverbal sensitivity on compliance: A speech accommodation theory explanation. *Human Communication Research, 14,* 301-332.

Buller, D. B., & Burgoon, J. K. (1986). The effects of vocalics and nonverbal sensitivity on compliance: A replication and extension. *Human Communication Research, 13,* 126-144.

Buller, D. B., LePoire, B. A., Aune, R. K., & Elroy, S. V. (1992). Speech perceptions as mediators of the effect of speech rate similarity on compliance. *Human Communication Research, 19,* 286-311.

Burgoon, J. K., Birk, T., & Pfau, M. (1990). Nonverbal behaviors, persuasion, and credibility. *Human Communication Research, 17,* 1140-1169.

Burgoon, J. K., Buller, D. B., & Woodall, W. G. (1989). *Nonverbal communication: The unspoken dialogue.* New York: Harper & Row.

Burgoon, J. K., Kelley, D. L., Newton, D. A., & Keeley-Dyreson, M. P. (1989). The nature of arousal and nonverbal indices. *Human Communication Research, 16,* 217-255.

Byrne, D. J. (1977). The speech spectrum—Some aspects of its significance for hearing aid selection and evaluation. *British Journal of Audiology, 11,* 40-46.

Cahn, J. E. (1990). The generation of affect in synthesized speech. *Journal of the American Voice I/O Society, 8,* 1-19.

Cantril, H., & Allport, G. W. (1971). *The psychology of radio.* New York: Arno Press.

Cappella, J. N. (Ed.). (1989). Linking the verbal and the nonverbal channels [Special issue]. *Journal of Language and Social Psychology, 8.*

Cappella, J. N., & Palmer, M. T. (1989). The structure and organization of verbal and nonverbal behavior: Data for models of production. In H. Giles & W. P. Robinson (Eds.), *Handbook of language and social psychology* (pp. 141-161). Chichester: John Wiley.

Caporael, L. R. (1981). The paralanguage of caregiving: Baby talk to the institutionalized aged. *Journal of Personality and Social Psychology, 40,* 876-884.

Catford, J. (1964). Phonation types: The classification of some laryngeal components of speech production. In D. Abercrombie, D. B. Fry, P. A. D. MacCarthy, N. C. Scott, & J. L. M. Trim (Eds.), *In honour of Daniel Jones* (pp. 26-37). London: Longmans.

Chevrie-Muller, C., Perbos, J., & Guilet, C. (1983). Automated analysis of the electro-glottographic signal: Application to the study of phonation in the elderly. *Aging Communication Bulletin Audiophonology, 16,* 121-144.

Coleman, L. M. (1976). Racial decoding and status differentiation: Who hears what? *Journal of Black Psychology, 3,* 34-46.

Coleman, R. F., & Markham, I. W. (1991). Normal variations in habitual pitch. *Journal of Voice, 5,* 173-177.

Colton, R. H. (1969). *Some acoustic and perceptual correlates of the modal and falsetto registers.* Unpublished doctoral dissertation, University of Florida.

Colton, R. H. (1988). Physiological mechanisms of vocal frequency control: The role of tension. *Journal of Voice, 2*, 208-220.

Cooke, M. P., & Brown, G. J. (1993). Computational auditory scene analysis: Exploiting principles of perceived continuity. *Speech Communication, 12*, 391-399.

Cooper, C. (1969). *The English teacher.* Menston, UK: Scolar Press. (Original work published 1687)

Cooper, D. S. (1989). Voice: A historical perspective. *Journal of Voice, 3*, 1-6.

Costanzo, F. S., Markel, N. N., & Costanzo, P. R. (1969). Voice quality profile and perceived emotion. *Journal of Counselling Psychology, 16*, 267-270.

Coupland, J., Coupland, N., & Robinson, J. D. (1992). "How are you?": Negotiating phatic communion. *Language in Society, 21*, 207-230.

Coupland, N., Coupland, J., & Giles, H. (1991). *Language, society and the elderly: Discourse, identity and ageing.* Oxford: Blackwell.

Coupland, N., Coupland, J., Giles, H., & Henwood, K. (1988). Accommodating the elderly: Invoking and extending a theory. *Language in Society, 17*, 1-41.

Cox, A. C., & Cooper, M. B. (1981). Selecting a voice for a specified task: The example of telephone announcements. *Language and Speech, 24*, 233-243.

Cramer, J. A. (1989). Radio: A woman's place is on the air. In P. J. Creedon (Ed.), *Women and mass communication: Challenging gender values* (pp. 214-226). Newbury Park, CA: Sage.

Crown, C. L. (1991). Coordinated interpersonal timing of vision and voice as a function of interpersonal attraction. *Journal of Language and Social Psychology, 10*, 29-46.

Crystal, D., & Quirk, R. (1964). *Systems of prosodic and paralinguistic features in English.* The Hague: Mouton.

Daly, E. M., Lancee, W. J., & Polivy, J. (1983). A conical model for the taxonomy of emotional experience. *Journal of Personality and Social Psychology, 45*, 443-457.

Davitz, J. R., & Davitz, L. J. (1959). The communication of feeling by content-free speech. *Journal of Communication, 9*, 6-13.

Deal, L. V., & Oyer, H. J. (1991). Ratings of vocal pleasantness and the aging process. *Folia Phoniatrica, 43*, 44-48.

Dubé-Simard, L. (1983). Genesis of social categorization, threat to identity and perception of social injustice: Their role in intergroup communication. *Journal of Language and Social Psychology, 3 & 4*, 183-205.

Ekman, P., & Friesen, W. V. (1969). The repertoire of nonverbal behavior: Categories, origins, usage and codings. *Semiotica, 1*, 49-97.

Ekman, P., & Friesen, W. V. (1974). Detecting deception from body and face. *Journal of Personality and Social Psychology, 29*, 288-298.

Ekman, P., Friesen, W. V., & Scherer, K. R. (1976). Body movement and voice pitch in deceptive interaction. *Semiotica, 16*, 23-27.

Ekman, P., O'Sullivan, M., Friesen, W. V., & Scherer, K. R. (1991). Invited article: Face, voice, and body in detecting deceit. *Journal of Nonverbal Behavior, 15*, 125-135.

Esling, J. (1978). *Voice quality in Edinburgh: A sociolinguistic and phonetic study.* Unpublished doctoral dissertation, Edinburgh University, Edinburgh.

Fairbanks, G. (1940). *Voice and articulation drill book.* New York: Harper.

Fanning, D. (1990, September 23). The executive life [Interview with J. Jacobi, voice coach]. *The New York Times*, section 3, p. 25.

Fay, P. J., & Middleton, W. C. (1939). Judgement of occupation from the voice as transmitted over a public address system and over a radio. *Journal of Applied Psychology, 23*, 586-601.

Feudo, P., Jr., Harvey, P. L., & Aronson, D. B. (1992). Objective analysis of actors' voices: Comparative development across training. *Journal of Voice, 6*, 267-270.

Firth, J. (1957). *Papers in linguistics, 1934-1951.* London: Oxford University Press.

Fiske, J. (1987). *Television culture.* London: Routledge & Kegan Paul.

Fitzgerald, F. Scott (1958). The great Gatsby. In *The Bodley Head Scott Fitzgerald* (Vol. 1). London: The Bodley Head.

Flanagan, J. L. (1957). Estimates of the maximum precision necessary in quantizing certain "dimensions" of vowel sounds. *Journal of the Acoustical Society of America, 24*, 533-534.

Forsyth, D. R. (1990). *Group dynamics* (2nd ed.). Pacific Grove, CA: Brooks/Cole.

Friedman, H. S., & Tucker, J. S. (1990). Language and deception. In H. Giles & W. P. Robinson (Eds.), *Handbook of language and social psychology* (pp. 257-270). Chichester: John Wiley.

Fritzell, B. (1992). Inverse filtering. *Journal of Voice, 6*, 111-114.

Fritzell, B., Hallén, O., & Sundberg, J. (1974). Evaluation of Teflon injection procedures for paralytic dysphonia. *Folia Phoniatrica, 26*, 414-421.

Frøkjaer-Jensen, B., & Prytz, S. (1976). Registration of voice quality. *Bruel and Kjaer Technical Review, 3*, 3-17.

Fry, D. B. (1979). *The physics of speech.* Cambridge: Cambridge University Press.

Furui, S. (1991). Speaker-dependent-feature extraction, recognition and processing techniques. In Speaker characterization in speech technology [Special issue]. *Speech Communication, 10*, 505-520.

Furui, S., Itakura, F., & Saito, S. (1972). Talker recognition by long-time average spectrum. *Electronics and Communication in Japan, 55*, 54-61.

Gallois, C. (1993). The language and communication of emotion. *American Behavioral Scientist, 36*, 309-338.

Gallois, C., & Callan, V. J. (1981). Personality impressions elicited by accented English speech. *Journal of Cross-Cultural Psychology, 12*, 347-359.

Gallois, C., & Callan, V. J. (1986). Decoding emotional messages: Influence of ethnicity, sex, message type, and channel. *Journal of Personality and Social Psychology, 51*, 755-762.

Gallois, C., & Callan, V. J. (1991). Interethnic accommodation: The role of norms. In H. Giles, J. Coupland, & N. Coupland (Eds.), *Contexts of accommodation* (pp. 245-269). Cambridge: Cambridge University Press.

Gallois, C., Callan, V. J., & Johnstone, M. (1984). Personality judgements of Australian Aborigine and white speakers: Ethnicity, sex and context. *Journal of Language and Social Psychology, 3*, 39-57.

Gallois, C., Franklyn-Stokes, A., Giles, H., & Coupland, N. (1988). Communication accommodation encounters in intercultural encounters. In Y. Y. Kim & W. B. Gudykunst (Eds.), *Theories in intercultural communication* (pp. 157-185). Newbury Park, CA: Sage.

Gallois, C., & Markel, N. N. (1975). Turn taking: Social personality and conversational style. *Journal of Personality and Social Psychology, 31*, 1134-1140.

Gauffin, J., & Sundberg, J. (1974). Masking effects of one's own voice. *Speech Transmission Laboratory Quarterly Progress Status Report, 1974, 1*, 35-41.

Genesee, F., & Bourhis, R. Y. (1982). The social psychological significance of code switching in cross-cultural communication. *Journal of Language and Social Psychology, 1,* 1-27.

Genesee, F., & Holobow, N. E. (1989). Change and stability in intergroup perceptions. *Journal of Language and Social Psychology, 8,* 17-38.

Giles, H. (1970). Evaluative reactions to accents. *Educational Review, 22,* 211-227.

Giles, H. (1973). Accent mobility, a model and some data. *Anthropological Linguistics, 15,* 87-105.

Giles, H., & Coupland, N. (1991a). *Language: Contexts and consequences.* Milton Keynes: Open University Press.

Giles, H., & Coupland, N. (1991b). Language attitudes: Discursive, contextual, and gerontological considerations. In A. G. Reynolds (Ed.), *Bilingualism, multiculturalism, and second language learning: The McGill Conference in Honour of Wallace E. Lambert* (pp. 21-42). Hillsdale, NJ: Lawrence Erlbaum.

Giles, H., Henwood, K., Coupland, N., Harriman, J., & Coupland, J. (1992). Language attitudes and cognitive mediation. *Human Communication Research, 18,* 500-527.

Giles, H., Mulac, A., Bradac, J. J., & Johnson, P. (1987). Speech accommodation theory: The next decade and beyond. In M. McLaughlin (Ed.), *Communication yearbook, Vol. 10* (pp. 13-48). Newbury Park, CA: Sage.

Giles, H., & Powesland, P.F . (1975). *Speech style and social evaluation.* London: Academic Press.

Giles, H., Robinson, W. P., & Smith, P. M. (1979). *Language: Social psychological perspectives.* Oxford: Pergamon Press.

Giles, H., & Ryan, E. B. (1982). Prolegomena for developing a social psychological theory of language attitudes. In E. B. Ryan & H. Giles (Eds.), *Attitudes toward language variation: Social and applied contexts* (pp. 208-223). London: Edward Arnold.

Giles, H., & Street, R. L., Jr. (1985). Communicator characteristics and behavior. In M. L. Knapp & G. R. Miller (Eds.), *Handbook of interpersonal communication* (pp. 205-261). Beverly Hills, CA: Sage.

Glaze, L. E., Bless, D. M., Milenkovic, P., & Susser, R. D. (1988). Acoustic characteristics of children's voices. *Journal of Voice, 2,* 312-319.

Goldbeck, T., Tolkmitt, F., & Scherer, K. R. (1988). Experimental studies on vocal communication. In K. R. Scherer (Ed.), *Facets of emotion* (pp. 119-138). Hillsdale, NJ: Lawrence Erlbaum.

Gregory, S., Webster, S., & Huang, G. (1993). Voice pitch and amplitude convergence as a metric of quality in dyadic interviews. *Language and Communication, 13,* 195-217.

Hall, E. T. (1959). *The silent language.* Garden City, NY: Doubleday.

Hall, E. T. (1963). A system for the notation of proxemic behavior. *American Anthropologist, 65,* 1003-1026.

Hall, E. T. (1966). *The hidden dimension.* Garden City, NY: Doubleday.

Hall, E. T. (1974). *Handbook for proxemic research.* Washington, DC: Society for the Anthropology of Visual Communication.

Hall, E. T. (1981). *Beyond culture.* Garden City, NY: Doubleday.

Hall, J. A. (1980a). *Nonverbal sex differences.* Baltimore, MD: Johns Hopkins University Press.

Hall, J. A. (1980b). Voice tone and persuasion. *Journal of Personality and Social Psychology, 38,* 924-934.

Hanley, T. D., Snidecor, J. C., & Ringel, R. L. (Eds.). (1966). Some acoustic differences among languages. *Phonetica, 14,* 97-107.

Harper, R. G., Wiens, A. N., & Matarazzo, J. D. (1978). *Nonverbal communication: The state of the art.* New York: John Wiley.

Hartman, D. (1979). The perceptual identity and characteristics of aging in normal adult speakers. *Journal of Communication Disorders, 12,* 53-61.

Hartshorne, C., & Weiss, P. (Eds.). (1960). *Collected papers of Charles Sanders Peirce: Vol. 2. Elements of logic.* Cambridge, MA: Belknap, Harvard University Press.

Haskell, J. A. (1987). Vocal self-perception: The other side of the equation. *Journal of Voice, 1,* 172-179.

Haskell, J. A. (1991). Adjusting adolescents' vocal self-perception. *Language, Speech and Hearing Services in Schools, 22,* 168-172.

Henton, C. G., & Bladon, R. A. (1985). Breathiness in normal female speech: Inefficiency versus desirability. *Language and Communication, 5,* 221-227.

Hermansky, H., & Cox, L. A., Jr. (1991). Perceptual linear predictive (PLP) analysis-resynthesis technique. In G. Pirani (Ed.), *Proceedings of the Second European Conference on Speech Communication and Technology* (pp. 329-332). Genoa, Italy: ESCA.

Higgins, M. B., & Saxman, J. H. (1991). A comparison of selected phonatory behaviors of healthy aged and young adults. *Journal of Speech and Hearing Research, 34,* 1000-1010.

Hill, A. A. (1958). *Introduction to linguistic structures.* New York: Harcourt Brace.

Hoare, Q., & Nowell-Smith, G. (Eds.). (1971). *Selections from the prison notebooks of Antonio Gramsci.* New York: International Publishers.

Hogg, M. A., & Abrams, D. (1988). *Social identifications.* London: Routledge & Kegan Paul.

Hollien, H. (1972). Three major vocal registers: A proposal. In A. Rigault & R. Charbonneau (Eds.), *Proceedings of the Seventh International Congress of Phonetic Sciences* (pp. 320-331). The Hague: Mouton.

Hollien, H. (1980). Vocal indicators of psychological stress. In F. Wright, C. Bahn, & R. W. Rieber (Eds.), *Forensic psychology and psychiatry* (pp. 47-72). New York: New York Academy of Sciences.

Hollien, H. (1987). "Old voices": What do we really know about them? *Journal of Voice, 1,* 2-17.

Hollien, H. (1990). *The acoustics of crime: The new science of forensic phonetics.* New York: Plenum.

Hollien, H., & Tolhurst, G. (1978). The aging voice. In V. Lawrence & B. Weinberg (Eds.), *Transactions of the 7th Symposium on the Care of the Professional Voice* (pp. 67-73). New York: Voice Foundation.

Honikman, B. (1964). Articulatory settings. In D. Abercrombie, D. B. Fry, P. A. D. MacCarthy, N. C. Scott, & J. L. M. Trim (Eds.), *In honour of Daniel Jones* (pp. 73-84). London: Longmans.

Hortaçsu, N., & Ekinci, B. (1992). Children's reliance on situational and vocal expression of emotions: Consistent and conflicting cues. *Journal of Nonverbal Behavior, 16,* 231-248.

Jaffe, J., & Feldstein, S. (1970). *Rhythms of dialogue.* New York: Academic Press.

Jakobson, R. (1960). Concluding statement: Linguistics and poetics. In T. Sebeok (Ed.), *Style in language* (pp. 350-377). Cambridge: MIT Press.

Jaworski, A. (1993). *The power of silence: Social and pragmatic perspectives.* Newbury Park, CA: Sage.

Johnson, C. J., Pick, H. L., Jr., Siegal, G. M., Cicciarelli, A. W., & Garber, S. R. (1981). Effects of interpersonal distance on children's vocal intensity. *Child Development, 52*, 721-723.

Johnson, W. F., Emde, R. N., Scherer, K. R., & Klinnert, M. D. (1986). Recognition of emotion from vocal cues. *Archives of General Psychiatry, 43*, 280-283.

Kendon, A., Harris, R. M., & Key, M. R. (1975). *Organization of behavior in face-to-face interaction*. The Hague: Mouton.

Kimble, C. E., Yoshikawa, J. C., & Zehr, H. D. (1981). Vocal and verbal assertiveness in same-sex and mixed-sex groups. *Journal of Personality and Social Psychology, 6*, 1047-1054.

Keider, A., Hurtig, R. R., & Titze, I. R. (1987). The perceptual nature of vocal register change. *Journal of Voice, 1*, 223-233.

Keith, M. C. (1989). *Broadcast voice performance*. Boston: Focal Press.

Kellermann, K. (1987). Information exchange in social interaction. In M. E. Roloff & G. R. Miller (Eds.), *Interpersonal processes: New directions in communication research* (pp. 188-219). Newbury Park, CA: Sage.

Kemp, J. A. (Ed.). (1972). *John Wallis: Grammar of the English language*. London: Longmans.

Kent, R. D. (1993). Vocal tract acoustics. *Journal of Voice, 7*, 97-117.

Klatt, D. H., & Klatt, L. C. (1990). Analysis, synthesis, and perception of voice quality variations among female and male talkers. *Journal of the Acoustical Society of America, 87*, 820-857.

Kramer, C. (1977). Perceptions of female and male speech. *Language and Speech, 20*, 151-161.

Kramer, E. (1964). Elimination of verbal cues in judgements of emotion from voice. *Journal of Abnormal and Social Psychology, 68*, 390-396.

Krauss, R. M., Apple, W., Morency, N., Wenzel, C., & Winton, W. (1981). Verbal, vocal, and visible factors in judgements of another's affect. *Journal of Personality and Social Psychology, 40*, 312-320.

Labov, W. (1966). *The social stratification of English in New York City*. Washington, DC: Center for Applied Linguistics.

Lacan, J. (1968). *The language of the self: The function of language in psychoanalysis*. New York: Dell.

Ladefoged, P. (1971). *Preliminaries to linguistic phonetics*. Chicago: University of Chicago Press.

Ladefoged, P. (1993). *A course in phonetics* (3rd ed.). New York: Harcourt Brace Jovanovich.

Lambert, W. E., Frankel, H., & Tucker, G. R. (1966). Judging personality through speech: A French-Canadian example. *Journal of Communication, 16*, 305-321.

Lambert, W. E., Hodgson, R. C., Gardner, R. C., & Fillenbaum, S. (1960). Evaluative reactions to spoken languages. *Journal of Abnormal and Social Psychology, 60*, 144-151.

Lass, N. J., Beverly, A. S., Nicosia, D. K., & Simpson, L. A. (1978). An investigation of speaker height and weight by means of direct observations. *Journal of Phonetics, 6*, 69-76.

Lass, N. J., Kelley, D. T., Cunningham, C. M., & Sheridan, K. J. (1980). A comparative study of speaker height and weight identification from voiced and whispered speech. *Journal of Phonetics, 8*, 195-204.

Lass, N. J., Trapp, D. S., Baldwin, M. K., Scherbick, K. A., & Wright, D. L. (1982). Effect of vocal disguise on judgements of speakers' sex and race. *Perceptual and Motor Skills, 54*, 1235-1240.

Laver, J. (1968). Voice quality and indexical information. *The British Journal of Disorders of Communication, 3,* 43-54.

Laver, J. (1974). Labels for voices. *Journal of the International Phonetic Association, 4,* 62-75.

Laver, J. (1975a). Communicative functions of phatic communion. In A. Kendon, R. M. Harris, & M. R. Key (Eds.), *The organization of behavior in face-to-face interaction* (pp. 215-238). The Hague: Mouton.

Laver, J. (1975b). *Individual features in voice quality.* Unpublished doctoral dissertation, Edinburgh University, Edinburgh.

Laver, J. (1976). The semiotic nature of phonetic data. *York Papers in Linguistics, 6,* 55-62.

Laver, J. (1977). Early writings on voice quality and tone of voice: From Cicero to Sweet. *Work in Progress, Department of Linguistics, University of Edinburgh, 10,* 92-111.

Laver, J. (1978). The concept of articulatory settings: An historical survey. *Historiographia Linguistica, 5,* 1-14.

Laver, J. (1980). *The phonetic description of voice quality.* Cambridge: Cambridge University Press.

Laver, J. (1981a). The analysis of vocal quality: From the classical period to the twentieth century. In R. E. Asher & E. J. A. Henderson (Eds.), *Towards a history of phonetics* (pp. 79-99). Edinburgh: Edinburgh University Press.

Laver, J. (1981b). Linguistic routines and politeness in greeting and parting. In F. Coulmas (Ed.), *Conversational routine* (pp. 289-304). The Hague: Mouton.

Laver, J. (1991). *The gift of speech.* Edinburgh: Edinburgh University Press.

Laver, J. (1993). *Principles of phonetics.* Cambridge: Cambridge University Press.

Laver, J., Jack, M., & Gardiner, A. (Eds.). (1990). *Proceedings of the Tutorial and Research Workshop on Speaker Characterization in Speech Technology.* Edinburgh: CSTR.

Laver, J., & Trudgill, P. (1979). Phonetic and linguistic markers in speech. In K. R. Scherer & H. Giles (Eds.), *Social markers in speech* (pp. 1-32). Cambridge: Cambridge University Press.

Laver, J., Wirz, S., MacKenzie, J., & Hiller, S. (1981). A perceptual protocol for the analysis of vocal profiles. *Work in Progress, Department of Linguistics, University of Edinburgh, 14,* 139-155.

Leventhal, H., & Scherer, K. R. (1987). The relationship of emotion to cognition: A functional approach to a semantic controversy. *Cognition and Emotion, 1,* 3-28.

Li, K.-P., Hughes, G. W., & House, A. S. (1969). Correlation characteristics and dimensionality of speech spectra. *Journal of the Acoustical Society of America, 46,* 1019-1025.

Liberman, M. V. (1978). *The intonational system of English.* Bloomington: Indiana University Linguistics Club.

Lindblom, B. (1983). Economy of speech gestures. In P. F. MacNeilage (Ed.), *The production of speech* (pp. 217-246). New York: Springer.

Linke, C. E. (1973). A study of pitch characteristics of female voices and their relationship to vocal effectiveness. *Folia Phoniatrica, 25,* 173-185.

Little, C. E. (Ed.). (1951). *The institutio oratoria of Marcus Fabius Quintilianus.* Nashville, TN: George Peabody College for Teachers.

Lyczak, R., Fu, G. S., & Ho, A. (1976). Attitudes of Hong Kong bilinguals toward English and Chinese speakers. *Journal of Cross-Cultural Psychology, 7,* 425-438.

Lykken, D. (1981). *A tremor in the blood.* New York: McGraw-Hill.

Lyons, J. (1977). *Semantics.* Cambridge: Cambridge University Press.

Mackiewicz-Krassowska, H. (1976). Nasality in Australian English. *Working Papers, Macquarie University, Speech and Language Research Centre, 1,* 27-40.

MacLachlan, J. (1979, November). What people really think of fast talkers. *Psychology Today,* pp. 113-117.

Malinowski, B. (1923). Phatic communication. Supplement to C. K. Ogden & I. A. Richards, *The meaning of meaning.* London: Routledge & Kegan Paul.

Mattingly, I. C. (1969). Speaker variation and vocal tract size. *Journal of the Acoustical Society of America, 39,* 1219.

McGlone, R. E., & Hollien, H. (1963). Vocal pitch characteristics of aged women. *Journal of Speech and Hearing Research, 6,* 164-170.

Mehrabian, A. (1969). Some referents and measures of nonverbal behavior. *Behavior Research Methods and Instrumentation, 1,* 203-207.

Mehrabian, A., & Russell, J. A. (1974). *An approach to environmental psychology.* Cambridge: MIT Press.

Mencel, E., Moon, J. B., & Leeper, H. A. (1988). Speaker race identification of North American Indian children. *Folia Phoniatrica, 40,* 175-182.

Michel, J., Hollien, H., & Moore, P. (1966). Speaking fundamental frequency characteristics of 15-, 16-, and 17-year old girls. *Language and Speech, 9,* 46-51.

Michel, J. F., & Hollien, H. (1968). Perceptual differentiation in vocal fry and harshness. *Journal of Speech and Hearing Research, 11,* 439-443.

Miller, N., Maruyama, G., Beaber, R. J., & Valone, K. (1976). Speed of speech and persuasion. *Journal of Personality and Social Psychology, 34,* 615-624.

Milmoe, S. (1965). *Characteristics of speakers and listeners as factors in nonverbal communication.* Senior Honors Thesis, Harvard University.

Mitchell, A. G., & Delbridge, A. (1965). *The pronunciation of English in Australia.* Sydney: Angus & Robertson.

Monsen, R. B., & Engebretson, A. M. (1977). Study of variations in the male and female glottal wave. *Journal of the Acoustical Society of America, 62,* 981-991.

Montepare, J. M., & Vega, C. (1988). Women's vocal reaction to intimate and casual male friends. *Personality and Social Psychology Bulletin, 14,* 103-113.

Montepare, J. M., & Zebrowitz-McArthur, L. (1987). Perceptions of adults with child-like voices in two cultures. *Journal of Experimental Social Psychology, 23,* 331-349.

Moore, B. C. J. (1982). *An introduction to the psychology of hearing* (2nd ed.). Orlando, FL: Academic Press.

Morner, M., Fransson, N., & Fant, G. (1964). Voice register terminology and standard pitch. *Speech Transmission Laboratory Quarterly Progress Status Report, 4,* 17-23.

Moses, P. J. (1954). *The voice of neurosis.* New York: Grune & Stratton.

Mulac, A. (1976). Assessment and application of the Revised Dialect Attitudinal Scale. *Communication Monographs, 43,* 238-245.

Mulac, A., Hanley, T. D., & Prigge, D. Y. (1974). Effects of phonological speech foreignness upon dimensions of attitude of selected American listeners. *The Quarterly Journal of Speech, 60,* 411-420.

Mulac, A., Incontro, C. R., & James, M. R. (1985). A comparison of the gender-linked language effect and sex-role stereotypes. *Journal of Personality and Social Psychology, 49,* 1099-1110.

Nolan, F. (1983). *The phonetic bases of speaker recognition.* Cambridge: Cambridge University Press.

Noller, P. (1984). *Nonverbal communication and marital interaction.* Oxford: Pergamon.

O'Shaughnessy, D. (1987). *Speech communication: Human and machine.* Reading, MA: Addison-Wesley.

Orlikoff, R. F. (1989). Vocal jitter at different fundamental frequencies: A cardiovascular-neuromuscular explanation. *Journal of Voice, 3,* 104-112.

Osgood, C. E., May, W. H., & Miron, M. S. (1975). *Cross-cultural universals of affective meaning.* Urbana: University of Illinois Press.

Osgood, C. E., Suci, G. J., & Tannenbaum, P. H. (1957). *The measurement of meaning.* Urbana: University of Illinois Press.

Painter, C. (1973). Cineradiographic data on the feature "covered" in Twi vowel harmony. *Phonetica, 28,* 97-120.

Patterson, M. L. (1976). An arousal model of interpersonal intimacy. *Psychological Review, 83,* 235-245.

Patterson, M. L. (1983). *Nonverbal behavior: A functional perspective.* New York: Springer.

Patterson, M. L. (1990). Functions of non-verbal behavior in social interaction. In H. Giles & W. P. Robinson (Eds.), *Handbook of language and social psychology* (pp. 101-120). New York: John Wiley.

Pear, T. H. (1931). *Voice and personality.* New York: John Wiley.

Pear, T. H. (1933). *The psychology of effective speaking.* London: Kegan Paul, Trench, Trubner.

Pearce, W. B., & Brommell, B. J. (1971). Vocalic communication in persuasion. *Quarterly Journal of Speech, 58,* 298-306.

Pike, K. (1943). *Phonetics.* Ann Arbor: University of Michigan Press.

Pittam, J. (1986). *Voice quality: Its measurement and functional classification.* Unpublished doctoral dissertation, The University of Queensland, Brisbane.

Pittam, J. (1987a). Listener's evaluations of voice quality in Australian English speakers. *Language and Speech, 30,* 99-113.

Pittam, J. (1987b). The long-term spectral measurement of voice quality as a social and personality marker: A review. *Language and Speech, 30,* 1-12.

Pittam, J. (1990). The relationship between perceived persuasiveness of nasality and source characteristics for Australian and American listeners. *The Journal of Social Psychology, 130,* 81-87.

Pittam, J., & Gallois, C. (1987). Predicting impressions of speakers from voice quality: Acoustic and perceptual measures. *Journal of Language and Social Psychology, 5,* 233-247.

Pittam, J., Gallois, C., & Callan, V. J. (1990). The long-term spectrum and perceived emotion. *Speech Communication, 9,* 177-187.

Pittam, J., & Millar, J. B. (1989). *Long-term spectrum of the acoustics of voice: An annotated and classified research bibliography.* Bloomington: Indiana University Linguistics Club.

Pittam, J., & Scherer, K. R. (1992). The encoding of affect: A review and directions for further research. In J. Pittam (Ed.), *Proceedings of the Fourth Australian International Conference on Speech Science and Technology* (pp. 744-749). Canberra: ASSTA.

Pittam, J., & Scherer, K. R. (1993). Vocal expression and communication of emotion. In M. Lewis & J. Haviland (Eds.), *The handbook of emotion* (pp. 185-197). New York: Guilford.

Popov, V. A., Simonov, P. V., Frolov, M. V., & Khachatur'yants, L. S. (1971). Frequency spectrum of speech as an indicator of the degree and nature of emotional stress. *Zurnal Vysey Nervnoy Deyatel'nosti, 1,* 104-109 (U.S. Department of Commerce JPRS52698).

Poyatos, F. (1991). Paralinguistic qualifiers: Our many voices. *Language and Communication, 11,* 181-195.

Ptacek, P. H., Sander, E. K., Manoley, W., & Jackson, C. (1966). Phonatory and related changes with advanced age. *Journal of Speech and Hearing Research, 9,* 353-360.

Ramig, L. A., & Ringel, R.L . (1983). Effects of physiological aging on selected acoustic characteristics of voice. *Journal of Speech and Hearing Research, 26,* 22-30.

Raphael, B. N., & Scherer, R. C. (1987). Voice modifications of stage actors: Acoustic analysis. *Journal of Voice, 1,* 83-87.

Robinson, W. P. (1972). *Language and social behaviour.* Harmondsworth: Penguin.

Robinson, W. P. (1978). *Language management in education: The Australian context.* Sydney: George Allen & Unwin.

Robinson, W. P. (1985). Social psychology and discourse. In T. A. van Dijk (Ed.), *Handbook of discourse analysis: Vol. 1. Disciplines of discourse* (pp. 107-144). London: Academic Press.

Rogers, P. L., Scherer, K. R., & Rosenthal, R. (1971). Content-filtering human speech: A simple electronic system. *Behavioural Research Methods and Instrumentation, 3,* 16-18.

Rosenthal, R., Hall, J. A., DiMatteo, M. R., Rogers, P. L., & Archer, D. (1979). *Sensitivity to nonverbal communication: The PONS test.* Baltimore, MD: Johns Hopkins University Press.

Rubin, A. M., & Rubin, R. B. (1986). Contextual age as a life-position index. *The International Journal of Aging and Human Development, 23,* 27-45.

Russell, D. A. (1983). *Greek declamation.* Cambridge: Cambridge University Press.

Russell, J. A. (1980). A circumplex model of affect. *Journal of Personality and Social Psychology, 39,* 1161-1178.

Russell, J. A., Lewicka, M., & Niit, T. (1989). A cross-cultural study of a circumplex model of affect. *Journal of Personality and Social Psychology, 57,* 848-856.

Ryan, E. B., Bourhis, R. Y., & Knops, U. (1991). Evaluative perceptions of patronizing speech addressed to elders. *Psychology and Aging, 6,* 442-450.

Ryan, E. B., & Bulik, C. M. (1982). Evaluations of middle class speakers of standard American and German-accented English. *Journal of Language and Social Psychology, 1,* 51-61.

Ryan, E. B., & Carranza, M. A. (1975). Evaluative reactions of adolescents toward speakers of standard English and Mexican American accented English. *Journal of Personality and Social Psychology, 31,* 855-863.

Ryan, E. B., Carranza, M. A., & Moffie, R. W. (1977). Reactions toward varying degrees of accentedness in the speech of Spanish-English bilinguals. *Language and Speech, 20,* 267-273.

Ryan, E. B., & Giles, H. (1982). *Attitudes towards language variation: Social and applied contexts.* London: Edward Arnold.

Ryan, E. B., Giles, H., Bartolucci, G., & Henwood, K. (1986). Psycholinguistic and social psychological components of communication by and with the elderly. *Language and Communication, 6,* 1-24.

Ryan, E. B., & Sebastian, R. J. (1980). The effects of speech style and social class background on social judgements of speakers. *British Journal of Social and Clinical Psychology, 19,* 229-233.

Ryan, W. J., & Burk, K. W. (1974). Perceptual and acoustic correlates of aging in the speech of males. *Journal of Communication Disorders, 7,* 181-192.

Sachs, J., Lieberman, P., & Erickson, D. (1973). Anatomical and cultural determinants of male and female speech. In R. Shuy & R. Fasold (Eds.), *Language attitudes: Current trends and prospects* (pp. 74-84). Washington, DC: Georgetown University Press.

Sacks, H., Schegloff, E. A., & Jefferson, G. (1974). A simplest systematics for the organisation of turn-taking for conversation. *Language, 50,* 696-735.

Sapir, E. (1927). Speech as a personality trait. *American Journal of Sociology, 32,* 892-905.

Saxman, J. H., & Burk, K. W. (1967). Speaking fundamental frequency characteristics of middle-aged females. *Folia Phoniatrica, 19,* 167-172.

Schegloff, E. A. (1968). Sequencing in conversational openings. *American Anthropologist, 70,* 1075-1095.

Scherer, K. R. (1970). *Attribution of personality from voice: A cross-cultural study on dynamics of interpersonal perception.* Unpublished doctoral dissertation, Harvard University.

Scherer, K. R. (1971). Randomized splicing: A note on a simple technique for masking speech content. *Journal of Experimental Research in Personality, 5,* 155-159.

Scherer, K. R. (1978). Personality inference from voice quality: The loud voice of extroversion. *European Journal of Social Psychology, 8,* 467-487.

Scherer, K. R. (1979a). Personality markers in speech. In K. R. Scherer & H. Giles (Eds.), *Social markers in speech* (pp. 147-209). Cambridge: Cambridge University Press.

Scherer, K. R. (1979b). Voice and speech correlates of perceived social influence in simulated juries. In H. Giles & R. N. St. Clair (Eds.), *Language and social psychology* (pp. 88-120). Oxford: Blackwell.

Scherer, K. R. (1982). Methods of research on vocal communication: Paradigms and parameters. In K. R. Scherer & P. Ekman (Eds.), *Handbook of methods in nonverbal behaviour research* (pp. 136-198). Cambridge: Cambridge University Press.

Scherer, K. R. (1984a). The state of the art in vocal communication: A partial view. In A. Wolfgang (Ed.), *Nonverbal behavior: Perspectives, applications, intercultural insights* (pp. 41-74). New York: Hogrefe.

Scherer, K. R. (1984b). Vocal communication. *The German Journal of Psychology, 8,* 57-90.

Scherer, K. R. (1985a). Vocal affect signalling: A comparative approach. In J. S. Rosenblatt, C. Beer, M.-C. Busnel, & P. J. B. Slater (Eds.), *Advances in the study of behavior, Vol. 15* (pp. 189-244). New York: Academic Press.

Scherer, K. R. (1985b, September). Vocal assessment of affective disorders. *NIMH workshop on Behavioral Assessment of Affective Disorders.* Washington, DC.

Scherer, K. R. (1986a). Vocal affect expression: A review and a model for future research. *Psychological Bulletin, 99,* 143-165.

Scherer, K. R. (1986b). Voice, stress, and emotion. In M. H. Appley & R. Trumbull (Eds.), *Dynamics of stress: Physiological, psychological, and social perspectives* (pp. 157-179). New York: Plenum.

Scherer, K. R. (1987). Vocal assessment of affective disorders. In J. D. Maser (Ed.), *Depression and expressive behavior* (pp. 57-82). Hillsdale, NJ: Lawrence Erlbaum.

Scherer, K. R. (1988). On the symbolic functions of vocal affect expression. *Journal of Language and Social Psychology, 7,* 79-100.

Scherer, K. R. (1989). Vocal correlates of emotional arousal and affective disturbance. In H. Wagner & A. Manstead (Eds.), *Handbook of psychophysiology* (pp. 165-197). New York: John Wiley.

Scherer, K. R., Banse, R., Wallbott, H. G., & Goldbeck, T. (1991). Vocal cues in emotion encoding and decoding. *Motivation and Emotion, 15,* 123-148.

Scherer, K. R., & Ekman, P. (Eds.). (1982). *Handbook of methods in nonverbal behavior research.* Cambridge: Cambridge University Press.

Scherer, K. R., Feldstein, S., Bond, R. N., & Rosenthal, R. (1985). Vocal cues to deception: A comparative channel approach. *Journal of Psycholinguistic Research, 14,* 409-425.

Scherer, K. R., London, H., & Wolff, J. J. (1973). The voice of confidence: Paralinguistic cues and audience evaluation. *Journal of Personality and Social Psychology, 7,* 31-44.

Scherer, K. R., & Oshinsky, J. S. (1977). Cue utilization in emotion attribution from auditory stimuli. *Motivation and Emotion, 1,* 331-346.

Scherer, K. R., Titze, I. R., Raphael, B. N., Wood, R. P., Ramig, L. A., & Blager, F. B. (1987). Vocal fatigue in a trained and an untrained voice user. In T. Baer, C. Sasaki, & K. S. Harris (Eds.), *Laryngeal function in phonation and respiration* (pp. 533-555). Boston: Little, Brown.

Scherer, U., Helfrich, H., & Scherer, K. R. (1980). Paralinguistic behaviour: Internal push or external pull? In H. Giles, W. P. Robinson, & P. M. Smith (Eds.), *Language: Social psychological perspectives* (pp. 279-282). Oxford: Pergamon.

Schutte, H. K. (1992). Integrated aerodynamic measurements. *Journal of Voice, 6,* 127-134.

Sebastian, R. J., & Ryan, E. B. (1985). Speech cues and social evaluation: Markers of ethnicity, social class, and age. In H. Giles & R. N. St. Clair (Eds.), *Recent advances in language, communication, and social psychology* (pp. 112-143). London: Lawrence Erlbaum.

Shaw, M. E. (1981). *Group dynamics: The psychology of small group behavior* (2nd ed.). New York: McGraw-Hill.

Sherman, D. (1954). The merits of backward playing of connected speech in the scaling of voice-quality disorders. *Journal of Speech and Hearing Disorders, 19,* 312-321.

Shipp, T., & Hollien, H. (1969). Perception of the aging male voice. *Journal of Speech and Hearing Research, 12,* 704-710.

Shipp, T., Qi, Y., Huntley, R., & Hollien, H. (1992). Acoustic and temporal correlates of perceived age. *Journal of Voice, 6,* 211-216.

Siegman, A. W. (1987). The telltale voice: Nonverbal messages of verbal communication. In A. W. Siegman & S. Feldstein (Eds.), *Nonverbal behavior and communication* (2nd ed.) (pp. 351-434). Hillsdale, NJ: Lawrence Erlbaum.

Siegman, A. W., Anderson, R. A., & Berger, T. (1990). The angry voice: Its effects on the experience of anger and cardiovascular reactivity. *Psychosomatic Medicine, 52,* 631-643.

Silverman, K. (1983). *The subject of semiotics.* Oxford: Oxford University Press.

Smith, B. L., Brown, B. L., Strong, W. J., & Rencher, A. C. (1975). Effects of speech rate on personality perceptions. *Language and Speech, 18,* 145-152.

Smith, P. M. (1979). Sex markers in speech. In K. R. Scherer & H. Giles (Eds.), *Social markers in speech* (pp. 109-146). Cambridge: Cambridge University Press.

Sonninen, A., & Hurme, P. (1992). On the terminology of voice research. *Journal of Voice, 6,* 188-193.

Spender, D. (1985). *Man made language* (2nd ed.). London: Routledge & Kegan Paul.

Sprigg, R. K. (1978). Phonation types: A re-appraisal. *Journal of the International Phonetic Association, 8,* 2-17.

Stanford, W. B. (1967). *The sound of Greek.* Berkeley: University of California Press.

Starkweather, J. A. (1956). Content-free speech as a source of information about the speaker. *Journal of Personality and Social Psychology, 52,* 394-402.

St. Clair, R. N. (1982). From social history to language attitudes. In H. Giles & E. B. Ryan (Eds.), *Attitudes towards language variation: Social and applied contexts* (pp. 164-174). London: Edward Arnold.

Stewart, M. A., & Ryan, E. B. (1982). Attitudes toward younger and older adult speakers: Effects of varying speech rates. *Journal of Language and Social Psychology, 1,* 91-109.

Stone, M. (1991). Imaging the tongue and vocal tract. *British Journal of Disorders of Communication, 26,* 11-23.

Street, R. L., Jr. (1982). Evaluation of noncontent speech accommodation. *Language and Communication, 2,* 13-31.

Street, R. L., Jr. (1985). Participant-observer differences in speech evaluation. *Journal of Language and Social Psychology, 4,* 125-130.

Sweet, H. (1900). *The history of language.* London: Dent.

Sweet, H. (1932). *A primer of phonetics* (4th ed.). Oxford: Oxford University Press.

Tajfel, H. (1981). *Human groups and social categories.* Cambridge: Cambridge University Press.

Tarnóczy, T., & Fant, G. (1964). Some remarks on the average speech spectrum. Speech Transmission Laboratory: Quarterly progress and status report. *Royal Institute of Technology, Stockholm, 4,* 13-14.

Taylor, D. M., & McKirnan, D. J. (1984). A five-stage model of intergroup relations. *The British Journal of Social Psychology, 23,* 291-300.

'tHart, J., Collier, R., & Cohen, A. (1990). *A perceptual study of intonation: An experimental-phonetic approach to speech melody.* Cambridge: Cambridge University Press.

Thompson, L. C. (1965). *A Vietnamese grammar.* Seattle: University of Washington Press.

Titze, I. R. (1988). A framework for the study of vocal registers. *Journal of Voice, 2,* 183-194.

Titze, I. R. (1992). Vocal efficiency. *Journal of Voice, 6,* 135-138.

Trager, G. L. (1958). Paralanguage: A first approximation. *Studies in Linguistics, 13,* 1-12.

Trudgill, P. (1972). Sex, covert prestige, and linguistic change in the urban British English of Norwich. *Language in Society, 1,* 179-195.

Trudgill, P. (1974). *The social differentiation of English in Norwich.* Cambridge: Cambridge University Press.

Turner, J. C. (1987). *Rediscovering the social group: A self-categorization theory.* Oxford: Blackwell.

UPSID. (1981). *Working papers in phonetics, University of California at Los Angeles, Department of Linguistics, 53.*

van Bezooijen, R., & Boves, L. (1986). The effects of low-pass filtering and random splicing on the perception of speech. *Journal of Psycholinguistic Research, 15,* 403-417.

van Dommelen, W. A. (1993a). Does dynamic F0 increase perceived duration? *Journal of Phonetics, 21,* 367-386.

van Dommelen, W. A. (1993b). Speaker height and weight identification: A re-evaluation of some old data. *Journal of Phonetics, 21,* 337-341.

Walker, J. F., Archibald, L. M., Cherniak, S. R., & Fish, V. G. (1992). Articulation rate in 3- and 5-year-old children. *Journal of Speech and Hearing Research, 35,* 4-13.

Walker, M. B., & Trimboli, A. (1989). Communicating affect: The role of verbal and nonverbal content. *Journal of Language and Social Psychology, 8,* 229-248.

Watson, J. S. (Ed.). (1970). *Cicero on oratory and orators.* Carbondale: Southern Illinois University Press.

Watson, P. J., Hixon, T. J., & Maher, M. Z. (1987). To breathe or not to breathe—That is the question: An investigation of speech breathing kinematics in world class Shakespearean actors. *Journal of Voice, 1,* 269-272.

Watzlawick, P., Beavin, J. H., & Jackson, D. D. (1968). *Pragmatics of human communication: A study of interactional patterns, pathologies, and paradoxes.* London: Faber & Faber.

Webster, W. G., & Burgoon, J. K. (1981). The effects of nonverbal synchrony on message comprehension. *Journal of Nonverbal Behavior, 5,* 207-223.

Wendahl, R. W., Moore, P., & Hollien, H. (1963). Comments on vocal fry. *Folia Phoniatrica, 15,* 251-255.

White, P. (1961). *The tree of man.* Harmondsworth: Penguin.

Wiener, M., Devoe, S., Rubinow, S., & Geller, J. (1972). Nonverbal behavior and nonverbal communication. *Psychological Review, 79,* 185-214.

Wilkins, J. (1968). *An essay towards a real character, and a philosophical language.* Menston, UK: Scolar Press. (Original work published 1668)

Williams, A., Giles, H., Coupland, N., Dalby, M, & Manasse, H. (1990). The communicative contexts of elderly social support and health: A theoretical model. *Health Communication, 2,* 123-143.

Williams, C. E., & Stevens, K. N. (1972). Emotions and speech: Some acoustical correlates. *Journal of the Acoustical Society of America, 52,* 1238-1250.

Wodehouse, P. G. (1938). *The code of the Woosters.* London: Herbert Jenkins.

Wolfe, V. I., Ratusnik, D. L., Smith, F. H., & Northrop, G. (1990). Intonation and fundamental frequency in male-to-female transsexuals. *Journal of Speech and Hearing Disorders, 55,* 43-50.

Woodall, W. G., & Burgoon, J. K. (1981). The effects of nonverbal synchrony on message comprehension. *Journal of Nonverbal Behavior, 5,* 207-223.

Woodall, W. G., & Burgoon, J. K. (1984). Talking fast and changing attitudes: A critique and clarification. *Journal of Nonverbal Behavior, 8,* 126-142.

Zahn, C. J., & Hopper, R. (1985). Measuring language attitudes: The speech evaluation instrument. *Journal of Language and Social Psychology, 4,* 113-123.

Zajonc, R. B., Murphy, S. T., & Englehart, M. (1989). Feeling and facial efference: Implications of the vascular theory of emotion. *Psychological Review, 96,* 395-416.

Zemlin, W. R. (1964). *Speech and hearing science.* Champaign, IL: Stipes.

Zimmerman, D. H., & West, C. (1975). Sex roles, interruptions and silences in conversation. In B. Thorne & N. Henley (Eds.), *Language and sex: Difference and dominance* (pp. 105-129). Rowley, MA: Newbury House.

Zuckerman, M., & Driver, R. E. (1989). What sounds beautiful is good: The vocal attractiveness stereotype. *Journal of Nonverbal Behavior, 13,* 67-82.

Zuckerman, M., Hodgins, H., & Miyake, K. (1990). The vocal attractiveness stereotype: Replication and elaboration. *Journal of Nonverbal Behavior, 14,* 97-112.

Index

About the Author

Jeffery Pittam is a Senior Lecturer in Communication Studies in the Department of English at The University of Queensland, Australia. He gained his Ph.D. on the functional measurement of voice quality from the same institution in 1986. His first degree was in phonetics/linguistics and he has a research master's in social psychology. He teaches spoken and written language communication from an interdisciplinary perspective, spanning the social psychology of language, phonetics/linguistics, and media studies. His research interests span the perceptual and acoustic measurement of voice and speech, social identity and media representations, and conversational analysis. For many years he has researched various aspects of voice, speech, and language communication in the Vietnamese community in Australia, and more recently in the area of language and AIDS. These projects include studies of voice and accent change, assimilation, language maintenance, ethnolinguistic identity, and media representations. His work in all these areas is interdisciplinary and consequently has been published in a wide variety of academic journals and edited volumes within psychology, communication studies, phonetics, and speech science.